MacCormick's Scotland

EDINBURGH STUDIES IN LAW

Series Editor
Elspeth Reid (University of Edinburgh)

Editorial Board
David L Carey Miller (University of Aberdeen)
George L Gretton (University of Edinburgh)
Hector L MacQueen (University of Edinburgh)
Kenneth G C Reid (University of Edinburgh)
Reinhard Zimmermann (Max-Planck Institute of Comparative and International Private Law, Hamburg)

Volumes in the series:
Elspeth Reid and David L Carey Miller (eds), *A Mixed Legal System in Transition: T B Smith and the Progress of Scots Law* (2005)

Hector MacQueen and Reinhard Zimmermann (eds), *European Contract Law: Scots and South African Perspectives* (2006)

John W Cairns and Paul du Plessis (eds), *Beyond Dogmatics: Law and Society in the Roman World* (2007)

William M Gordon, *Roman Law, Scots Law and Legal History* (2007)

Kenneth G C Reid, Marius J de Waal and Reinhard Zimmermann, *Exploring the Law of Succession: Studies National, Historical and Comparative* (2007)

Vernon Valentine Palmer and Elspeth Christie Reid (eds), *Mixed Jurisdictions Compared: Private Law in Louisiana and Scotland* (2009)

J W Cairns and Paul du Plessis (eds), *The Creation of the* Ius Commune: *From* Casus *to* Regula (2010)

James Chalmers, Fiona Leverick and Lindsay Farmer (eds), *Essays in Criminal Law in Honour of Sir Gerald Gordon* (2010)

Elaine E Sutherland, Kay E Goodall, Gavin F M Little and Fraser P Davidson (eds), *Law Making and the Scottish Parliament* (2011)

euppublishing.com/series/esil

EDINBURGH STUDIES IN LAW
VOLUME 10

MacCormick's Scotland

Edited by
Neil Walker

EDINBURGH
University Press

© The Edinburgh Law Review Trust and the Contributors, 2012

Edinburgh University Press Ltd
22 George Square, Edinburgh EH8 9LF

www.euppublishing.com

Typeset in New Caledonia by
Koinonia, Manchester, and
printed and bound in Great Britain by
CPI Group (UK) Ltd, Croydon CR0 4YY

A CIP record for this book is available from the British Library

ISBN 978 0 7486 4380 6 (hardback)
ISBN 978 0 7486 4381 3 (webready PDF)
ISBN 978 0 7486 4930 3 (epub)
ISBN 978 0 7486 4929 7 (Amazon ebook)

The right of the contributors
to be identified as authors of this work
has been asserted in accordance with
the Copyright, Designs and Patents Act 1988.

Contents

Preface and Acknowledgements

The present volume began its life at a celebratory event held at Edinburgh Law School to mark the extraordinary contribution of Neil MacCormick, our dear colleague of thirty-six years, who retired in 2008 and died the following year. The main activity of that memorable June day in 2010 was a seminar on the Scottish themes in Neil's life and work, at which most of the contributors to the book we have before us spoke. This event was attended by a mix of friends and colleagues, mostly from the Law School itself, but also embracing a select number who had a particularly close connection with Neil or who had some special insights to offer on the issues that had engaged him for so many years. The seminar was followed by the unveiling of a memorial plaque for Neil in the new Neil MacCormick Room, a ceremony introduced by Neil's old friend, Sir David Edward, and performed by his widow Flora. A day of fond remembrance and of involvement in just the kinds of activities that Neil would have enjoyed to the full was fittingly capped by a convivial dinner at a local restaurant.

The title of the book speaks for itself. Such is the esteem in which Neil MacCormick is held and so great has been his influence that we can expect – and are already beginning to experience – a flood of memorial collections, of essays of tribute, and of general re-engagements with his life's work. By concentrating on MacCormick's *Scotland*, we have sought to do something distinctive – the importance of which seemed obvious to the denizens of Old College but is perhaps less well appreciated by many unfamiliar with the pattern of Neil's life. There has been no more cosmopolitan figure in the legal academic world over the past thirty years than Neil MacCormick. He lived and loved the life of the global intellectual, the champion of transnational academic collaboration, the dedicated European, the ever-curious traveller. Indeed, it is hard to imagine a less parochial World-view than that inhabited by Neil MacCormick. Yet he was also Scottish through and through. This was a matter of politics, and his brilliantly asserted and selflessly committed nationalism. But as anyone who knew him or who heard or read him at any length would confirm, it was also a question of culture and belief, of literature and lore, of landscape and memory, of family and familiarity, of a style and a tone that could only ever have been made in Scotland.

The essays that follow all, in their different ways, seek to represent the Scottish dimension which was so central to Neil's life and times and such an integral part of his distinctive and remarkable character. The opening Section, "Scotland's MacCormick", asks what it meant for Neil to belong to Scotland. Hector MacQueen examines how Neil's Scottishness informed various aspects of his work, providing a constant backdrop to his remarkably diverse and ever-evolving set of intellectual and political concerns and commitments. Maks Del Mar supplements this with a splendidly comprehensive bibliography of Neil's work, one that doubtless will surprise many by the sheer volume of Scottish material it reveals, together with a short but insightful essay on the various Scottish strands in his writing. One of these strands, of course, was the Scottish Enlightenment, and the second section brings together essays by John Cairns and Alexander Broadie on two of Neil's favourite Enlightenment thinkers, John Millar and Adam Ferguson. Both authors seek to bring out the continuities between the intellectual and practical concerns of these two towering eighteenth-century figures and the kinds of contemporary issues that Neil sought to address.

The third section turns its attention to MacCormick the lawyer and legal theorist. Gerry Maher and Julie Dickson take as their point of departure Neil's abiding concern with the nature and anatomy of a legal system, a concern that combined his interest in the character of legal order in general with his particular preoccupation with the distinctive properties and at least semi-autonomous quality of the Scottish legal system and Scots law. Both authors stress how elusive and multi-faceted the concept of legal system is, and how closely tied up with questions of identity as well as with the more familiar matters of coherence, order and effectiveness. Section 4, "Sovereignty and Beyond", continues the legal theme, but is explicitly concerned with those large constitutional questions of Scotland's relationship to the UK and to Europe which brought Neil's academic and political interests into such close alignment. Neil Walker traces the relationship between MacCormick's liberal nationalism and his well-known post-sovereignty perspective in the context of his views on Scottish independence, while Joanne Scott examines that same post-sovereignty nationalism against the backdrop of Scotland's shifting position as a region within supranational Europe.

The final section puts the various pieces of Neil back together again, asking not how Scotland influenced Neil, as did the opening section, but how Neil sought to influence Scotland. Drew Scott and Will Storrar both examine Neil as a prime example of the Scottish public intellectual. They describe his remarkably varied and effective role in the Scottish public sphere, and also ask what his career tells us about what is distinctive about the Scottish public intellectual more generally. And, in conclusion, Zenon Bańkowski, Neil's oldest colleague and friend in the Law School, offers a very personal perspective on what it meant for him, as a non-Scot indefinitely abroad and increasingly at home in Scotland, to engage with and be engaged by Neil's Scottishness over forty years.

Neither the original seminar nor the book that has followed would have seen the light of day without the generous support and excellent efforts of many people. Thanks are due, first and foremost, to Flora MacCormick, and also to Neil's sister Marion, for their warm encouragement and active involvement in the day of celebration. Thanks are also due to all the contributors from Edinburgh and beyond, with a special word for Maks Del Mar and Hector MacQueen who did not have the opportunity to present at the original event but were happy to work to tight timetables to make their own invaluable contribution to the final product. I am also obliged to the many other colleagues who supported and participated in the event. On the academic side, I would like to mention in particular Douglas Brodie, then Dean of the Law School, who was so generous with his time and financial support, and Claudio Michelon, Sharon Cowan, Stephen Tierney and Kenneth Reid, all of whom were closely involved in the preparation of the event or as academic commentators on the day. On the administrative side, too, I have a number of people to thank. Neil had a special bond with many of the administrative and secretarial staff of the Law School, and it was telling how many – past and present - were delighted to take a full part in the day's events, contributing greatly to the atmosphere of warm collegiality. Special thanks are due to Lisa Kendall for general planning and to the Research Office, and in particular Alison Stirling and Lorna Gallacher, for excellent hands-on organisation. Last but far from least, I would like to acknowledge my gratitude to Bonnie Holligan, who was a model of diligence and calm intelligence as an editorial assistant, and without whom I certainly could not have brought this project to timely fruition.

Neil Walker,
Old College, Edinburgh
August 2011

List of Contributors

PROFESSOR ZENON BAŃKOWSKI is Emeritus Professor of Legal Theory at the University of Edinburgh.

PROFESSOR ALEXANDER BROADIE is Emeritus Professor of Logic and Rhetoric at the University of Glasgow.

PROFESSOR JOHN W CAIRNS is Professor of Legal History at the University of Edinburgh.

DR MAKSYMILIAN DEL MAR is Lecturer in Legal and Social Philosophy at Queen Mary, University of London.

DR JULIE DICKSON is Fellow and Lecturer in Law at Somerville College, Oxford.

PROFESSOR HECTOR MACQUEEN is Professor of Private Law at the University of Edinburgh and a Scottish Law Commissioner.

PROFESSOR GERRY MAHER is Professor of Criminal Law at the University of Edinburgh.

PROFESSOR DREW SCOTT is Professor of European Union Studies at the University of Edinburgh.

PROFESSOR JOANNE SCOTT is Professor of European Law at University College London.

PROFESSOR WILLIAM STORRAR is Director of the Center of Theological Inquiry, Princeton.

PROFESSOR NEIL WALKER is Regius Professor of Public Law and the Law of Nature and Nations at the University of Edinburgh.

Scotland's MacCormick

1 A Post-Positivist Outlook from the Thistle

Hector MacQueen°

A. INTRODUCTION
B. SCOTTISH INDEPENDENCE, DEVOLUTION AND
   NATIONALISM
C. SCOTS LAW AND THE SCOTTISH LEGAL SYSTEM AS A
   SOURCE
D. STAIR, HUME, SMITH AND KANT: NATURAL LAW AND
   ENLIGHTENMENT
E. CONCLUSION

A. INTRODUCTION

You did not have to spend very much time in Neil MacCormick's company in the Faculty (later School) of Law at Edinburgh University to realise how well and how much he knew about Scotland. It was not just the Scottish Enlightenment philosophers such as David Hume (1711-1776) and Adam Smith (1723-1790), who were so important to his own thought, or the Scottish politics in which he played such a prominent and activist part. It was also the country's history (perhaps especially that of the West Highlands and Islands), geography, topography and general culture (including the Gaelic dimension inherited from his forebears in the Ross of Mull). Something of the flavour of Neil's conversation on these occasions can be detected in his introduction to the re-issue of his father's memoir, *The Flag in the Wind*,[1] where he recalls school holidays at Bunessan in Mull, Killin in Perthshire and Tayvallich in Argyll, picnics at Loch Lomond, Loch Lubnaig and Inverkip, and boating on Loch Sween and Loch na Lathaich. The introduction also mentions the views from the family flat at 2 Park Quadrant in Glasgow to the Kilpatrick Hills and the Campsie Fells and the more distant Argyll and Perthshire mountains. Also within more immediate eyeshot was "the magnificent side view of Gilbert Scott's Glasgow University"[2] (where Neil would in due course read English

° Scottish Law Commissioner and Professor of Private Law, University of Edinburgh. As so often, I am grateful to John Cairns for helpful comments on an earlier draft of this contribution.
1 J MacCormick, *The Flag in the Wind* (2008; first published 1955) xi.
2 MacCormick, *Flag in the Wind* xi. Influential for Neil was his Glasgow moral philosophy

and Philosophy). Elsewhere he said of Scott's fantastic edifice: "To this day, my unreflective paradigm of going to University is defined in terms of the path up over Queen Alexandra's bridge to Gilmorehill and the mullioned windows of its lecture halls."[3] But the view from Park Quadrant also took in the cityscape of industrial Glasgow and the cranes of the Clydeside docks shipyards. The whole was a perspective, Neil wrote, on Scotland in miniature; so an outlook was formed, in every sense of the word.[4]

There was also the observation of everyday life around him in his adopted city of Edinburgh, sometimes simply for the humour in it, intentional and unintentional alike; but also sometimes providing the means for illuminating serious points. There are examples of the latter in his published writings: for instance, the abusive drunk successfully turned off the bus by a determined Edinburgh lady passenger, both of them immediately recognisable characters who together illustrate the positive morality of the group in Neil's account of the jurisprudence of H L A Hart;[5] or, again, the brilliantly sustained analysis at the opening of *Institutions of Law* of the managed queue in the booking hall of Edinburgh's Waverley railway station as an institutionalised norma- tive order.[6] This sort of thing was also a feature of his lectures to Edinburgh undergraduates; and I have put on the Law School's web page tribute one example which has stayed vivid in my mind for thirty-five years and which I suspect I will always recall, not only for its extraordinary theatre, but also for the substance of the point that Neil was addressing, namely, the difference between legal and social norms.[7]

Discourse of this kind was never ostentatious even when, as in the lecture, it aimed primarily to amuse; never was conversation forced to take a Scottish turn so that the speaker's knowledge could be put on show. Neil enjoyed some of the more obvious aspects of what the world knows as Scottish – wearing

teacher Dr William D Lamont (1901-1983): see e.g. especially Lamont's *The Principles of Moral Judgment* (1946); also *The Value Judgement* (1955) and *Law and the Moral Order* (1981). Neil is acknowledged and his work discussed in the last of these books, while in the first Lamont demonstrates the technique of using reported case law to illustrate moral problems later used extensively by Neil. He also makes frequent reference to *Gloag & Henderson*, the standard survey work on Scots law, for discussion of concepts such as promise, real, personal and basic rights, obligation and duty. No doubt reinforcing his appeal to Neil's sensibilities, Lamont was also a scholarly historian of early and medieval Islay: see e.g. his *The Early History of Islay* (1970).

3 N MacCormick, "Doubts about the 'Supreme Court' and reflections on *MacCormick v Lord Advocate*" (2004) *Juridical Review* 237 at 238.

4 MacCormick, *Flag in the Wind*, xi.

5 N MacCormick, *H L A Hart*, 2nd edn (2008) 67; cf 1st edn (1981) 50.

6 *Institutions of Law: An Essay in Legal Theory* (2007) 1-2, 14-37.

7 See *http://www.law.ed.ac.uk/neilmaccormick/condolencesandtributes.aspx* (last checked 25 July 2011).

the kilt, playing the bagpipes,[8] drinking whisky and performing vigorously at Burns Suppers, for example – but mostly, so far as I saw, these performances took place when foreign visitors needed to be entertained in the way they expected from the country they were in. In the ordinary daily routines and social exchanges of law school life, the fact that Neil was imbued with Scottishness emerged simply because that was how it was. He could no more have avoided it than breathing.

This contribution will suggest that Scottishness is apparent in the same way in Neil's writings and the development of his thought. This is not to argue that Neil's work is essentially Scottish, or that only Scots with the same range of reference about their country that Neil had can truly understand it. Such claims Neil himself would have emphatically and rightly rejected. The suggestion here is rather that Scottishness emerges in his writings in the same way as it did in his conversation and teaching, naturally and appropriately to the point under discussion, and as un-self-consciously as is ever possible in the act of serious writing. Sometimes the point of departure was Scotland in some aspect or other (usually political), and quite frequently what he wanted to say was about and for Scotland; but it was all part of a wider picture in the end at least European in its overall scope and ambition. Scottishness is thus part of the texture, the woof and warp, of Neil's work: not to be over-emphasised, but, equally, not to be overlooked or underplayed. I do not know whether this observation has any wider significance than as an aspect of Neil's contribution to legal thought; it is not customary, I think, to ask whether Englishness is important for Hart's jurisprudence or what being Austrian meant for Kelsen, although perhaps for both men their Jewish identities might present more questions similar to those raised here about Neil and Scotland.[9] But I do think that it reveals something about why Neil's contribution to jurisprudence took the form it did.

Most of this present piece is derived from repeated readings of the mighty quartet on "Law, State, and Practical Reason" in which Neil brought his life's

---

8 For Neil's account of how he was taught to play the pipes by two great-uncles on Mull, see *Practical Reason in Law and Morality* (2008) 83.

9 The index to Nicola Lacey's *A Life of H L A Hart: The Nightmare and the Noble Dream* (2004) contains numerous references under the entry "Hart, Herbert – Jewish identity" but there is no similar entry for English (or British) identity. The only book-length biography of Kelsen of which I am aware, but which has not been available to me, is R A Métall, *Hans Kelsen: Leben und Werk* (1969). See however N B Ladavac, "Hans Kelsen (1881-1973): a biographical note and bibliography" (1998) 9 *European Journal of International Law* 391. Kelsen's Jewish origins were of great significance in the events of his life, notably in 1930s Germany, but he had converted to Catholicism in 1905 and was, in Ladavac's words, "resolutely agnostic" in his spiritual beliefs. National identity may not have mattered much to someone born in Prague, raised in Vienna and thereafter working in, successively, Austria, Germany, Switzerland and the USA.

work and thought together in what turned out, alas, to be a grand finale.[10] But the paper tries to place itself in relation to Neil's claim, made throughout the quartet, that over the course of his career his intellectual position shifted from the positivism he took from Hart at Oxford in the 1960s to what he called "post-positivism".[11] This built from his delineation of law as institutional fact and as a normative order characterised by an institutional commitment to practical reason as well as formal reasoning. He was led on to challenge the view that there was any necessary correlation between law and state as institutions; and the development of European Union law as a legal order, with its claim to supremacy over the laws of its member states, however contested, reinforced that perspective. The member states were no longer, if they ever had been, complete masters of the law in their own houses, while the Union, although a legal order, was equally clearly not a state in its own right. These post-sovereign entities pointed to the need for a post-positivist theory of law. Finally, while law's institutional character continued to differentiate the phenomenon from the normative orders of morality (which depended instead on the judgement of the autonomous individual actor), law's parallel commitment to practical reason meant that its content was not arbitrary or dependent solely on the will of the law-making institution. Law being a normative order meant that there were limits upon what could be called law. It is perhaps not too much of an exaggeration to say that by the end of his life Neil was seeking a rapprochement between positivism and natural law.

In what follows, I will seek to show how Neil's Scottishness played its part in the intellectual path that culminated in the "Law, State and Practical Reason" quartet.

B. SCOTTISH INDEPENDENCE, DEVOLUTION AND NATIONALISM

The most obvious way in which Neil's work was Scottish was in his writing about Scotland's constitutional position in the United Kingdom and, later, in the European Union. Maksymilian Del Mar's bibliography in Chapter 2 of this volume shows that amongst Neil's earliest incursions into print was editing and contributing to a collection entitled *The Scottish Debate*, published in 1970. The editor explained his purpose:

10 *Questioning Sovereignty: Law, State, and Nation in the European Commonwealth* (1999) (henceforth *Questioning Sovereignty*); *Rhetoric and the Rule of Law: A Theory of Legal Reasoning* (2005) (henceforth *Rhetoric*); *Institutions of Law: An Essay in Legal Theory* (2007) (henceforth *Institutions*); *Practical Reason in Law and Morality* (2008) (henceforth *Practical Reason*).
11 The shift in Neil's thinking can also be perceived in the second edition of his book on Hart (MacCormick, *H L A Hart* (n 5)).

This book is founded on the supposition that the present demand for greater political independence in Scotland is not merely a nine days' wonder but will remain a live issue in British politics in the foreseeable future. The objectives which the book is aimed are ... to facilitate rational judgment of the issues at stake by presenting a debate on the arguments for and against home rule in one form or another ... No doubt politics is in the end founded in large part upon prejudice and emotion, but these ought to be tempered and tested in the fire of critical discussion.[12]

Neil went on to declare his own "editorial bias":

I am myself convinced by the arguments in favour of creating some sort of parliament and government in Scotland, but I remain unsure as to what sort would, on the whole, be best ... Despite being unconvinced that independence would be the best course for Scotland or for the rest of Britain, I am a member of the Scottish National Party, since it seems to me abundantly clear that neither of the two large parties is likely to take the smallest step towards any worthwhile form of self-government for Scotland ... unless they are subjected to powerful electoral pressures of a quite unequivocal kind. The Liberal Party, whose policies are at least as attractive to me, seems likely to remain a minority party; and Liberal successes are not unequivocal pointers to a demand for home rule, as those of the National Party are.[13]

He added, summarising the thrust of his own contribution to the volume:

[I]t seems perfectly obvious that devolution would have to precede independence, so that if devolution worked well we could abandon the notion of proceeding to independence.[14]

As the Del Mar bibliography amply demonstrates, Neil went on writing about these matters for the rest of his life. But whereas in 1970 his contribution was essentially designed to influence political discussion and events, later on he wrapped the issue more and more into his legal philosophy. Perhaps he would have argued that his evolving legal philosophy was more and more wrapped into his political beliefs. In *Questioning Sovereignty*, the first of the four volumes in which Neil drew together the threads of his life's work on law, state and practical reason, the case of Scotland and the United Kingdom was where he began to test his general arguments about the relationship between law and state.[15] What exactly had happened at the Union of Scotland and England in 1707, when a single Crown and Parliament had been established at the head of the new United Kingdom but two laws and judicial systems had

12 N MacCormick (ed), *The Scottish Debate: Essays on Scottish Nationalism* (1970) 1-2.
13 MacCormick (ed), *The Scottish Debate* 2.
14 MacCormick (ed), *The Scottish Debate* 2. For Neil's own contribution, entitled "Independence and Constitutional Change", see MacCormick (ed), *The Scottish Debate* 52-64.
15 See MacCormick, *Questioning Sovereignty* ch 4.

very largely been left to carry on as before (the situation which had continued to prevail down to the present day)? "Scotland has been the anomaly that has made an ostensibly unitary state, an archetype of nation state in certain political-theoretical terms, function internally in a markedly federal way."[16] The great case of *MacCormick v Lord Advocate*,[17] brought by Neil's father in 1953 to test whether the new Queen could style herself "Elizabeth II" when her United Kingdom had never known an Elizabeth I, had at least raised, if it did not answer, the question of whether the Scottish legal system now subscribed in full to the English doctrine of sovereignty or supremacy of Parliament, or whether the Union of 1707 constituted some kind of fundamental law for the United Kingdom. At any rate, the continuing identity of Scotland, and the existence of Scots law and the Scottish legal system, demonstrated very clearly the lack of a necessary correlation between law, state and nation, the heart of Neil's argument in *Questioning Sovereignty*. The development of the Scottish Parliament in 1999 merely made more visible the anomaly in the United Kingdom's conception of its own sovereignty. Indeed, that conception was undermined not only by Scottish separateness but also by the United Kingdom's membership from 1973 of the European Union and the entry into force of the Human Rights Act 1998.[18]

Questioning Sovereignty also shows Neil's acceptance of the idea that in the pre-1707 Scottish constitution "sovereignty belonged to the people, to the community of the realm, rather than to Parliament, or, strictly, King or Queen in Parliament".[19] For that idea he could refer to the *De Iure Regni Apud Scotos* of George Buchanan (1506-1582), first published in 1579 but written in 1567 to justify the deposition of Mary Queen of Scots,[20] and, still earlier, the Declaration of Arbroath, addressed to the Pope in 1320 to support the argument that Robert Bruce had been made King of Scots by, amongst other things, "the due consent and assent" of the people.[21] Alexander Broadie's recent detailed argument that the Declaration here draws on the thought of

16 MacCormick, *Questioning Sovereignty* 60.
17 1953 SC 396. Neil defends the significance of the case in "Doubts about the 'Supreme Court' and reflections on *MacCormick v Lord Advocate*" (n 3).
18 The anomaly is further deepened by the advancing process of devolution in Northern Ireland and Wales as well as under the Scotland Bill before the Westminster Parliament at the time of writing.
19 MacCormick, *Questioning Sovereignty* 55; see also 59-60. The idea of the "community of the realm" springs from medieval sources and is most famously explored for Scotland in G Barrow, *Robert Bruce and the Community of the Realm of Scotland*, 4th edn (2005). See also A Duncan, *The Kingship of the Scots 842-1292: Succession and Independence* (2002).
20 See R A Mason (ed), *A Dialogue on the Law of Kingship among the Scots: A critical edition and translation of George Buchanan's "De Iure Regni apud Scotos Dialogus"* (2004).
21 On the Declaration see E J Cowan, *"For Freedom Alone": The Declaration of Arbroath, 1320* (2003); G Barrow (ed), *The Declaration of Arbroath: History, Significance, Setting* (2003).

Scotland's greatest medieval philosopher, John Duns Scotus (c.1265-1308), would have pleased Neil greatly.[22]

There is of course room for controversy as to the extent to which popular sovereignty was indeed the fundamental underpinning of the historical Scottish constitution.[23] Neil did not go so far as to argue for that position categorically, but rather acknowledged it as one among various streams of thought in Scotland over time. It was probably important that James Dalrymple, Viscount Stair (1619-1695), the foundational institutional writer of Scots law whom, as we shall see repeatedly in what follows, Neil much admired, could be read as supportive of the view that the sovereignty of the legislature was subject to that of the law.[24] Also of significance was the history of the Edinburgh University chair held by Neil from 1972 until 2008, the Chair of Public Law and of the Law of Nature and Nations. In particular, James Lorimer (1818-1890), who occupied the chair and revived its intellectual focus from 1862 until his death, rejected both Austinian positivism and Benthamite utilitarianism in favour of natural law.[25] (It might incidentally also have interested Neil in this context that his immediate predecessor, Archibald Hunter Campbell (1902-1989), who held the chair from 1945 to 1972, at some point supplied to his friend Lord President Cooper (1892-1955), leader of the court in *MacCormick v Lord Advocate*, a note strongly criticising the Diceyan view that the Act of Union is simply a statute like any other, changeable by Parliament as it wills.)[26]

22 A Broadie, "The past as propaganda: the Declaration of Arbroath", unpublished lecture given on 18 November 2010 at the Royal Society of Edinburgh as part of the British Academy Medieval Week 2010; also given on 8 January 2011 at the Annual Conference of Scottish Medievalists.

23 See e.g. R A Mason, *Kingship and the Commonweal: Political Thought in Renaissance and Reformation Scotland* (1998); C Kidd, "Sovereignty and the Scottish constitution before 1707" (2004) *Juridical Review* 225. More legalistic analyses are R Sutherland, "Aspects of the Scottish constitution prior to 1707", in J P Grant (ed), *Independence and Devolution: The Legal Implications for Scotland* (1976) 15-44; J W Cairns, T D Fergus and H L MacQueen, "Legal humanism and the history of Scots Law: John Skene and Thomas Craig", in J MacQueen (ed), *Humanism in Renaissance Scotland* (1990) 48-74, especially at 60-66.

24 See J Dalrymple, Viscount Stair, *Institutions of the Law of Scotland* I.1.10-17 (1681,1693; 6th edn, 1981). Note in particular the doctrine of the desuetude of Acts of the pre-1707 Scottish Parliament. But see further J D Ford, *Law and Opinion in Scotland During the Seventeenth Century* (2007).

25 See N MacCormick, "On public law and the law of nature and nations" (2007) 11 *Edinburgh Law Review* 149 at 154-155. This text was Neil's lecture to celebrate the tercentenary of the chair and the foundation of the Edinburgh Law School in 1707. Neil also noted the Glasgow-based contribution of Lorimer's pupil, William Galbraith Miller (1848-1904), for whom see D M Walker, *A History of the School of Law: The University of Glasgow* (1990) 45, 64-66; E Attwooll, "William Galbraith Miller, humanitarian intervention and international law" (1994) *Juridical Review* 36.

26 The note survives among the Cooper papers in the National Library of Scotland (NLS Acc 6188/10). See further G Little, "A Flag in the Wind: *MacCormick v Lord Advocate*", in J P Grant and E E Sutherland (eds), *Scots Law Tales* (2010) 23-44 at 35-36.

But, whatever the historical position before 1707, there can be little doubt about the political appeal of the idea of popular sovereignty in a modern and democratic age. Popular lack of support for the status quo in the Anglo-Scottish Union, as manifested at the ballot box in successive UK general elections, was thus for Neil the constitutional justification for re-examination of Scotland's governance arrangements. *Questioning Sovereignty* concludes with an analysis of how the issue of Scotland's position in the United Kingdom may be resolved, and how best a transition to Scottish independence might be handled.[27] A referendum would be a necessary precursor, as it was in 1997 for devolution; and indeed holding such a referendum has been, and remains, the policy and aim of the SNP Scottish Government, albeit one frustrated in the Scottish Parliament of 2007-2011 by that government's lack of an overall parliamentary majority. This looks like a departure from Neil's 1970 position that, if devolution worked well, there would be no need to go on to independence; but the really vital difference was, and is, in the overall context. An independent Scotland would remain a member of the European Union which the United Kingdom had joined in 1973 and in which, subject to the vital principle of subsidiarity, post-sovereign states had agreed to go forward together in pursuit of certain common goals.

Scotland is not the only issue with which *Questioning Sovereignty* is concerned, of course; but this reader remains struck by the extent to which it lies at the core of the book's argument alongside the question of the European Union's "new constellation of institutional authority".[28] Also of fundamental importance to the whole discussion is the book's restatement of Neil's defence of nationalism in its "civic" and "liberal" forms, which is clearly crucial if Scotland's continuation as a separate unit (in whatever form, and within whatever overall constitutional arrangements) is to be justified.[29] But vitally the argument here is not just about Scotland: it is an argument about when it is legitimate for groups to claim some sort of entitlement to some sort of self-government, taking us back once more to the question of popular sovereignty. Many other cases from across the European Union show that this is an important general question becoming steadily more pressing for both the countries concerned and the Union itself.[30] The experience of Scotland (and England) might however provide the best sort of example of how to go forward in this area:

27 MacCormick, *Questioning Sovereignty* ch 12.
28 MacCormick, "On public law and the law of nature and nations" (n 25) 157.
29 MacCormick, *Questioning Sovereignty* chs 10 and 11.
30 Notably Belgium and Spain.

It is a matter of satisfaction, that ought to be more commented on than it has been, that England and Scotland achieved a union in peace and by negotiation, and they have now revised it by introduction of wide-ranging devolution in total peace and good will. The question of independence has been brought to the centre of the public agenda without the scratching of a finger or the shedding of even one drop of blood. Whatever comes next, it can be achieved and surely will be achieved in the same way. It can be done well with mutual good will, and there is no sign that mutual good will is lacking.[31]

C. SCOTS LAW AND THE SCOTTISH LEGAL SYSTEM AS A SOURCE

Throughout Neil's academic career, one of the most powerful forces in the Scottish legal academy was what has become known as "legal nationalism". This is probably still most associated with the name of T B (later Sir Thomas) Smith (1915-1988), Professor of Scots Law at Edinburgh University when Neil himself was appointed to that institution's Chair of Public Law and of the Law of Nature and Nations in 1972.[32] Smith contributed a thoughtful and insightful piece to *The Scottish Debate* in 1970, so clearly the two men were already well acquainted by that time.[33] Smith's article makes plain that his legal nationalism was far from the caricature in which it is sometimes presented: it was not a simple matter of "Scots law is best", or of a special link between Scots law and the Scottish people, or of a restoration of the law as it had been in some previous golden age. "Legal nationalism in the sense of parochialism," wrote Smith, "is to be deplored".[34] The question was rather a matter of avoiding as far as possible an unreflective drift into becoming simply a version of English law; not because Smith was anti-English but because, in his view, English law was not invariably the best or most just law available for assimilation into the Scottish (or any other) legal system. In a straight comparison, Scots law, properly understood, and especially Scots private law, had many advantages over English law; and most of these strengths came from the continental European or Civil Law influences that historically had gone into the making of the law. Smith's argument was for a renewal of these influences: in 1970, however, as his contribution to *The Scottish Debate* makes clear, he was pessimistic about this ever happening, even if there was

31 MacCormick, *Questioning Sovereignty* 204.
32 See in general E Reid and D L Carey Miller (eds), *A Mixed Legal System in Transition: T B Smith and the Progress of Scots Law* (2005).
33 T B Smith, "Scottish nationalism, law and self-government", in MacCormick, *The Scottish Debate* (n 12) 34-51.
34 Smith, "Scottish nationalism" 49.

to be a greater degree of Scottish self-government.[35]

Smith's pessimism here reflects a truism that legal nationalism, however defined, and political nationalism do not necessarily sit happily together. Despite Neil's connection with Smith,[36] there is no sign in the former's writings that he subscribed to any version of legal nationalism; rather the opposite. The promotion of a distinctive Scots law was not a reason for pursuing Scottish self-government. In a review of another collection of essays entitled *Independence and Devolution: The Legal Implications for Scotland* and published in 1976 as the then Labour Government half-heartedly attempted to provide for a measure of Scottish home rule, Neil wrote approvingly of a comment made by one of the contributors (Eric Clive) that "a distinctive legal system is about as desirable as a distinctive system of weights and measures",[37] and added:

> If the Scots identity is manifested in outward and visible form only in banknotes, tartans, legal doctrines and forms of religious observance, to these Scots must cleave or lose all sense of identity. If legislative and political power returns to Edinburgh, it can cheerfully be used in pursuit of quite new goals, and with a traditional eclecticism of borrowing, since it will be the Scots' own choice, not something foisted on Scotland from without. It is as though we no longer need the symbolic nationalism of a Walter Scott now that the political nationalism at least of an Andrew Fletcher is gaining ground.[38]

However, in the reference here to "traditional eclecticism of borrowing", there is at least a nod in the direction of Smith's brand of legal nationalism, and this is reinforced in an important further sentence of the same review:

35 For discussion see H L MacQueen, "Two Toms and an ideology for Scots law: T B Smith and Lord Cooper of Culross", in Reid and Carey Miller, *A Mixed Legal System in Transition* (n 32) 44-72 at 63-72.

36 And the friendship of Neil's father with Andrew Dewar Gibb, prominent legal and political nationalist, for whom see L Farmer, "Under the shadow over Parliament House: the strange case of legal nationalism", in L Farmer and S Veitch (eds), *The State of Scots Law* (2001) 151-164; H MacQueen, "'A picture of what will be some day the law of the civilised nations': comparative law and the destiny of Scots law", in *Towards Europeanization of Private Law: Essays in Honour of Professor Jerzy Rajski* (2007) 521-538 at 522-526.

37 E M Clive, "Scottish family law", in J P Grant (ed), *Independence and Devolution: The Legal Implications for Scotland* (1976) 162-174 at 173.

38 Neil MacCormick, "Book review" (1976) *Scots Law Times (News)* 303. The reference to Walter Scott is to (1) his well-known defence (under the pseudonym "Malachi Malagrowther") of the continuation of Scottish banknotes in 1826; (2) the tartan in which he draped Scotland and George IV when the king visited Edinburgh in 1823; and perhaps also (3) his famous line challenging the introduction of civil jury trial in Scotland in 1806: "No, no – 'tis no laughing matter; little by little, whatever your wishes may be, you will destroy and undermine, until nothing of what makes Scotland Scotland shall remain." See generally now S Kelly, *Scott-land: The Man Who Invented a Nation* (2010). For Andrew Fletcher, Scottish patriot and opponent of the 1707 Union, see most recently J Robertson, "Fletcher, Andrew, of Saltoun (1653?-1716)", *Oxford Dictionary of National Biography* (2004; online edn, Jan 2008, *http://www.oxforddnb.com/view/article/9720*, accessed 25 July 2011).

Nevertheless, a concentration not necessarily on the principles of the past, but on the need for a lucid, principled and rationally presented legal system, will surely remain a worthy goal of legal endeavour – not because it is our tradition only, but because in this respect the tradition is good if nowadays more honoured in the breach than in the observance.[39]

This casts suggestive backlight upon some of Neil's earliest writings, which were actually focused on substantive Scots law. In the first of two pieces published in the News section of the *Scots Law Times* in 1967, he discussed the law of the foreshore in Scotland in the course of commenting critically on a recent English court decision denying any right to gather sea coal from beaches near Hartlepool.[40] The article draws on older Scottish legal writings, such as Thomas Craig's early seventeenth-century *Jus Feudale*, Stair's *Institutions* (first published 1681), John Erskine's *Institute* (published 1773), Green's *Encyclopaedia of Scots Law*, and a number of Scottish cases. Scots law's relative clarity and promotion of liberty is contrasted favourably with the restrictive uncertainty of English law.

By contrast, the second piece, at first blush, appears alarmingly open to converting Scots into English law, since it argues that the then recently passed and England-only Misrepresentation Act 1967 "could with profit be applied to Scotland".[41] But on closer inspection, Neil's point turns out to be that the "principles" rather than the *ipsissima verba* of the statute should be extended into Scots law. He is perfectly well aware, under reference to the earlier work of T B Smith and J J Gow, that the concept of misrepresentation has no independent status in Scots law, which focuses instead on the error induced by the misrepresentation as a ground for the reduction of the contract. But what the principles of the Act offer is the idea that damages can be used as an alternative to reduction with its prerequisite of *restitutio in integrum*, the limitations and potential injustice of which had long before been exposed in *Boyd & Forrest v Glasgow & South Western Railway Company*.[42] There are Smithian (and indeed Roman law) echoes in Neil's observation:

[I]t is at least arguable that such provisions as those of the Act would in some measure restore the principles of the older Scots law. They would go far to restoring the bona fide character of the consensual contracts; they achieve a similar, if wider, effect to that of the old rule that culpa lata dolo aequiparatur; and lastly, while they do not quite restore the seller's liability for latent defects they do much to mitigate

---

39 MacCormick, "Book review" at 304.
40 "Seabathing, sunbathing and sea coal" (1967) *Scots Law Times (News)* 69.
41 N MacCormick, "The Misrepresentation Act, 1967" (1967) *Scots Law Times (News)* 190 (quotation at 191). There is a striking contrast with contemporary criticism of the Act in England: see P S Atiyah and G H Treitel, "The Misrepresentation Act 1967" (1967) 30 *Modern Law Review* 369.
42 1915 SC (HL) 20.

the worst effects of caveat emptor. Not for the first time, we may observe the irony of English law seeking, as pastures new, fields once happily grazed by Scots.[43]

Neil again followed a trail over which Smith had previously passed when in 1970 he contributed to a major debate on the subject of *jus quaesitum tertio* – that is, third party rights in contract.[44] This was one of the classic subjects illustrative of the fundamental differences between Scots and English law, with the former recognising third party rights and the latter applying a strict doctrine of privity of contract to deny them.[45] The foundational text on the subject in Scots law was a passage in Stair's *Institutions*,[46] which had however been reinterpreted by the courts, and in particular by Lord Dunedin in a House of Lords case in 1920,[47] in such a way as to narrow its scope very considerably. Smith had urged the restoration of the law to the position espoused by Stair; others, while recognising that Lord Dunedin had distorted Stair's meaning, argued that Stair's position did not cover all the subsequent authorities on *jus quaesitum tertio*. Neil's contribution was basically in support of the Stair as against the Dunedin position, on the grounds that the former was more clearly in line with general legal principles, and was also, unlike the Dunedin view, internally coherent and consistent. As a position, Neil's conclusion on Stair's meaning was to be the subject of later criticism.[48] But the significant point for us to observe is the importance he attached to a principled, reasoned and coherent approach to a problem of Scots law.

We shall return later to the importance of Stair for Neil more generally. Here the point I want to develop is that Neil's commitment to a rational law and legal system based on principle was in fact deeply congruent with the

43 MacCormick, "The Misrepresentation Act 1967" 192. It is beyond the scope of the present article (and the powers of the present writer) to comment in any detail on Neil's knowledge of Roman law as an influence in his thinking; but it should not be forgotten that he was the published translator of Book I of the Digest. See further below, e.g. at n 59. The authority of Roman law in Europe (including Scotland) from the Middle Ages on is another interesting example of living law's non-dependence upon sovereign power: see further N Jansen, *The Making of Legal Authority: Non-legislative Codifications in Historical and Comparative Perspective* (2010), especially ch 1. Jansen also discusses medieval canon law, the American Restatements, the Unidroit Principles of International Commercial Contracts, and recent European private law texts in this context.

44 D N MacCormick, "Jus quaesitum tertio: Stair v Dunedin" (1970) *Juridical Review* 228. For the contemporary debate on the subject see H L MacQueen, "Third party rights in contract", in K Reid and R Zimmermann (eds), *A History of Private Law in Scotland*, 2 vols (2000) vol 2, 220-251 at 247.

45 English law has since changed with the passage of the Contracts (Rights of Third Parties) Act 1999.

46 Stair, *Inst* I.10.5.

47 *Carmichael v Carmichael's Executrix* 1920 SC (HL) 95.

48 Geoffrey MacCormack, "A note on Stair's use of the term 'Pollicitatio'" (1976) JR 121; Stipulations in Favour of Third Parties (Scot Law Com Memorandum No 38, 1977) para 12; W W McBryde, *The Law of Contract in Scotland*, 3rd edn (2007) para 10.30.

aspect of Scottish legal nationalism that argued that a fundamental feature of Scots private law was its sense of internal structure and coherence. But I think it fair to say that after 1970 it would be many years before Neil returned to the substance of Scots private law. It remained a point of reference in the sense that classic Scots private law (and other) cases were treated in all his major writings, but it was not usually their Scottishness that mattered. Rather, it was the way in which they (along with many other cases from England, albeit most often of a public rather than a private law nature) could be used to illustrate the judges' commitment to rationality in arguing out and justifying their decisions. At the same time, however, he continued to be alive to ongoing academic debate about these cases. For example, he treated *Donoghue v Stevenson* at length throughout *Legal Reasoning and Legal Theory* in 1978;[49] by the time he came back to it in *Practical Reason in Law and Morality* thirty years later, his thinking about it was fully informed by much work done during that intervening time on the background of the case and its participants by such scholars as Lord Rodger of Earlsferry and Professor Bill McBryde.[50] Indeed, their work enabled him to plunge more deeply into the moral as distinct from the legal questions posed by the case.

Neil's awareness of the continuing commitment of Scots private law to a sense of its own systematic and rational nature must have been at least sharpened by the work he did for T B Smith's last great project, *The Laws of Scotland: Stair Memorial Encyclopaedia*, the many volumes of which began to appear in the later 1980s. Neil's contribution, published in 1990, was a long article on "General Legal concepts", the aim of which he explained as follows:

> The task of this title in the Encyclopaedia is to provide an exhaustive explanation and analysis of the general normative concepts in their legal application, and to give such an account of the specialised legal concepts (most of them the subject of special discussion in other titles) as will facilitate locating them in the general conceptual framework of a legal system.[51]

Neil's chosen starting point was Stair's famous definition of law as "the dictate of reason" and the contrast between that and the Austinian positivism which identified law as the command of a sovereign.[52] "Stair's conception of

---

49 N MacCormick, *Legal Reasoning and Legal Theory* (1978; reissued with a new foreword, 1994). See the book's Table of Cases for references to *Donoghue v Stevenson* 1932 SC (HL) 31.

50 The relevant works are cited in *Practical Reason* at 182 n 15. For Neil's discussion see *Practical Reason* 181-192. The whole literature on the story of the case is now thoroughly surveyed in E Reid, "The snail in the ginger beer float: *Donoghue v Stevenson*", in Grant and Sutherland (n 26) 83-99.

51 N MacCormick, "General legal concepts", in *The Laws of Scotland: Stair Memorial Encyclopaedia* vol 11 (1990) paras 1001-1136 at para 1005.

52 MacCormick, "General legal concepts" para 1001. See Stair, *Inst* I.1.1.

law," Neil wrote, "is preferable to those which stress the merely imperative and voluntaristic aspects of law".[53] He also observed that if law was necessarily linked to the concept of a state, "[i]t will be noted by inference from this that the legal system of Scotland for the moment exists as a system of positive law only by virtue of being a sub-system of that which constitutes the United Kingdom of Great Britain and Northern Ireland".[54] He did not pursue the point further, but it was clearly implicit, both in the immediate and the wider context, that Neil did not accept its truth. (Had he done so, it would also have been a necessary conclusion that English law was likewise but a sub-system within the United Kingdom.)

What followed in the Encyclopaedia article was an analysis of the core ideas of a legal system – lawful and unlawful conduct, duties, obligations, persons and personality, capacity, status, rights, things and institutions, rules and principles, and (particularly interesting) good faith – as manifested in and illustrated by Scots law, and in particular (although not exclusively) private law. Scots law Neil saw as "founded on principles" more than upon precedents or other kinds of rules, and this was a good thing so long as the Scots lawyer had a "clear conception of the nature of such principles ... grounded in human values, drawing reasonable lines between the tolerable and the unacceptable in terms of these values, and providing a rationalisation of existing customary rules, case law rules (precedents) and statutory provisions".[55] Hence the criminal courts' then recent decision, that a shopkeeper's supply of materials for purposes of solvent abuse by children was criminal, was justified although no specific rule had existed before to criminalise such conduct.[56] Later on in the article Neil also argued for the general validity of a master distinction of Scots law between real and personal rights, rejecting the Hohfeldian notion of "multital rights", which was then the subject of serious debate in the (as it now seems) unlikely forum provided by the *Journal of the Law Society of Scotland*.[57]

The Encyclopaedia article was later re-worked to become Part 2 of *Institutions of Law*, published in 2007. That title for the book did not simply flow from Neil's theory of law as institutional normative order or institutional fact; nor was it by way of a tribute to Stair's great work or, indeed, to the *Institutes of Natural Law* published in 1872 by Neil's predecessor

---

53 MacCormick, "General legal concepts" para 1002.
54 MacCormick, "General legal concepts" para 1004.
55 MacCormick, "General legal concepts" para 1011.
56 *Khaliq v Her Majesty's Advocate* 1984 JC 43.
57 See MacCormick, "General legal concepts" paras 1099-1112; for the debate (involving Gerry Maher, George Gretton and Scott Styles), see para 1106 n 2.

Lorimer.[58] Part 2 is labelled "Persons, Acts and Relations", and the treatment is generalised rather than rooted in Scots law (although traces of its Scottish origin can still be detected in the footnotes). It begins, however, in Roman law: "Even in the twenty-first century, one can still say rather as Gaius said twenty centuries ago, that all law concerns persons, things and actions."[59] This is, of course, the institutional scheme of law, set out most influentially in Justinian's *Institutes* and followed not only in many of the European civil codes, but also (although not uncritically) in the early Scottish institutional writers – Stair, Lord Bankton (1685-1760) and John Erskine (1695-1768) – as well as by Professor David Hume (1757-1838; nephew of the philosopher) in his influential lectures to the law students of Edinburgh University between 1786 and 1822.[60] Neil's order of treatment of his subject accordingly changes from that in the Encyclopaedia article: he begins with persons and personality. "There can," he says, "be no normative order without persons, for what is ordered is the conduct of persons and the treatment they are to receive".[61] From there he can move on to wrongs and duties, personal rights and obligations, and property, i.e. all together, things. Into this he could draw, additionally, discussions of the concept of intellectual property and the "splitting" of ownership between trustee and beneficiary in the English law of trusts as institutional legal facts. With the latter he cited, but did not discuss in any detail, important comparative and analytical work by an Edinburgh colleague, Professor George Gretton, developing the notion of the trustee's "dual patrimony" as another way to resolve the difficulties of split ownership in the trust.[62] But perhaps more surprisingly the Encyclopaedia discussion of good faith referred to above was not carried into *Institutions of Law*, and I have found no reference to the subject in any of the other volumes of the "Law, State and Practical Reason" series.[63] Nor, I think, does he deal at any point with the law of actions.

A vital observation in Neil's discussion of persons and personality in law is that "[i]nstitutional normative order itself institutionalizes the concept of the

---

58 On this latter work, reprinted in Germany as recently as 1987, see J W Cairns, "Lorimer, James (1818–1890)", *Oxford Dictionary of National Biography* (2004; online edn, Jan 2008, *http://www.oxforddnb.com/view/article/17016*, accessed 25 July 2011).

59 MacCormick, *Institutions* 77.

60 See generally J W Cairns, "Institutional writings in Scotland reconsidered" (1983) 4 *Journal of Legal History* 76.

61 MacCormick, *Institutions* 77.

62 See G L Gretton, "Trusts without equity" (2000) 49 *International and Comparative Law Quarterly* 599.

63 For the discussion of good faith, see MacCormick, "General legal concepts" (n 50) paras 1125-1135.

person".[64] This led him to be critical of any cack-handed distinction in law between "natural" persons, i.e. human beings, and "juristic" persons such as corporations. The latter concept was not a legal "fiction":

> The key fact to note is that human beings are in their very nature collaborative and social beings and that there are some acts which can only be joint acts of collaborating individuals ... Likewise, there are some harms and misfortunes which are necessarily corporate ... Acting corporately, or group-wise, is entirely natural to human beings, although indeed it is dependent on human convention, contrivance and organization. Convention, contrivance, and organization are also natural to human beings ... The fact of the matter surely is that the law's *non-personification* of certain types of social collectivity is far more a matter of fiction than its conferment of personality is in the case of others.[65]

Scots law thus earned praise for its recognition (contrasting with the English law position) of the personality of a partnership as distinct from those of the individual partners, albeit perhaps it did not press the concept far enough.[66] It would have interested Neil that in recent years the Scottish Law Commission has recommended not only extension of the personality of the partnership but also its recognition in the case of unincorporated associations.[67] He would probably have shared the Commission's frustration and disappointment that neither of these recommendations looks likely to be implemented soon, since, thanks to the current reservations in the devolution settlement, each can only be enacted in the Westminster Parliament and the relevant United Kingdom government department (the Department for Business, Innovation and Skills, or BIS) has declared its unwillingness to take either any further for the moment.[68] Within a clearly devolved area, however, the Commission has also discussed but ultimately rejected the possibility of giving trusts legal personality as a preferable solution to the problems currently addressed by the dual patrimony theory.[69] The Commission's discussion drew on Neil's

---

64 MacCormick, *Institutions* 77.
65 MacCormick, *Institutions* 84.
66 Neil cited on this P Hemphill, "The personality of partnerships in Scotland" (1984) *Juridical Review* 208. For the personality of the firm in Scots law, see Partnership Act 1890 s 4(2). The concept pre-existed the 1890 Act, however: see Hemphill, "Personality of partnerships" 209-216.
67 Joint Report on Partnership Law (Law Com No 283; Scot Law Com No 192, 2003) pt V; Report on Unincorporated Associations (Scot Law Com No 217, 2009). The recommendations of the Report on Partnership with regard to personality apply also to English law.
68 Annual Report 2009 (Scot Law Com No 220, 2010) 7; Annual Report 2010 (Scot Law Com No 223, 2011) 11. The disappointment about non-implementation of the unincorporated associations Report is somewhat tempered by the introduction on 1 April 2011 of the Scottish Charitable Incorporated Organisation which enables unincorporated charities to gain legal personality. See further the website of the Office of the Scottish Charities Regulator at *http://www.oscr.org.uk/ news-and-events/latest-news/first-scio-approved/*, accessed 25 July 2011.
69 Discussion Paper on The Nature and Constitution of Trusts (Scot Law Com DP No 133, 2006), pt 2.

concept of law as institutional fact but not, unfortunately, on his specific comments about the law of persons;[70] and perforce it could not take note of his later published difficulties with the dual patrimony idea.[71] Meantime the Scottish Parliament has plugged some but not all of the gaps in the criminal law with the Criminal Justice and Licensing (Scotland) Act 2010, sections 65-68 of which enable the solemn prosecutions of organisations as such, including partnerships and unincorporated associations.[72]

That thinking through the idea of personality systematically is important is confirmed by the recent Scottish case of *Balmer v Her Majesty's Advocate*.[73] A partnership ran a nursing home that was destroyed by fire, killing fourteen of the forty residents. The partnership was subsequently dissolved and the business transferred to a limited company. The three partners were charged on indictment with a number of health and safety offences under statute. The prosecutions were dismissed because the offences could be committed only by an employer, and the partners argued successfully that the partnership was the employer. When a prosecution was then brought against the partnership, the case was again dismissed since the firm no longer existed; another attempt to prosecute the partners as surviving partners of the dissolved firm was also dismissed. The Scottish Law Commission has published proposals on how the difficulty exposed by this case may best be addressed, involving some limited continuation of a partnership's personality, despite dissolution, for the purpose of establishing criminal liability.[74] This is similar to a proposal with regard to continuing the civil liabilities of a dissolved partnership already made by the Commission jointly with the Law Commission of England and Wales in 2003.[75]

A reviewer of *Institutions of Law*, generally favourable to the book, described its Part 2 as "certainly solid, with some interesting points raised, but perhaps inevitably largely unexciting".[76] This fairly downbeat assessment may

---

70 As stated in MacCormick, "General legal concepts" (n 51) paras 1040-1044.

71 MacCormick, *Institutions* 151.

72 Previously there was specific legislative provision only for summary prosecutions of partnerships. See also s 53 of the 2010 Act, which allows a partner to be found guilty of a "corporate offence" committed by the partnership where it is proved that the offence was committed with the consent or connivance, or through the neglect, of the partner concerned (whether alone or with others).

73 2008 SLT 799. More detail on the background to the case can be found in the report of the Fatal Accident Inquiry into the deaths at the Rosepark Nursing Home, available on the Scottish Courts website at *http://www.scotcourts.gov.uk/opinions/2011FAI18.pdf*, accessed 25 July 2011.

74 See Discussion Paper on Criminal Liability of Partnerships (Scot Law Com DP No 150, 2011).

75 Joint Report on Partnership Law (n 67) para 7.32; implemented by clauses 39 and 45 of the draft Bill appended to the Report.

76 D Dwyer, "Beyond Kelsen and Hart? MacCormick's *Institutions of Law*" (2008) 71(5) *Modern Law Review* 823 at 827.

be valid from the perspective of the legal philosopher; but the book certainly feels different to a private lawyer struggling to understand and justify the basic concepts and structure of his subject. Jurisprudence too often seems to the private lawyer to be pre-occupied above all with public and criminal law, and to neglect – or be unexcited by – the overall structure of that part of the law that is at the core of most ordinary social life as well as legal practice.[77] Further, as Nils Jansen has recently observed, private law's own conceptual and intellectual structures make it at least stand somewhat apart from the general political process.[78] Although Neil never studied Scots private law in the formal setting of a law degree programme, he could not be accused of neglecting it and in *Institutions of Law* he put it close to the centre of law as institutional normative order. One can perhaps suggest that it was a growing insight into the significance of private law that helped him to articulate ever more fully the intellectual position that he came to term "post-positivism". In turn, Scots private lawyers armed with Neil's analyses can come fully to grips with their subject as a system of thought, develop an intelligent critique where necessary, and propose principled reform where and when appropriate. It is a substantial legacy.

D. STAIR, HUME, SMITH AND KANT: NATURAL LAW AND ENLIGHTENMENT

In the foreword to *Institutions of Law*, Neil mentioned that he had written the book in Scotland and was "mindful of the inspiration to be drawn from the great writers of our Enlightenment".[79] But, in point of fact, the influence of Scottish Enlightenment thought on Neil's work is most evident not in *Institutions of Law*, but in the last and perhaps the most personal and deeply felt of the "Law, State, and Practical Reason" series, *Practical Reason in Law and Morality*. The book opens with David Hume's negative answer to the question "Can reason be practical?"[80] Neil had long before published a detailed critique of Hume's perception of reason as the slave of the passions[81]

---

77 A notable exception is E J Weinrib, *The Idea of Private Law* (1995). This reader was helped less by W Lucy, *The Philosophy of Private Law* (2007). There are excellent studies of the private law institutions of property, contract and delict (tort), but when in the English language these are often coloured more than they perhaps realise by Common Law concepts of these subjects.
78 Jansen, *The Making of Legal Authority* (n 43) 19.
79 MacCormick, *Institutions* v.
80 MacCormick, *Practical Reason* 1.
81 MacCormick, *Legal Reasoning and Legal Theory* 2-8, 265-274. Here and elsewhere (see e.g. MacCormick, *Legal Right and Social Democracy: Essays in Legal and Political Philosophy* (1982) 67; *Questioning Sovereignty* 6; *Institutions* 286, 299; *Practical Reason* 72), Neil drew on the work

– "Hume has indeed too passive a view of reason"[82] – but came, I think, to feel a need to reconsider the statement also made in that critique that nonetheless Hume was "not wrong in contending that our affectively valuing anything belongs to the realm of our attitudes and pre-dispositions; even in the case of reason, it is not *reason* which is expressed if we set value on rationality".[83] *Practical Reason in Law and Morality* is that reconsideration. But while in some sense Hume provided the point for departure in the book, Neil thereafter referred to him in it only infrequently (perhaps characteristically kindly in relation to those with whom he disagreed, even when they had been dead for over 200 years). Instead, he found the answer to the problem in a fascinating amalgam based upon the thought of Stair, Adam Smith and Immanuel Kant (1724-1804). Neil probably knew, as I did not before starting the research for this paper, that the last-named of these believed himself to be both the grandson of a Scot who had abandoned his native heath for East Prussia and the son of a Königsberg man who spelled his surname "Cant" in the Scottish fashion.[84] But since Kant apparently never moved further than ten miles from his native town, it is probably too much to claim him as yet another enlightened Scotsman with decisive influence upon Neil's final statement on practical reason as a fundamental of both morality and law.

No one, it should be noted, has done more than Neil to bring Stair's name to the attention of the modern world, even if Neil himself always gracefully acknowledged the extent of his own indebtedness to the insights upon Stair's work provided by a lecture given in Glasgow by Archie Campbell as long ago as 1954.[85] This is not the place for a detailed exposition of what Neil drew from Stair, Smith and Kant to produce his concluding views. They can be best understood in the pages where they were expressed; so far as Stair is

---

of Hume's contemporary opponent Thomas Reid (1710-1796), Adam Smith's successor in the Chair of Moral Philosophy at Glasgow University 1764-1781. Further on Reid, see T Cuneo and R van Woudenberg (eds), *The Cambridge Companion to Thomas Reid* (2000).

82 MacCormick, *Legal Reasoning and Legal Theory* 269.

83 See the foreword to the 1994 reprint of *Legal Reasoning and Legal Theory*, xvi ("the Humean stance taken in my last chapter needs to be radically reconsidered").

84 M Kuehn, *Kant: A Biography* (2001) 427-428.

85 A Hunter Campbell, *The Structure of Stair's Institutions* (1955). Also influential for Neil here was Dr W Lamont (see n 2), "sometime Reader in Moral Philosophy in this [*Glasgow*] university, from whom as a student here I learned of Stair's hitherto neglected qualities as a moral and political philosopher" ("The rational discipline of law", 1981 *Juridical Review* 146). For Neil's other major writings on Stair apart from this just-cited article and *Practical Reason*, see his *Legal Right and Social Democracy* (n 81) ch 4 (a re-working of a 1979 article on Stair and Locke); "Stair as analytical jurist", in D M Walker, *Stair Tercentenary Studies*, Stair Society vol 33 (1981) 187-199; "Stair and the natural law tradition: still relevant?", in H L MacQueen (ed), *Miscellany Six*, Stair Society vol 54 (2009) 1-10.

concerned, they were also luminously drawn together in the 2007 Annual Lecture of the Stair Society published in the Society's sixth Miscellany volume.[86] It is sufficient for present purposes first to suggest the significance of his decision to christen the offspring of the marriage of Smith's impartial spectator to Kant's categorical imperative the "Smithian categorical imperative" rather than the "Kantian impartial spectator". Neil preferred the relative concreteness of giving full weight to human sentiment and emotion in moral judgements against the transcendentalism of trying without reference to emotion to rationalise one's action as though it embodied a universal rule. Kant had at least had the opportunity to think about the impartial spectator; what would Smith have made of the categorical imperative had he had a similar opportunity? Neil boldly gave his fellow Scot the chance to do what he could not have done for himself.

I have also already quoted, as Neil himself did frequently too, Stair's vital dictum that law is the dictate of reason.[87] I think Neil does not quote in *Practical Reason* (although he does elsewhere)[88] another interesting passage in Stair which in essence prefers judge-made to legislative law:

> [T]he nations are more happy whose laws have entered by long custom, wrung out from their debates upon particular cases, until it come to the consistence of a fixed and known custom … [*In contrast*] In statutes the law giver must at once balance … conveniences and inconveniences, wherein he may, and often doth, fall short … [T]hose statutes are best which are approbatory, or correctory, of experienced customs.[89]

Here, it may be suggested, was the process underpinning the Smithian categorical imperative by which law might be determined through the exercise of human reason upon the decisions of many particular cases. Also crucial to the exposition in *Practical Reason* was what Neil called "Stair's Three Steps", the principles of obedience, freedom and engagement, under which, "[p]utting it simply, we have to do what is right, keep our engagements, and act for the best within the sphere of discretion bestowed on us by the principle of freedom".[90] For positive law, the dictates of reason produced three principles – society, property and commerce – all aimed "at the maintenance, flourishing, and peace of society, the security of property,

---

86 MacCormick, "Stair and the natural law tradition".
87 Stair, *Inst* I.1.1.
88 E.g. in "Rational discipline of law" (n 85) 148; see also "Stair as analytical jurist" (n 83) 190, and *H L A Hart* (n 5) 149.
89 Stair, *Inst* I.1.15.
90 MacCormick, *Practical Reason* 107.

and the freedom of commerce".[91] So, although Stair was in many ways a classic exponent of the Protestant natural law theory against which the enlightened Smith and Kant (and Hume) reacted, his thinking was actually very largely congruent with that of Smith in *The Theory of Moral Sentiments* and *The Wealth of Nations*. Natural law and Enlightenment thought could make common cause together.

Also noteworthy is the way in which Neil illustrates by reference to Scottish historical experience the inadequacies of Stair and Smith's thinking in dealing with problems of distributive, environmental and inter-generational justice. It was in pursuit of the principles of society, property and commerce that the massacre of Glencoe took place in 1691, with Stair's eldest son as the minister of government whose signature sealed the fate of the unfortunate MacDonalds.[92] Enlightenment thinking and values also underlay the Highland Clearances of the eighteenth and nineteenth centuries, of which deep memories were still being handed down on Mull in Neil's childhood.[93] But, Neil argued, the reworking of that Enlightenment thought into the Smithian categorical imperative had at least the potential to enable issues of distributive justice to be addressed in a more satisfying way. Had he lived longer, he might have wished to apply the imperative to the debate about bankers' continuing contractual entitlements to enormous financial bonuses despite the banks' even more enormous losses and taxpayer-funded bailouts in the period 2008-2010.[94]

Rejection of Hume's position on reason did not entail rejection on all other fronts. In a lecture to the David Hume Institute in Edinburgh in 2006 Neil suggested that Hume's conceptualisation of the "Perfect Commonwealth" was apt to describe the structure of the European Union and to meet the criticism of "democratic deficit" so often laid against the Union.[95] Again, that argument must be left to speak for itself; but Neil confessed himself during the lecture "a still rather star-struck fan of David Hume".[96] Alas, Neil's death dashed the hopes of the David Hume Institute for more from him on Hume, when it

---

91 Stair, *Inst* I.1.18.
92 MacCormick, *Practical Reason* 130.
93 MacCormick, *Practical Reason* 131-134.
94 See the comments in *Practical Reason* (134-135) attacking the large payout received by the departing chief executive of the failed Northern Rock bank in 2008 while other employees would be made redundant with little or no pay-off and shareholders went uncompensated for the losses inflicted on them following the board's disastrous decision to enter sub-prime mortgage markets.
95 Sir N MacCormick, *The European Union and the Idea of a Perfect Commonwealth*, David Hume Institute, Hume Occasional Papers No 68 (2006), drawing upon D Hume, *The Idea of a Perfect Commonwealth*, last of the *Political Discourses* first published in 1752.
96 MacCormick, *The European Union and the Idea of a Perfect Commonwealth* 9.

appointed him its President for a term of office that should have covered the tercentenary of the great man's birth. Perhaps, however, my hunch that Neil would have preferred the company of the gregarious and convivial Hume to that of the more reclusive figures of either Smith or Kant, or that of his fellow Glasgow alumnus and philosopher, the rather unbending and formidable Stair, is not altogether without foundation in experience.[97] Certainly Hume and Neil both faced impending death in the same way, resolutely and sorrowing only for those whom they would leave behind.[98]

E. CONCLUSION

I hope that the observations offered here are not merely trivial pluckings of Scottish references from the body of Neil's work but have rather highlighted something that is significant and substantial for the full understanding and use of that work in future. Once again, in writing about a departed friend and colleague, I am left with feelings of both awe and gratitude for his achievements, example and, above all, friendship. Like Bill Wilson and Peter Birks before him, Neil MacCormick seems never to have stopped thinking or been afraid to change his mind.[99] He has left us with an ordered heap of good learning,[100] institutional in the best senses of that heavily laden word, and we must now make of it what we can without him. As we take up that task, let us remember that his was the work of a great Scotsman, and try to ensure that it continues to be appreciated and applied, in Scotland and beyond.

97 For the characters of Hume, Smith and Kant, see respectively R Graham, *The Great Infidel: A Life of David Hume* (2004); N Phillipson, *Adam Smith: An Enlightened Life* (2010); Kuehn, *Kant: A Biography* (n 84), all passim. Hume's letter seeking to prise the reclusive Smith out of Kirkcaldy to Edinburgh (or some mid-point) is surely one of the most entertaining communications ever made by one philosopher to another: see Phillipson, *Adam Smith* 202. Stair, not widely popular in his lifetime, awaits a modern full-length biography but in the meantime see J D Ford, "Dalrymple, James, first Viscount Stair (1619-1695)", *Oxford Dictionary of National Biography* (2004; online edn, Oct 2009 *http://www.oxforddnb.com/view/article/7050*, accessed 24 July 2011).

98 Compare James Boswell's famous account of his visit to the dying Hume (H Milne (ed), *Boswell's Edinburgh Journals 1767-1786* (2001) 256-258) with MacCormick, *Practical Reason* 207-209.

99 See my contributions to the memorial volumes for Professors Bill Wilson and Peter Birks: H L MacQueen (ed), *Scots Law into the Twenty-first Century* (1996), chs 1 and 2; A Burrows and Lord Rodger of Earlsferry (eds), *Mapping the Law: Essays in Memory of Peter Birks* (2006), ch 21.

100 Cf T Wood, *An Institute of the Laws of England, or the Lawes of England in their Natural Order* (1720), Preface, ii (referring to English Common Law as a "heap of good learning" in need of institutional (in the classical legal sense) ordering).

2 The Works of Neil MacCormick: A Bibliography and a Bibliographical Essay on Scottish Themes

Maksymilian Del Mar[*]

A. BIBLIOGRAPHY

(1) Preliminary remarks

The following bibliography proceeds in chronological order, listing publications under each year (where a publication covers two years, for example 1997-1998, the publication has been catalogued under the first year but the two years are noted in parentheses). All translations and reprints of MacCormick's works are catalogued immediately after and indented below

[*] Lecturer in Legal and Social Philosophy, Department of Law, Queen Mary, University of London.

the relevant publication. Although an attempt was made to list as many reprints and translations of MacCormick's works as could be located, it is unlikely that all are included here. Where the same piece, with the same title, has appeared in two different sources (sometimes with very minor modifications), the other source is noted and catalogued separately. Not all publications in languages other than English could be accessed to check if they were translations of previously or subsequently published work in English – where this is so, there is an asterisk ° next to the source. Under each year, the following order of publications is followed: (1) books; (2) lectures published as standalone pamphlets; (3) edited books; (4) special journal issues; (5) chapters; (6) articles; (7) reviews in journals; (8) reviews in newspapers; (9) translations of the works of others by MacCormick; (10) newspaper articles (any that could be found are listed here, but it is likely that there are others); (11) films; and (12) audio interviews. MacCormick's unpublished archives contain finalised drafts of three book reviews, published versions of which could not be found: (1) J Stone, *Human Law and Human Justice* (1965); (2) D Szechi (ed), *"Scotland's Ruine": Lockhart of Carnwath's Memoirs of the Union* (1995); and (3) H J Spaeth, *Supreme Court Policy-Making* (1979). Also included in the archives are drafts of short pieces on John MacCormick and Adam Smith commissioned by the *Scottish Review* as part of its "Greatest Scots" series; *Scottish Review* is an online journal, and despite best attempts, the published version of these pieces could not be located (it is likely that the pieces appeared in 2000).

(2) Note on parliamentary work

MacCormick was a Member of the European Parliament (MEP) from 1999 to 2004. Citing his parliamentary work, including official newsletters, reports, newspaper articles and other relevant documentation, falls outside the scope of this bibliography. This parliamentary work has, however, been preserved and catalogued by the Special Collections of the University of Edinburgh Library (Reference: GB 237 Coll-1049). Those interested in investigating MacCormick's parliamentary work can profitably begin by considering the following four documents: (1) "Subsidiarity, common sense, and local knowledge" (Contribution to the European Convention, Brussels, 18 September 2002, CONV 275/02, CONTRIB 94); (2) "Democracy at many levels: European constitutional reform" (Contribution to the European Convention, Brussels, 24 September 2002, CONV 298/02, CONTRIB 101); 3) "Stateless nations and the Convention's debate on regions" (Contribution to the European Convention, Brussels, 31 January 2003, CONV 525/03, CONTRIB

220); and 4) "Report on the communication from the Commission entitled 'A framework for target-based tripartite contracts and agreements between the Community, the States and regional and local authorities'" (Report as Rapporteur of the Committee of Constitutional Affairs, also known as the "MacCormick Report", 11 November 2003, A5-0401/2003).

(3) Acknowledgements

Many people have helped me to obtain and confirm the details included in this bibliography. As grateful as I am for all the help received, I hasten to add that any mistakes are my responsibility. I would like to thank (in alphabetical order): Maureen Allen, at the *Times Literary Supplement*; Fernando Atria; Aulis Aarnio; Peter Cane; Mathilde Cohen; Paolo Comanducci; Enrico Diciotti; Randy Gordon; Riccardo Guastini; Marcus Hahn-Lorber; Jaap Hage; Vincent Hendricks; Conrado Hübner Mendes; Hent Kalmo; Massimo La Torre; Óscar A. Lema Bouza, at the European Law Students" Association; Rebecca MacLeod; Hector MacQueen; Claudio Michelon; Nicola Moncur, at the Law and Europa Library, University of Edinburgh; Margaret Morrison and Rosemary O"Hare, at *The Herald Times*; Kimmo Nuotio; Giorgio Pino; Gerard Power and Katherine Read, at the Institute for Advanced Legal Studies, University of London; Raimo Siltala; Leonor Moral Soriano; Magnus Ulväng; Ros Wallington, at Oxford University Press; Sue Watters, from the Pi Gamma Mu International Honour Society for Social Sciences; and Bei Yang. Special thanks are also due to Zenon Bańkowski, Douglas Brodie, Flora MacCormick, William Twining and Neil Walker. This bibliography was completed while I was a Visiting Research Fellow and a European Visiting Fellow funded by the Royal Society of Edinburgh (RSE) and the Caledonian Research Fund (CRF) at the Institute for Advanced Studies in the Humanities in Edinburgh (IASH). My most sincere thanks go to the RSE, CRF and IASH, as well as to the School of Law, University of Edinburgh; without their support, completing this bibliography would have been impossible.

(4) Bibliography

1966

"Can *Stare Decisis* be abolished?" 11 *Juridical Review (New Series)* 197-213.
"Review of *Legal Systems and Lawyers' Reasonings* by J Stone" 11 *Juridical Review (New Series)* 187-191.
"Review of *Sovereignty within the Law* by A Larson, C W Jenks and others" 11 *Juridical Review (New Series)* 283-286.

1967

"Seabathing, sunbathing and sea coal" *Scots Law Times (News)* 69-71.

"The Misrepresentation Act, 1967" *Scots Law Times (News)* 190-192.

"Review of *Other People's Law* by Lord Kilbrandon" 12(2) *Journal of the Law Society of Scotland* 77-79.

1969

"Balliol's experimental summer school" 4 (Michaelmas) *Oxford Magazine* 44-46.

1970

The Scottish Debate (ed), London: Oxford University Press.

"Introduction", in N MacCormick (ed), *The Scottish Debate*, London: Oxford University Press, 1-3.

"Independence and constitutional change", in N MacCormick (ed), *The Scottish Debate*, London: Oxford University Press, 52-64.

"Delegated legislation and civil liberty" 86 *Law Quarterly Review* 171-180.

"Ius Quaesitum Tertio: Stair v Dunedin" 15 *Juridical Review* 228-246.

"Review of *Morality and the Law* by S E Stumpf" 20(80) *The Philosophical Quarterly* 300-301.

"Review of *The Ethics of Punishment* by W Moberly" 20(80) *The Philosophical Quarterly* 301-302.

1971

"Social services and controls", in H W R Wade (ed), *Annual Survey of Commonwealth Law*, London: Butterworths, 666-685.

"Review of *The Concept of a Legal System: An Introduction to the Theory of Legal System* by J Raz", 21(85) *The Philosophical Quarterly* 380-381.

"Review of *The Constitutional Decisions of John Marshall* ed by J P Cotton" 18(10) *Notes and Queries* 394-395.

1972

"Voluntary obligations and normative powers", 46 *Aristotelian Society (Supplementary Volume)* 59-78 (symposium with J Raz) (also published with modification as ch 10 in *Legal Right and Social Democracy* (1982)).

"Review of *Constitutional and Administrative Law* by S A de Smith" Summer, *Public Law*, 174-179.

1973

Law as Institutional Fact, Edinburgh University Inaugural Lecture, No 52, Edinburgh: Edinburgh University Press (also published in the *Law Quarterly Review* in 1974, and as ch 2 of *An Institutional Theory of Law* in 1986).

"Legal obligation and the imperative fallacy", in A W B Simpson (ed), *Oxford Essays in Jurisprudence, 2nd Series*, Oxford: Clarendon Press, 100-130.

"A note upon privacy", 89 *Law Quarterly Review* 23-27.

"Justice according to Rawls" 89 *Law Quarterly Review* 393-417.

1974

"Law as institutional fact" 90 *Law Quarterly Review* 102-129 (also published by Edinburgh University Press in 1973, and as ch 2 of *An Institutional Theory of Law* in 1986).

"Privacy: a question of definition", 1(1) *British Journal of Law and Society* 75-78.

"Principles of Law" 19 *Juridical Review (New Series)* 217-226.

"The rise of Scottish nationalism: a case of too little too late?" 64(256) *The Round Table* 425-438.

"Jurisprudence in the law course: a footnote" 13 *Journal of the Society of Public Teachers of Law (New Supplement)* 359-362 (1974-1975).

"A filial look at Home Rule's founding father" 20 November 1974, *The Scotsman* 13.

1975

Independence and Federalism After the Referendum, presented to the Andrew Fletcher Society in June 1975, Dundee: Andrew Fletcher Society, 10 pages.

"Rapports introductifs de la responsabilité considérée comme un droit" 2 *Revue de Sciences Criminelle et Droit Pénal Comparé* 484-497 (translated into French by D Chast) (presented at 21 Journées de défense sociales: Journées Franco-Ecossaises, Edinburgh, 25-27 September 1974).

"We need a new politics" February, *Life and Work* 12-18.

1976

Lawyers in their Social Setting (ed), Edinburgh: W Green & Son.

"Editor's Foreword" in N MacCormick (ed), *Lawyers in their Social Setting*, Edinburgh: W Green & Son, vii-ix.

"Accountability, professionalism and the Scottish judiciary", in M G Clarke and H M Drucker (eds), *Our Changing Scotland*, Edinburgh: Polygon Press, 79-86.

"Minority report" with I Aitken, T Brinton and J Haviland, *Report of the Committee on Financial Aid to Political Parties*, Cmnd 6601, 75-81.

"Justice: an un-original position" 3 *Dalhousie Law Journal* 367-384 (presented as a lecture at the Institut für Rechts- und Sozialphilosophie der Universität des Saarlandes, 1 June 1975) (also published with modification as ch 5 in *Legal Right and Social Democracy*, 1982).

"Children's rights: a test case for theories of right" 52(3) *Archiv für Rechts- und Sozialphilosophie* 305-316 (also published with modification as ch 8 in *Legal Right and Social Democracy*, 1982).

Translated into Spanish as "Los derechos de los niños: una prueba de fuego para las teorías de los derechos" (1988) 5 *Anuario de Filosofía del Derecho* 293-306.

Reprinted in C Nino (ed), *Rights*, The International Library of Essays in Law and Legal Theory, New York: New York University Press, 1992, 75-86.

"Formal justice and the form of legal arguments" 6 *Etudes de Logique Juridique* 103-118.

Excerpts included in M D A Freeman (ed), *Lloyd's Introduction to Jurisprudence*, London: Sweet & Maxwell, multiple editions, including 1994 and 2001.

"The mandate question" 12 *Question* (The Independent Political Review for Scotland) 8-9.

"Review of *How to Do Things with Rules* by W Twining and D Miers" 3(2) *British Journal of Law and Society* 279-282.

"Two-stranded support for legislative devolution" 5-6 February 1976, *The Scotsman* 7.

1977

Civil Liberties and the Law, presented at Heriot-Watt University on 25 October 1977, Edinburgh: Heriot-Watt University Special Lecture Series, 20 pages (also published with modification as ch 3 in *Legal Right and Social Democracy*, 1982).

"Rights in legislation", in P M S Hacker and J Raz (eds), *Law, Morality and Society*, Oxford: Clarendon Press, 189-209.

Translated into German by D Jaber, as "Rechte in der Gesetzgebung", in M Stepanians (ed), *Individuelle Rechte*, Paderborn: Mentis, 164-183.

"Challenging sociological definitions" 4(1) *British Journal of Law and Society* 87-94.

"Iudex qui litem suam fecit" *Acta Juridica* 149-165.

"The obligation of reparation" 78 *Proceedings of the Aristotelian Society (New Series)* 175-193 (1977-1978) (presented at a meeting of the Aristotelian Society, London, 20 March 1978) (also published with modification as ch 11 in *Legal Right and Social Democracy*, 1982).

"Review of *Political Alienation and Political Behavior* by D C Schwartz" 10(3) *Canadian Journal of Political Science* 673-674.

1978

Legal Reasoning and Legal Theory, Oxford: Clarendon Press (2nd edition in 1994 with Oxford University Press).

Excerpts, mainly from the "Introduction" reprinted under the title "Legal reasoning and legal theory", in N Kuenssberg (ed), *Argument Amongst Friends: Twenty Five Years of Sceptical Enquiry*, Edinburgh: The David Hume Institute, 2010, 28-34.

Translated into Chinese by J Feng yi, as *Fa lü tui li yu fa lü li lun*, Beijing: Fa lü chu ban she (2005).

Translated into French by J Gagey, as *Raisonnement Juridique et Théorie du Droit*, Paris: P U F, 1996.

Translated into Italian by A Schiavello, ed by V Villa, as *Ragionamento giuridico e teoria del diritto*, Torino: G Giappichelli, 2001.

Translated into Portuguese by W Barcellos, as *Argumentação jurídica e teoria do direito*, São Paulo: Martins Fontes, 2006.

Excerpts included in H Davies and D Holdcroft (eds), *Jurisprudence: Texts and Commentary*, London: Butterworths, 1991.

"The Motivation of judgement in the common law", in Ch Perelman and P Foriers (eds), *La Motivation des Décisions de Justice*, Brussels: Bruylant, 167-194 (presented as a lecture at the Centre National de Recherches de Logique, Brussels, 18 May 1976).

"Privacy and obscenity", in R Dhavan and C Davies (eds), *Censorship and Obscenity*, Oxford: Martin Robertson & Co, 76-97 (also published with modification as ch 9 in *Legal Right and Social Democracy* 1982).

"Does the United Kingdom have a constitution? Reflections on *MacCormick v Lord Advocate*" 29(1-2) *Northern Ireland Legal Quarterly* 1-20.

"Dworkin as pre-Benthamite" 87(4) *Philosophical Review* 585-607 (extended review essay of R Dworkin, *Taking Rights Seriously*) (also published with modification as ch 7 in *Legal Right and Social Democracy*, 1982).

Reprinted in M Cohen (ed), *Ronald Dworkin and Contemporary Juris-prudence*, London: Duckworth (1984) 182-201.

"Review of *Canadian Society in Historical Perspective* by S D Clark, and *The Canadian Class Structure* by D Forcese" 11(3) *Canadian Journal of Political Science* 676-677.

"Review of A Smith, *Lectures on Jurisprudence*, ed by R L Meek, D D Raphael, P G Stein" 88(352) *The Economic Journal* 837-839.

1979

"Constitutional points", in D I Mackay (ed), *Scotland: The Framework for Change*, Edinburgh: Paul Harris, 47-67.

"Nation and nationalism", in C MacLean (ed), *The Crown and the Thistle*, Edinburgh: Scottish Academic Press, 97-111 (also published with modification as ch 13 in *Legal Right and Social Democracy*, 1982).

"Constitution", in C MacLean (ed), *The Crown and the Thistle*, Edinburgh: Scottish Academic Press, 149-155 (also published in a modified version, by SUNY Press, in 1999).

"Law, obligation and consent: reflections on Stair and Locke" 65(3) *Archiv für Rechts- und Sozialphilosophie* 387-411 (presented as the Austin Lecture, UK Association for Legal and Social Philosophy in 1978) (also published with modification as ch 4 in *Legal Right and Social Democracy*, 1982).

"Review of *Law and Society: Crisis in Legal Ideals*, by E Kamenka, R Brown and E R S Tay" 27(3) *Political Studies* 525.

1980

"The coherence of a case and the reasonableness of doubt" 2 *Liverpool Law Review* 45-50.

Translated into German, as "Die Kohärenz eines Falles und die Vernünft-igkeit eines Zweifels", in M Martinek et al (eds), *Festschrift für Günther Jahr zum 70 Geburtstag*, Tübingen: J C B Mohr, 119-126.

"Wie ernst soll man Rechte Nehmen?", 11(1) *Rechtstheorie* 1-7 (review essay of R Dworkin, *Taking Rights Seriously*, 1978).

"Review of *Natural Law and Natural Rights*, by J Finnis", 28(4) *Political Studies* 651.

1981

H L A Hart, London: Edward Arnold (2nd edition, with substantive revisions, in 2008 with Stanford University Press).

Translated into Japanese by T Tsunoda, as *Hāto Hórigaku no zenizō*, Kōyō: Shobō (1996) (includes new preface).

Translated into Spanish by J M Pérez Bermejo, as *H L A Hart*, Madrid: Marcial Pons, 2010.

Chapter 4, "Social rules", translated into Spanish by L Emilfork, as "Reglas sociales" (1986) 28 *Revista de Ciencias Sociales* 297-319.

Excerpts included in H Davies and D Holdcroft (eds), *Jurisprudence: Texts and Commentary*, London: Butterworths, 1991.

"Stair as analytical jurist", in D M Walker (ed), *Stair Tercentenary Studies*, Edinburgh: Stair Society, 276-288.

"The artificial reason and judgement of law", in A Aarnio, I Niiniluoto and J Uusitalo (eds), *Methodologie und Erkenntnistheorie der Juristischen Argumentation*, *Rechtstheorie Beiheft* [Supplement] 2, Berlin: Duncker & Humblot, 105-120.

Reprinted in A Aarnio and N MacCormick (eds), *Legal Reasoning* vol I, Aldershot: Dartmouth, 1992, 167-182.

"Adam Smith on law" 15(2) *Valparaiso University Law Review* 243-263 (also published with modification as ch 6 in *Legal Right and Social Democracy*, 1982).

"Natural law reconsidered" 1(1) *Oxford Journal of Legal Studies* 99-109.

"Law, morality and positivism" 1(2) *Legal Studies* 131-145 (also published as ch 6 of *An Institutional Theory of Law* in 1986).

"The limits of reason: a reply to Dr Knud Haakonssen" 67 *Archiv für Rechts- und Sozialphilosophie* 504-509 (also published with modification as part of chs 6 and 13 in *Rhetoric and the Rule of Law*, 2005).

"The rational discipline of law" 26 *Juridical Review (New Series)* 146-160 (presented at the Stair Tercentenary Conference, University of Glasgow, 28 March 1981).

"A political frontier of jurisprudence: John Chipman Gray on the state" 66(5) *Cornell Law Review* 973-985.

"Review of *Justice and Liberty* by D D Raphael)" 67(4) *Archiv für Rechts- und Sozialphilosophie* 557-558.

"Review of *Judging Justice: An Introduction to Political Philosophy* by P Pettit, and *Justice*, ed by E Kamenka and A Erh-Soon Tay" 1(2) *Legal Studies* 213-216.

1982

Legal Right and Social Democracy: Essays in Legal and Political Philosophy, Oxford: Oxford University Press.

Translated into Spanish by L G Soler, as *Derecho Legal y Socialdemocracia: Ensayos Sobre Filosofia Juridica y Política*, Madrid: Tecnos, 1990.

Chapter 2, "Against moral disestablishment", translated into Spanish as "En contra de la ausencia de fundamento moral", in R Vásquez (ed), *Derecho y Moral: Ensayos Sobre un Debate Contemporáneo*, Barcelona: Gedisa, 1998, 160-182.

Chapter 13, "Nation and nationalism", translated into Catalan by A Colomer and A Monzon, as "Nació i nacionalismo" (1988-1989) 8(4) *Afers: fulls de recerca i pensament* 379-398.

Excerpts included in H Davies and D Holdcroft (eds), *Jurisprudence: Texts and Commentary*, London: Butterworths, 1991.

"Law and Enlightenment", in R H Campbell and A S Skinner (eds), *The Origins and Nature of the Scottish Enlightenment*, Edinburgh: John Donald, 150-166.

"On analytical jurisprudence", in P Trappe (ed), *Conceptions Contemporaires du Droit* vol I, Wiesbaden: *Archiv für Rechts- und Sozialphilosophie (Supplementa)*, 29-41 (also published as ch 4 of *An Institutional Theory of Law* in 1986).

"Coercion and law", in P Trappe (ed), *Conceptions Contemporaires du Droit* vol II, Wiesbaden: *Archiv für Rechts- und Sozialphilosophie Supplementa*, 259-271 (also published with modification as ch 12 in *Legal Right and Social Democracy*, 1982).

"Legal reasoning and practical reason", in P A French, T E Uehling Jr and H K Wettstein (eds), *Midwest Studies in Philosophy* vol 7, Minneapolis: University of Minnesota Press, 271-286.

"Rights, claims and remedies", in M A Stewart (ed), *Law, Morality and Rights*, Dordrecht: D Reidel, 161-181 (also published in *Law and Philosophy*, 1982).

"Rights, claims and remedies" 1(2) *Law and Philosophy* 337-357 (also published by Reidel in 1982).

"The nature of legal reasoning: a brief reply to Dr Wilson" 2(3) *Legal Studies* 286-290.

"Legal right and social democracy" 89(2) *Queen's Quarterly* 209-304 (presented as the Corry Lecture at Queen's University, March 1981) (also published with modification as ch 1 in *Legal Right and Social Democracy*, 1982).

"The polity and values: The question of moral disestablishment" 57(1) *International Social Science Review* 32.

"Review of *Social Order and the Limits of Law: A Theoretical Essay*, by I

Jenkins" 30(1) *Political Studies* 153-154.

"Review of *The Science of a Legislator*, by K Haakonssen" 30(2) *Political Studies* 328-329.

"Dr W D Lamont" 20 November 1982, *The Times*.

"Boldness on the bench. Review of *What Next in the Law*, by Lord Denning" 4148 *Times Literary Supplement*, 1 October 1982, 1076.

1983

"Contemporary legal philosophy: the rediscovery of practical reason" 10(1) *Journal of Law and Society* 1-18 (also published by Dartmouth in 1996). Excerpts included in M D A Freeman (ed), *Lloyd's Introduction to Jurisprudence*, London: Sweet & Maxwell, multiple editions, including 1994 and 2001.

"Jurisprudence and the constitution" 36 *Current Legal Problems* 13-30 (also published as ch 8 of *An Institutional Theory of Law* in 1986).

"Legal decisions and their consequences: from Dewey to Dworkin" 58 *New York University Law Review* 239-258 (presented as the Dewey Lecture in Jurisprudence, School of Law, New York University, 5 October 1982) (also published with modification as ch 6 of *Rhetoric and the Rule of Law*, 2005). Reprinted in A Aarnio and N MacCormick (eds), *Legal Reasoning* vol II, Aldershot: Dartmouth, 1992, 83-102.

"What is wrong with deceit?" 10(1) *Sydney Law Review* 5-19 (presented as a public lecture at the School of Law, University of Sydney, 22 July 1981).

"Reply to Mr Tur" 24(4) *Philosophical Books* 205-208.

"Gewirth's fallacy" 9(2) *Queen's Law Journal* 345-351 (1983-1984) (review of A Gewirth, *Human Rights*).

"At the side of the accused. Review of *Not Without Prejudice*, by D Napley" 4164 *Times Literary Supplement*, 21 January 1983, 66.

1984

"The idea of liberty: some reflections on Lorimer's Institutes", in V Hope (ed), *Philosophers of the Scottish Enlightenment*, Edinburgh: Edinburgh University Press, 233-248.

"On reasonableness", in C Perelman and R Vander Elst (eds), *Les Notions à Contenu Variable en Droit*, Brussels: Bruylant, 233-248 (also published with modification by *Notre Dame Law Review* in 1999, and as ch 9 of *Rhetoric and the Rule of Law*, 2005).

"Coherence in legal justification", in W Krawietz, H Schelsky, H Winkler and A Schramm (eds), *Theorie der Normen: Festgabe für Ota Weinberger zum 65. Geburtstag*, Berlin: Duncker & Humblot, 37-53 (also published by Reidel in 1984 and Jurisdiska Fakulteten i Uppsala in 1992).

Translated into Italian by M La Torre as "La congruenza nella giustificazione giuridica", ch 13 of N MacCormick and O Weinberger, *Il diritto come istituzione*, Milan: Dott A Giuffrè, 1990, 335-357.

Translated into Italian by P Comanducci, in P Comanducci and R Guastini (eds), *L'analisi del ragionamento giuridico. Materiali ad uso degli studenti*, Torino: G Giappichelli, 1987, 243-263.

"Coherence in legal justification", in A Peczenik, L Lindahl and B van Roermund (eds), *Theory of Legal Science: Proceedings of the Conference on Legal Theory and Philosophy of Science, Lund, Sweden, December 11-14 1983*, Dordrecht: D Reidel, 235-251 (also published by Duncker & Humblot in 1984 and Jurisdiska Fakulteten i Uppsala in 1992).

"Der Rechtsstaat und die Rule of Law" 39 *Juristenzeitung* 65-70.

Translated into English as "'Rechtsstaat' and Rule of Law", in J Thesing (ed), *The Rule of Law*, Sankt Augustin: Konrad Adenauer Stiftung, 68-77.

"Analytical jurisprudence and the possibility of legal knowledge" 49 *Saskatchewan Law Review* 1-13 (1984-1985).

"Review of *Max Weber*, by A T Kronman" 32(3) *Political Studies* 512-513.

"Review of *Ethics and the Rule of Law*, by D Lyons" 32(4) *Political Studies* 695-696.

"Between the one and the many. Review of *Public and Private in Social Life*, by S I Benn and G F Gaus" 4216 *Times Literary Supplement*, 20 January 1984, 58.

1985

Grundlagen des Institutionalistischen Rechtspositivismus, with O Weinberger, Berlin: Duncker & Humblot (Schriften zur Rechtstheorie, Heft 113) (published in English in 1986 by Reidel).

Conditions of Validity and Cognition in Modern Legal Thought [*Geltungs- und Erkenntnisbedingungen im modernen Rechtsdenken*], with S Panou and L Lombardi Vallauri (eds), Stuttgart: Franz Steiner Verlag (*Archiv für Rechts- und Sozialphilosophie, Beiheft* [Supplement] 25).

"Alcuni problemi circa l'ordine spontaneo", in S Ricossa and E Robilant (eds), *Libertà giustizia e persona nella società tecnologica*, Milan: Dott A Giuffré, 51-68 (presented in Turin in April 1984) (also published, with modifications, under the title "Spontaneous order and the Rule of Law:

some problems", in 1986 (*Jahrbuch des Öffentlichen Rechts der Gegenwart*) and 1989 (*Ratio Juris*)).

"The limits of rationality in legal reasoning", in A-J Arnaud, R Hilpinen and J Wróblewski (eds), *Juristic Logic, Rationality and Irrationality in Law*, (*Rechtstheorie, Beiheift* [Supplement] 8), Berlin: Duncker & Humblot, 161-177 (also published as ch 9 of *An Institutional Theory of Law* in 1986).

Translated into Spanish as "Los límites de la racionalidad en el razonamiento jurídico", in J Betegón and J R de Páramo (eds), *Derecho y Moral: Ensayos Analíticos*, Barcelona: Ariel, 9-22.

"The idea of a free government", *Occasional Paper of the Wilson Center*, Washington: The Wilson Center 7-17 (presented at Johns Hopkins University, 12 September 1985).

"The democratic intellect and the law" 5(2) *Legal Studies* 177-183 (Presidential address to the Society of Public Teachers of Law, 19 September 1984).

Reprinted in M Del Mar, W Twining and M Giudice (eds), *Legal Theory and the Legal Academy* vol III, Library of Essays in Contemporary Legal Theory, 2010, Surrey: Ashgate, 43-54.

"A moralistic case for a-moralistic law?" 20(1) *Valparaiso University Law Review* 1-41 (presented as the Seegers Lectures at the Valparaiso School of Law, 26 and 27 March 1985).

"A too brief reply to D'Amato, Boyle, Cullison and Stith" 20(1) *Valparaiso University Law Review* 77-82.

"Review of *Good Law: Towards a Rational Lawmaking Process*, by H J M Boukema" 16 *Rechtstheorie* 503-504.

Translator of "The Digest of Justinian: Book One", in T Mommsen and P J Krueger (eds) (English translation ed by A Watson), *The Digest of Justinian*, Philadelphia: University of Pennsylvania Press, 1-39.

1986

An Institutional Theory of Law: New Approaches to Legal Positivism, with O Weinberger, Dordrecht: D Reidel (originally published in German in 1985 by Duncker & Humblot).

Translated into Chinese by Y Zhou, as *Zhi Du Fa Lun, Zhong Guo Zheng Fa Da Xue Chu Ban She* (Press of China University of Political Science and Law), 1994 (2nd edition in 2004).

Translated into French by O Nerhot and P Coppens, as *Pour une théorie institutionnelle du droit*, Bruxelles: Story Scientia LGDG, 1992.

Translated into Italian by M La Torre, as *Il diritto come istituzione*, Milan: Dott A Giuffrè, 1990.

The Legal Mind: Essays for Tony Honoré, with P Birks (eds), Oxford: Oxford University Press.

"Editors' Preface", with P Birks, in P Birks and N MacCormick (eds), *The Legal Mind: Essays for Tony Honoré*, Oxford: Oxford University Press, v-vi.

"Speech acts, legal Institutions and real laws", with Z Bańkowski, in P Birks and N MacCormick (eds), *The Legal Mind: Essays for Tony Honoré*, with P Birks (eds), Oxford: Oxford University Press, 121-134.

Translated into French, as "La théorie des actes de langage et la théorie des actes juridiques", with Z Bańkowski, in P Amselek (ed), *Théorie des actes de langage, éthique et droit*, Paris: P U F, 1986, 195-209.

Translated into Spanish by J Calvo González, as "La teoría de los actos de habla y la teoría de los actos jurídicos", with Z Bańkowski, (1991) 8 *Anuario de Filosofía del Derecho* 219-238.

"The interest of the state and the Rule of Law", in P Wallington and R Merkin (eds), *Essays in Memory of Professor F H Lawson*, London: Butterworths, 169-187 (originally presented as the 5th annual Lawson Lecture, Lancaster University, 12 March 1985) (also published with modification as ch 3 in *Questioning Sovereignty*, 1999).

"Theory in the law curriculum", with W Twining, in W Twining (ed), *Legal Theory and Common Law*, Oxford: Oxford University Press, 238-254.

"Spontaneous order and the Rule of Law: some problems" 35 *Jahrbuch des Öffentlichen Rechts der Gegenwart* 1-13 (presented at Liberty Fund conference at Gleneagles, Scotland, July 1986) (also published in *Ratio Juris* in 1989; earlier version in Italian published by Dott A Giuffré in 1985).

Reprinted in the *Hume Reprints Series*, No 2, Edinburgh: The David Hume Institute, 1987, 13 pages.

Reprinted in S Ratnapala and G Moens (eds), *Jurisprudence of Liberty*, Sydney: Butterworths, 1996, 67-80 (2nd edition published by LexisNexis in 2010).

Translated into Spanish by F Laporta, as "Orden espontáneo e imperio de la ley: algunos problemas" (1989) 6 *Doxa: Cuadernos de filosofía del derecho* 309-327.

1987

"Hans Kelsen", in V Bogdanor (ed), *The Blackwell Encyclopaedia of Political Institutions*, Oxford: Basil Blackwell, 309-310.

"Law", in V Bogdanor (ed), *The Blackwell Encyclopaedia of Political Institutions*, Oxford: Basil Blackwell, 319-321.

"Sovereignty", in V Bogdanor (ed), *The Blackwell Encyclopaedia of Political Institutions*, Oxford: Basil Blackwell, 583-584.

"Comment on G Postema's 'The Normativity of Law'", in R Gavison (ed), *Issues in Contemporary Legal Philosophy*, Oxford: Clarendon Press, 105-113.

"Universalisation and induction in law", in C Faralli and E Pattaro (eds), *Reason in Law*, Milan: Seminario Giuridico della Università di Bologna, 91-106 (also published with modification as part of ch 5 of *Rhetoric and the Rule of Law*, 2005).

"Smashing the two-way mirror", in E Simpson (ed), *Anti-Foundationalism and Practical Reasoning: Conversations between Hermeneutics and Analysis*, Edmonton, Alberta: Academic Printing and Publishing, 201-216.

"Why cases have rationes and what these are", in L Goldstein (ed), *Precedent in Law*, Oxford: Clarendon Press, 155-182 (also published with modification as ch 8 of *Rhetoric and the Rule of Law*, 2005).

"Law", in D Miller (ed), *The Blackwell Encyclopaedia of Political Thought*, Oxford: Basil Blackwell, 274-294.

"John Austin", in D Miller (ed), *The Blackwell Encyclopaedia of Political Thought*, Oxford: Basil Blackwell, 27-28.

"William Blackstone", in D Miller (ed), *The Blackwell Encyclopaedia of Political Thought*, Oxford: Basil Blackwell, 47.

"Changing waterfront uses on the River Clyde, Scotland: a preliminary survey", O T Magoon et al (eds), *The Coastal Zone '87*, Proceedings of the Fifth Symposium on Coastal and Ocean Management, Seattle, May 26-29 1987, 4022-4031

"Review of *The Ivory Tower: Essays in Philosophy and Public Policy*, by A Kenny" 35(4) *Political Studies* 702.

"Review of *A Matter of Principle*, by R Dworkin" 35(3) *Political Studies* 533.

"Review of *Essays on Kelsen*, by R Tur and W Twining (eds)" 28(3) *Philosophical Books* 183-186.

"Review of *Philosophy and the Criminal Law*, ed by A Duff and N E Simmonds" 7(5) *Canadian Philosophical Reviews* 190-192.

"Review of *Precedent and Law: Dynamics of Common Law Growth*, by J Stone" Summer *Public Law* 297-299.

"Access to the goods. Review of *The Morality of Freedom*, by J Raz" 4392 *Times Literary Supplement*, 5 June 1987, 599.

1988

Constitutionalism and Democracy, presented as the 3rd Lecture at the Scottish National Party annual national conference, Inverness, September 1988, Edinburgh: SNP Publications Department, 16 pages.

"Persons as institutional facts", in E Weinberger and W Krawietz (eds), *Reine Rechtslehre im Speiegel Ihrer Fortsetzer und Kritiker*, Vienna and New York: Springer-Verlag, 371-393 (also published with modification as ch 5 in *Institutions of Law*, 2007).

"The ethics of international intervention: reply to Mr McMahan", in A Ellis (ed), *Ethics and International Relations*, Manchester: Manchester University Press, 82-85.

"On the interpretation and understanding of case law", in S Panou, G Bozonis, D Georgas and P Trappe (eds), *Theory and Systems of Legal Philosophy* vol III, Stuttgart: *Archiv für Rechts- und Sozialphilosophie Supplementa*, 134-144.

"The determinacy of selves", in W J A Macartney (ed), *Self-Determination in the Commonwealth*, Aberdeen: Aberdeen University Press, 112-118.

"Institutions, arrangements and practical reason" 1(1) *Ratio Juris* 73-82. Japanese translation in (1988) 105 *Hogaku Kyokai Zassi* 389-408.

"Le raisonnement juridique" 33 *Archives de Philosophie du Droit* 99-112 (also published by Editions Yvonne Blais in 1992).

"Courage in costume. Review of *A "Life is Too Short" – Autobiography, Vol 1*, by N Fairbairn" 4426 *Times Literary Supplement*, 29 January 1988, 107.

1989

Enlightenment, Rights and Revolution: Essays in Legal and Social Philosophy, with Z Bańkowski (eds), Aberdeen: Aberdeen University Press.

"Editors' Preface", with Z Bańkowski, in Z Bańkowski and N MacCormick (eds), *Enlightenment, Rights and Revolution: Essays in Legal and Social Philosophy*, Aberdeen: Aberdeen University Press, ix-xii.

"La texture ouverte des règles juridiques", in P Amselek (ed), *Controverses autour de l'Ontologie Juridique*, Paris: P U F, 109-126 (also published in English by Edinburgh University Press in 1991).

"Law, morality and discursive rationality: foreword", with J Wróblewski, in A Aarnio and K Tuori (eds), *Law, Morality and Discursive Rationality*, Helsinki: Department of Public Law, University of Helsinki, 1-7.

"Some principles of statutory interpretation", with Z Bańkowski, in J van Dunné (ed), *Legal Reasoning and Statutory Interpretation*, Arnhem:

Youda Quint, 41-53 (presented as one of the Rotterdam Lectures in Jurisprudence, 1 June 1988).

"Unrepentant gradualism", in O D Edwards (ed), *A Claim of Right for Scotland*, Edinburgh: Polygon Press, 99-109.

Reprinted in L Paterson (ed), *A Diverse Assembly: The Debate on a Scottish Parliament*, Edinburgh: Edinburgh University Press, 1998, 174-182.

"Constitutionalism and constitutions", in D McCrone (ed), *What Scotland Wants: Ten Years On*, Proceedings of a One Day conference on 25 February 1989, Edinburgh: Unit for the Study of Government in Scotland, 3-8.

"Constitutionalism and democracy", in O Weinberger (ed), *Aktuelle Probleme Der Demokratie* [Actual Problems of Democracy], *Internationales Jahrbuch für Rechtsphilosophie und Gesetzgebung*, Vienna: Manzsche Verlags- und Universitätsbuchhandlung, 17-28.

"Discretion and rights" 8(1) *Law and Philosophy* 23-36.

"Spontaneous order and Rule of Law: some problems" 2(1) *Ratio Juris* 41-54 (also published in *Jahrbuch des Öffentlichen Rechts der Gegenwart* in 1986; translation into Spanish referred to under 1986; earlier version in Italian published by Dott A Giuffré in 1985).

"Preface" 62 *Southern California Law Review* 743-745 (Symposium: The Works of Joseph Raz).

"The ethics of legalism" 2 *Ratio Juris* 184-193.

Reprinted in M Del Mar, W Twining and M Giudice (eds), *Legal Theory and the Legal Academy* vol III, Library of Essays in Contemporary Legal Theory, 2010, Surrey: Ashgate, 177-186.

Excerpts included in M D A Freeman (ed), *Lloyd's Introduction to Jurisprudence*, London: Sweet & Maxwell, multiple editions, including 1994 and 2001.

Translator, with R Alder, of R Alexy, *A Theory of Legal Argumentation*, Oxford: Clarendon Press.

1990

"Universalisation and induction in law", in South Korean IVR (eds), *Philosophy of Law and Social Philosophy East and West: Festschrift for Dr Ton-Kak Suh's 70th Birthday*, Seoul, 105-118.

"General legal concepts", in T B Smith and R Black (eds), *The Laws of Scotland: Stair Memorial Encyclopaedia* vol 11, Edinburgh: The Law Society of Scotland and Butterworths, 359-419 (also published with modification as chs 5 to 9 in *Institutions of Law*, 2007).

"Reconstruction after deconstruction: a response to CLS" 10 *Oxford Journal of Legal Studies* 539-558 (also published, in a shorter version, by Edinburgh University Press in 1993).

"Of self-determination and other things" 15 *Bulletin of the Australian Society of Legal Philosophy* 1-20.

"Commentary on 'The Future of Legal Systems' by Thijmen Koopmans", Edinburgh: David Hume Institute (response to the Presidential Address to the David Hume Institute delivered at Royal Society of Edinburgh, November 1989), 13-18.

1991

Interpreting Statutes: A Comparative Study, with R S Summers (eds), Aldershot: Dartmouth.

Controversies About Law's Ontology, with P Amselek (eds), Edinburgh: Edinburgh University Press.

"On method and methodology", with Z Bańkowski, R S Summers and J Wróblewski, in N MacCormick and R S Summers (eds), *Interpreting Statutes: A Comparative Study*, Aldershot: Dartmouth, 9-28.

"Statutory interpretation in the United Kingdom", with Z Bańkowski, in N MacCormick and R S Summers (eds), *Interpreting Statutes: A Comparative Study*, Aldershot: Dartmouth, 359-406.

"Interpretation and justification", with R S Summers, in N. MacCormick and R S Summers (eds), *Interpreting Statutes: A Comparative Study*, Aldershot: Dartmouth, 511-544.

"On 'open texture' in law", in P Amselek and N MacCormick (eds), *Controversies About Law's Ontology*, Edinburgh: Edinburgh University Press, 72-83 (also published in French by P U F in 1989).

"Foreword to English edition", in P Amselek and N MacCormick (eds), *Controversies About Law's Ontology*, Edinburgh: Edinburgh University Press, vii-x.

"An idea for a Scottish constitution", in W Finnie, C Himsworth and N Walker (eds), *Edinburgh Essays in Public Law*, Edinburgh: Edinburgh University Press, 159-181.

"Moral disestablishment and rational discourse", in H Jung, H Müller-Dietz and U Neumann (eds), *Recht und Moral*, Baden-Baden: Nomos Verlag, 219-234.

Translated into German, as "Entrechtlichung der Moral und Rationaler Diskurs", in A Aarnio et al (eds), *Rechtsnorm und Rechtswirklichkeit*, Berlin: Duncker & Humblot, 1993, 547-561.

"Preface", with W Twining, in W Twining (ed), *Issues of Self-Determination*, Aberdeen: Aberdeen University Press, xi-xvii.

"Is nationalism philosophically credible?", in W Twining (ed), *Issues of Self-Determination*, Aberdeen: Aberdeen University Press, 8-19 (also published with modification as ch 10 in *Questioning Sovereignty*, 1999). Translated into Spanish as "¿Es filosóficamente creíble el nacionalismo?" (1994) 31 *Anales de las Cátedra Francisco Suárez* 61-71.

"*Donoghue v Stevenson* and legal reasoning", in P T Burns and S J Lyons (eds), *Donoghue v Stevenson and the Modern Law of Negligence*, Vancouver, BC: Continuing Legal Education of British Columbia, 191-214.

"Philosophy in legal education" March *Scots Philosophical Newsletter* 5-9.

"Notes on narrativity and the normative syllogism" 4(2) *International Journal for the Semiotics of Law* 163-174 (also published with modification as part of ch 4 of *Rhetoric and the Rule of Law*, 2005).

"Citizens' legal reasoning and its importance for jurisprudence" *Archiv für Rechts- und Sozialphilosophie (Beiheft* [Supplement] *40)* 15-21 (ed by E Dais, S Jorgensen and A Erh-Soon Tay).

"Neil Gunn and nationalism: a memoir" 67 (Winter) *Chapman* 63-64 (1991-1992).

"Law, state and feminism: MacKinnon's theses considered. Review of C MacKinnon, *Toward a Feminist Theory of the State*" 10(4) *Law and Philosophy* 447-452.

"Llewellyn revisited. Review of *The Case Law System in America*, by K Llewellyn", with Z Wiseman, 70 *Texas Law Review* 771-779 (1991-1992).

"Review of D Lieberman: *The Province of Legislation Determined*" 3(2) *Utilitas* 313-317.

"Doing and discussing. Review of *General Theory of Norms*, by H Kelsen" 4607 *Times Literary Supplement*, 19 July 1991, 22.

1992

Legal Reasoning vols I and II, with A Aarnio (eds), Aldershot: Dartmouth.

The Judicial Application of Law by J Wróblewski, with Z Bańkowski (eds), Dordrecht: Kluwer Publishing.

"Introduction", with A Aarnio, in A Aarnio and N MacCormick (eds), *Legal Reasoning* vol I, Aldershot: Dartmouth, ix-xvii.

"Introduction", with A Aarnio, in A Aarnio and N MacCormick (eds), *Legal Reasoning* vol II, Aldershot: Dartmouth, xi-xvii.

"Republicanism and Enlightenment thought: observations from Scotland", in

A E Dick Howard (ed), *The United States Constitution: Roots, Rights and Responsibilities*, Washington and London: Smithsonian Inst Press, 97-114.

"Coherence in legal justification", in *De Lege: Skrifter av Fakultetens Hedersdoktorer*, Jurisdiska Fakulteten i Uppsala, Yearbook 2, 311-30 (also published by D Reidel in 1984).

"La raisonnement juridique en Common Law: la motivation comme justification", in P Legrand (ed), *Common Law: d'un siècle à l'autre*, Cowansville, Québec: Editions Yvonne Blais, 309-332 (also published in *Archives de philosophie du droit* in 1988).

"Natural law and the separation of law and morals", in R P George (ed), *Natural Law Theory*, Oxford: Clarendon Press, 105-133.

"Further thoughts on institutional facts" 5(1) *International Journal for the Semiotics of Law* 3-15.

"Legal deduction, legal predicates and expert systems" 5(2) *International Journal for the Semiotics of Law* 181-202 (also published with modification as part of ch 4 of *Rhetoric and the Rule of Law*, 2005).

"A deductivist rejoinder to a semiotic critique" 5(2) *International Journal for the Semiotics of Law* 215-224 (also published with modification as part of ch 4 of *Rhetoric and the Rule of Law*, 2005).

"The North Star: Scotland in Europe" 1 *Edit: University of Edinburgh Magazine* 26-27.

"Time to tear ourselves away" Thursday 6 February 1992, *The Scotsman*.

1993

"Law", in P H Scott (ed), *Scotland: A Concise Cultural History*, Edinburgh: Mainstream Publishing, 343-355.

"Reconstruction after deconstruction: closing in on critique", in A Norrie (ed), *Closure or Critique: New Directions in Legal Theory*, Edinburgh: Edinburgh University Press, 142-156 (also published, in a longer version, in *Oxford Journal of Legal Studies* in 1990).

"Constitutionalism and democracy", in R Bellamy (ed), *Theories and Concepts of Politics*, Manchester: Manchester University Press, 124-147.

"Beyond the sovereign state", 56(1) *Modern Law Review* 1-18.

"Argumentation and interpretation in law" 6(1) *Ratio Juris* 16-29 (also published in *Argumentation* in 1995, and with modification as ch 7 of *Rhetoric and the Rule of Law*, 2005).

Translated into Spanish by J Bengoetxea as "La argumentación y la interpretación en el derecho" (1993) 36 *Revista Vasca de Administración Publica* 201-217.

Translated into German by J Jung, as "Argumentation und Interpretation im Recht; "Rule-Consequentialism" und Rationale Rekonstruktion", in G Teubner (ed), *Entscheidungsfolgen Als Rechtsgründe: Folgenorientiertes Argumentieren in Rechtsvergleichender Sicht*, Baden-Baden: Nomos Verlag, special issue of *Arbeiten zur Rechtsvergleichung* 169, 1995, 39-53.

Translated into French by Le Centre de Philosophie du Droit, with the collaboration of E Soubrenie, as "Argumentation et interprétation en droit", in P Amselek (ed), *Interprétation et droit*, Bruxelles: Bruylant, 1995, 213-226.

Reprinted in J Bjarup (ed), *Allmän Rättslära. Texter till Rättskällor*, Juridicum: Stockholms Universitet VT, 2005, 73-79.

"H L A Hart: in memoriam" 6(3) *Ratio Juris* 337-338.

"Can a law be bad? Review of *Norm and Nature*, by R Shiner" 4696 *Times Literary Supplement*, 28 April 1993, 23.

"With due respect: ties of sentiment and the vindication of rights. Review of *What's Wrong with Rights?* by E F Kingdom, and *Toward a Feminist Theory of the State*, by C MacKinnon" 4686 *Times Literary Supplement*, 22 January 1993, 3-4.

1994

Legal Reasoning and Legal Theory, 2nd edn, Oxford: Oxford University Press (includes new "Foreword", ix-xvi).

Prescriptive Formality and Normative Rationality in Modern Legal Systems, with W Krawietz and G H von Wright (eds), Berlin: Duncker and Humblot.

"Four quadrants of jurisprudence", in W Krawietz, N MacCormick and G H von Wright (eds), *Prescriptive Formality and Normative Rationality in Modern Legal Systems*, Berlin: Duncker and Humblot, 53-70.

"Legal concepts", in R Asher (ed) and J W Simpson (exec ed), *Encyclopaedia of Language and Linguistics*, Oxford: Pergamon Press, 2069-2074.

"Diritto, 'Rule of Law', e democrazia", translated into Italian by E Diciotti and R Guastini, in P Comanducci and R Guastini (eds), *Analisi e Diritto*, Torino: Giappichelli, 189-209*.

"What place for nationalism in the modern world?", in H MacQueen (ed), *In Search of New Constitutions, Hume Papers in Public Policy*, No 2, Edinburgh: The David Hume Institute, 79-95 (presented as the Stevenson Lecture in Citizenship, University of Glasgow, 18 June 1994; also published by Westview Press in 1996, and with modification as part of ch 11 in *Questioning Sovereignty*, 1999).

"Constitutionalism, democracy and welfare", in M Adler (ed), *Democracy and Social Security*, Proceedings of the 5th Annual Erasmus / Tempus Course on "Social Security in Europe", Edinburgh: University of Edinburgh, 5-8.

"Legal reasoning and the institutional theory of law", in P Koller, W Krawietz and P Strasser (eds), *Institution und Recht*, Berlin: Duncker & Humblot (*Rechtstheorie Beiheft* [Supplement] *14*), 117-139 (also published with modification as ch 4 of *Rhetoric and the Rule of Law*, 2005).

"*The Concept of Law* and the concept of law" 14(1) *Oxford Journal of Legal Studies* 1-23 (also published by Clarendon Press in 1996) (presented as the Hart Lecture, University of Oxford, 11 May 1993).

"Sovereignty, democracy and subsidiarity" 2 *Juridisk Tidskrift vid Stockholms universitet* 290-297 (also published by Lothian Foundation Press in 1995; by Sakkoulas Publications in 1994; by Schäffer-Poeschel in 1997; and in *Rechtstheorie* in 1994) (presented as a lecture on the occasion of receiving a Doctor Juris honorary degree at the University of Saarland).

"Sovereignty, democracy and subsidiarity", in L Kotsiris (ed), *Law at the Turn of the 20th Century*, Thessaloniki: Sakkoulas Publications, 1994, 185-197 (also published by Lothian Foundation Press in 1995; by Schäffer-Poeschel in 1997; in *Juridisk Tidskrift vid Stockholms universitet* in 1994; and in *Rechtstheorie* in 1994).

"Sovereignty, democracy and subsidiarity" 25 *Rechtstheorie* 281-290 (also published by Lothian Foundation Press in 1995; by Sakkoulas Publications in 1994; by Schäffer-Poeschel in 1997; and in *Juridisk Tidskrift vid Stockholms universitet* in 1994).

"On justification and interpretation", with J Wróblewski, 53 *Archiv für Rechts- und Sozialphilosophie* 255-268.

"John Smith: an appreciation" 8 *Scottish Affairs* 5-8.

"In memoriam: Eugene Kamenka" 17 *IVR Newsletter* 1-2.

"Review of *Interpretation and Legal Theory* by A Marmor" 105(1) *Ethics* 195-196.

"Names can hurt people: should 'shameless indecency' be an exception to free speech? Review of *Only Words* by C A MacKinnon" 4757 *Times Literary Supplement*, 3 June 1994, 3-4.

"Free under the law. Review of *Ethics in the Public Domain*, by J Raz" 4787 *Times Literary Supplement*, 30 December 1994, 11.

Contemporary Questions in Legal Theory: Intensive Course (ed), Course Reader for the Faculty of Law, University of Toronto, 202 pages.

1995

"Defeasibility in law and logic", in Z Bańkowski, I White and U Hahn (eds), *Informatics and the Foundations of Legal Reasoning*, Dordrecht: Kluwer

Academic Publishers, 99-117 (also published with modification as ch 12 in *Rhetoric and the Rule of Law*, 2005).

"Argumentation und Interpretation im Recht: 'Rule consequentialism' und rationale Rekonstruktion", in G Teubner (ed), *Entscheidungsfolgen als Rechtsgrunde*, Baden-Baden: Nomos Verlagsgesellschaft, 39-53 (draws on passages from "On Method and Methodology" in *Interpreting Statutes*, 1991) (translated into German with the assistance of H Jung).

"Sovereignty, democracy and subsidiarity", in R Bellamy, V Bufacchi and D Castliglione (eds), *Democracy and Constitutional Culture in Europe*, London: Lothian Foundation Press, 95-106 (also published in *Juridisk Tidskrift vid Stockholms universitet* in 1994, and in *Rechtstheorie* in 1994, both in slightly different versions).

"Time, narratives and law", in J Bjarup and M Blegvad (eds), *Time, Law and Society, Archiv für Rechts- und Sozialphilosophie, Bieheft* [Supplement] *64*, Stuttgart: Franz Steiner Verlag, 111-125 (also published with modification as ch 11 in *Rhetoric and the Rule of Law*, 2005).

"Sovereignty: myth and reality", in *De Lege: Uppsala University Law Faculty Yearbook* (special issue ed by N Jareborg, "Towards universal law: trends in national, European and international lawmaking"), Uppsala: Iustus Förlag, 227-248 (also published with modification in *Scottish Affairs* in 1995, and as ch 8 in *Questioning Sovereignty*, 1999).

"Sovereignty: myth and reality" 11 *Scottish Affairs* 1-13 (also published with modifications by Iustus Förlag in 1995, and as ch 8 in *Questioning Sovereignty*, 1999).

"The *Maastricht-Urteil*: sovereignty now" 1(3) *European Law Journal* 259-266.

Translated into German by the editorial team with the assistance of C Starck, as "Das *Maastricht-Urteil*: Souveränität heute" 50 *Juristenzeitung* 797-800.

Translated into Spanish, as "La sentencia de Maastricht: soberanía ahora" 55 *Debats: Revista trimestral editada por la Institució Alfons el Magnànim* 25-30.

Reprinted in F Fleerackers, E van Leeuwen, and B van Roermund (eds), *Law, Life and the Image of Man: Modes of Thought in Modern Legal Theory, Festschrift for Jan M Broekman*, Berlin: Duncker & Humblot, 1996, 447-453.

Excerpts reprinted in D Chalmers, C Hadjiemmanuil, G Monti and A Tomkins (eds), *European Union Law: Texts and Materials*, Cambridge: Cambridge University Press, 2006.

"The relative heteronomy of law" 3(1) *European Journal of Philosophy* 69-85 (presented at the Legal Theory Workshops Series, Faculty of Law, University of Toronto, 23 September 1994) (also published with modification as ch 14 in *Institutions of Law*, 2007).

"Argumentation and interpretation in law" 9(3) *Argumentation* 467-480 (also published in *Ratio Juris* in 1995).

"Eugene Kamenka 1928-1994" 20 *Bulletin of the Australian Society of Legal Philosophy* 1-3.

"The European Union?", with Z Bańkowski and A Scott, RUSEL Working Paper No 22, Department of Politics, University of Exeter, last accessed online at *http://www.huss.ex.ac.uk/politics/research/rusel/rusel22.pdf* on 7 November 2010, 10 pages.

"Professor Barrie Wilson: a tribute by the Provost of Law and Social Sciences", in 5 *Bulletin: The University of Edinburgh News* 1 and 24.

"Review of H Kelsen, *General Theory of Norms*. Trans by M Hartney" 43(4) *Political Studies* 784.

"Evils that Mann did. Review of *Crossing Over the Line, Legislating Morality and the Mann Act*, by D J Langum", 4800 *Times Literary Supplement*, 31 March 1995, 10.

1996

"What place for nationalism in the modern world?", in S Caney, D George and P Jones (eds), *National Rights, International Obligations*, Boulder: Westview Press, 34-52 (also published by the David Hume Institute in 1994, and with modification as part of ch 11 in *Questioning Sovereignty*, 1999).

"*The Concept of Law* and the concept of law", in R P George (ed), *The Autonomy of Law: Essays on Legal Positivism*, Oxford, Clarendon Press, 163-194 (also published in the *Oxford Journal of Legal Studies* in 1994) (presented as the Hart Lecture at the University of Oxford, 11 May 1993).

"Law and philosophy: the rediscovery of practical reason", in P A Thomas (ed), Legal Frontiers, Aldershot: Dartmouth, 41-65 (also published in the *Journal of Law and Society* in 1983).

"Liberalism, nationalism and the post-sovereign state" 44(3) *Political Studies* 553-567 (special issue edn by R Bellamy and D Castiglione) (also published with modification as part of ch 11 in *Questioning Sovereignty*, 1999).

Reprinted in R Bellamy and D Castiglione (eds), *Constitutionalism in Transformation: European and Theoretical Perspectives*, Oxford: Blackwell, 1996, 141-155.

"Libertad, igualdad y nacionalismo" 130 *Sistema: Revista de ciencas sociales* 31-49 (translated into Spanish by L R Abascal).

"Institutional normative order: a conception of law" 82 *Cornell Law Review* 1051-1070 (1996-1997) (also published with modification as ch 1 in *Questioning Sovereignty*, 1999).

"Justice as impartiality: assenting with anti-contractualist reservations. Review of *Justice as Impartiality* by B Barry" 44(2) *Political Studies* 305-310.

"The law is a mongrel: how a separate legal tradition underpins Scottish nationhood. Review of *A Legal History of Scotland, Volume 2*, by D M Walker" 4845 *Times Literary Supplement*, 9 February 1996, 3-4.

1997

Interpreting Precedents: A Comparative Study, with R S Summers and A L Goodhart (eds), Aldershot: Dartmouth.

Constructing Legal Systems: "European Union" in Legal Theory, (ed), Dordrecht: Kluwer Academic Publishing.

"Democracy, subsidiarity and citizenship in the 'European Commonwealth'", in N MacCormick (ed), *Constructing Legal Systems: "European Union" in Legal Theory*, Dordrecht: Kluwer Academic Publishing, 1-26 (also published in *Law and Philosophy* in 1997, in *Diritto Pubblico* in 1999, and with modification as ch 9 in *Questioning Sovereignty*, 1999).

"Introduction", with R S Summers, in N MacCormick, R S Summers and A L Goodhart (eds), *Interpreting Precedents: A Comparative Study*, Aldershot: Dartmouth, 1-15.

"Precedent in the United Kingdom", with Z Bańkowski and G Marshall, in N MacCormick, R S Summers and A L Goodhart (eds), *Interpreting Precedents: A Comparative Study*, Aldershot: Dartmouth, 315-354.

"Further general reflections and conclusions", with R S Summers, in N MacCormick, R S Summers and AL. Goodhart (eds), *Interpreting Precedents: A Comparative Study*, Aldershot: Dartmouth, 531-550.

"The ideal and the actual of law and society", in J Tasioulas (ed), *Law, Values and Social Practices*, Aldershot: Dartmouth, 15-37.

"Universal and Particular: the problem with precedent", in A Aarnio, R Alexy and G Bergholtz (eds), *Justice, Morality and Law: A Tribute to Aleksander Peczenik on the Occasion of his 60th Birthday, 16 November 1997*, Lund: Juristförklaget i Lund, 261-271.

"On institutional normative order: an idea about law", in E G Valdés, W Krawietz, G H von Wright and R Zimmerling (eds), *Normative Systems in*

Legal and Moral Theory: Festschrift for Carlos E Alchourrón and Eugenio Bulygin, Berlin: Duncker & Humblot, 1997, 411-425.

"Sovereignty, democracy and subsidiarity", in M Herberger, A-W Scheer and J Zentes, *Entwicklungslinien in Recht und Wirtschaft*, Stuttgart: Schäffer-Poeschel, 247-254 (also published by Lothian Foundation Press in 1995; by Sakkoulas Publications in 1994; by Schäffer-Poeschel in 1997; in *Juridisk Tidskrift vid Stockholms universitet* in 1994; and in *Rechtstheorie* in 1994) (presented as a lecture on the occasion of receiving a Doctor Juris honorary degree at the University of Saarland).

"Estado de derecho y *rule of law*", in J Thesing (ed), *Estado de Derecho y Democracia*, Buenos Aires: Konrad Adenauer Stiftung, 101-117.

"Democracy, subsidiarity and citizenship in the 'European Commonwealth'" 16(4) *Law and Philosophy* 331-356 (also published by Kluwer Academic Publishing in 1997, in *Diritto Pubblico* in 1999, and with modification as ch 9 in *Questioning Sovereignty*, 1999).

"Law as institutional normative order" 28 *Rechtstheorie* 219-234 (contribution to special issue, ed. by A Aarnio and W Krawietz, "New approaches and ways of legal thinking: the Otto Brusiin Lectures 1982-1997") (also published with modification as ch 1 in *Questioning Sovereignty*, 1999).

"Speaking volumes: J M MacCormick's *The Flag in the Wind*" *The Times Higher Education Supplement*, 26 December 1997.

"Scottish National Party" April *Round&About* 6.

1998

Laws, Institutions and Facts, with H de Jong (eds), 17(3) *Law and Philosophy* 213-345 (special issue).

"Sovereignty or subsidiarity? Some comments on Scottish devolution", in A Tomkins (ed), *Devolution and the British Constitution*, London: Key Haven Publications, 1-18.

"Sovereign states and vengeful victims: The problem of the right to punish", with D Garland, in A Ashworth and M Wasik (eds), *Fundamentals of Sentencing Theory: Essays in Honour of Andrew von Hirsch*, Oxford: Oxford University Press, 11-30.

"Weinberger, O", in E Craig (ed), *Routledge Encyclopaedia of Philosophy*, London: Routledge, 701-702.

"Villey, M", in E Craig (ed), *Routledge Encyclopaedia of Philosophy*, London: Routledge, 614-615.

"Savigny, F K von", in E Craig (ed), *Routledge Encyclopaedia of Philosophy*, London: Routledge, 482-483.

"Renner, K", in E Craig (ed), *Routledge Encyclopaedia of Philosophy*, London: Routledge, 267-268.

"Pound, R", in E Craig (ed), *Routledge Encyclopaedia of Philosophy*, London: Routledge, 609-610.

"Pothier, R J", in E Craig (ed), *Routledge Encyclopaedia of Philosophy*, London: Routledge, 608-609.

"Llewellyn, K N", in E Craig (ed), *Routledge Encyclopaedia of Philosophy*, London: Routledge, 661-662.

"Hohfeld, W N", in E Craig (ed), *Routledge Encyclopaedia of Philosophy*, London: Routledge, 476-477.

"Hart, H L A", in E Craig (ed), *Routledge Encyclopaedia of Philosophy*, London: Routledge, 234-236.

"Frank, J", in E Craig (ed), *Routledge Encyclopaedia of Philosophy*, London: Routledge, 725-726.

"Legal reasoning and argumentation", in E Craig (ed), *Routledge Encyclopaedia of Philosophy*, London: Routledge, 525-531.

"Law, Philosophy of", with B Brown, in E Craig (ed), *Routledge Encyclopaedia of Philosophy*, London: Routledge, 464-468.

"The English constitution, the British state, and the Scottish anomaly" *Scottish Affairs* (special issue "Understanding Constitutional Change", Edinburgh (The British Academy Lecture 1997), 129-146 (also published in *Proceedings of the British Academy* in 1999, and with modification as ch 4 in *Questioning Sovereignty*, 1999).

"The dialectic of might and right: legal positivisms and constitutional change" 51 *Current Legal Problems* 37-63 (special issue, ed by MDA Freedman, "Legal Theory at the End of the Millennium", Oxford: Oxford University Press) (also published with modification as ch 5 in *Questioning Sovereignty*, 1999).

"Raimo Siltala, *A Theory of Precedent: From Analytical Positivism to A Post-Analytical Philosophy of Law*, Opponent's Review" 4 *Oikeus* 424-432.

"Norms, institutions and institutional facts" 17(3) *Law and Philosophy* 301-345 (also published with modification as chs 1 and 2 in *Institutions of Law*, 2007).

"After sovereignty: understanding constitutional change" 9 *The King's College Law Journal* 20-38 (also published with modification as ch 6 in *Questioning Sovereignty*, 1999).

"Precedent as a source of law" 60 *Archiv für Rechts- und Sozialphilosophie* 177-185 (special issue ed by E Attwooll and P Comanducci).

"The significance of precedent" *Acta Juridica* 174-187.

Reprinted in G Bradfield and D van der Merwe (eds), *"Meaning" in Legal Interpretation*, Cape Town: Juta & Co Ltd, 174-187.

"Reasonableness and objectivity" 74(5) *Notre Dame Law Review* 1575-1603 (1998-1999) (also published with modification by Bruylant in 1984, and as ch 9 of *Rhetoric and the Rule of Law*, 2005).

Translated into Spanish by F Atria, as "Razonabilidad y objetividad" (2002) 45 *Revista de Ciencias Sociales* 399-436.

Reprinted in F Atria and N MacCormick (eds), *Law and Legal Interpretation*, Aldershot: Ashgate, 2003, 527-555.

"The Scottish Parliament as law-maker: laws for an Information Age?" 29(3) *Law Librarian* 152-156 (presented as the annual lecture of the Scottish Group of the Society for Computers and Law, Edinburgh, 18 June 1998).

Also published, in a shorter version, in (1998) 9(4) *Computers and Law* 22-23.

"Preface", with H de Jong, 17(3) *Law and Philosophy* 213.

"A parliament once again?" 4976 *Times Literary Supplement*, 14 August 1998, 11-12.

"Risking constitutional collision in Europe?" 18(3) *Oxford Journal of Legal Studies* 517-532 (review of D Rossa Phelan, *Revolt or Revolution: The Constitutional Boundaries of the European Community*) (also published with modification as ch 7 in *Questioning Sovereignty*, 1999).

"Jurisprudence, democracy, and the death of the Weimar Republic. Review of *Popular Sovereignty and the Crisis of German Constitutional Law* by P C Caldwell and *Legality & Legitimacy* by D Dyzenhaus" 77(4) *Texas Law Review* 1095-1106 (1998-1999).

"To 'ought' from 'is'. Review of *The Disintegration of Natural Law: Aquinas to Finnis*, by P C Westerman" 4980 *Times Literary Supplement*, 11 September 1998, 26.

"Independence has to be transformed from abstract ideal to concrete proposal" *The Herald*, 14 November 1998.

1999

Questioning Sovereignty: Law, State and Nation in the European Commonwealth, Oxford: Oxford University Press.

Translated into Italian by A Torre, as *La sovranità in discussione*, Bologna: Società editrice il Mulino, 2003.

Excerpts from ch 6 included in M D A Freeman (ed), *Lloyd's Introduction to Jurisprudence*, London: Sweet & Maxwell, 2001.

Laws, Facts and Values, ed, *Law and Philosophy*, 18(5) 443-577 (special issue).

"My philosophy of law", in L Wintgens (ed), *The Law in Philosophical Perspective: My Philosophy of Law*, Dordrecht: Kluwer Academic Publishers, 121-145 (also published with modification as part of ch 1 in *Questioning Sovereignty*, 1999).

"Nation and nationalism", in R Beiner (ed), *Theorizing Nationalism*, Albany: SUNY Press, 189-204 (also published, in an earlier version, by the Scottish Academic Press, in 1979, and with modification as ch 13 in *Legal Right and Social Democracy*, 1982).

"Does a nation need a state? Reflections on liberal nationalism", in E Mortimer and R Fine (eds), *People, Nation and State: The Meaning of Ethnicity and Nationalism*, London: I B Tauris, 125-137.

"Rhetoric and the Rule of Law", in D Dyzenhaus (ed), *Recrafting the Rule of Law: The Limits of Legal Order*, Oxford: Hart Publishing, 163-177 (also published by the Philosophy Documentation Center in 2001, and with modification as ch 2 of *Rhetoric and the Rule of Law*, 2005) (presented at the Perelman Symposium, 20th World Congress of Philosophy, Boston, 1998).

Translated into Spanish by I Linfante, as "Retórica y estado de derecho" (1999) 21 *Isegoría: Revista de filosofía moral y política*, 5-21.

"Can judges make mistakes?", in H Jung and E Neumann (eds), *Rechtsbegründung – Rechtsbegründungen*, Baden-Baden: Nomos Verlagsgesellschaft, 76-89 (presented as the annual lecture of the Centre for Law and Society, University of Edinburgh, 1986) (also published with modification as ch 13 in *Rhetoric and the Rule of Law*, 2005).

Translated into Basque by J Bengoetxea Caballero, as "Akatsik egin al dezakete epaileek?" (2003) 10 *Eleria: Euskal Herriko Legelarien Aldizkaria* 113-123 (republished in the same journal (2006) 15, 145-155).

"Powers and power-conferring norms", in S Paulson (ed), *Normativity and Norms: Critical Perspectives on Kelsenian Themes*, Oxford: Oxford University Press, 493-506 (an earlier and narrower version was presented at the 5th Siena Kelsen Symposium, June 1993) (also published with modification as ch 9 in *Institutions of Law*, 2007).

"Decentralisation, devolution and confederal independence", in E Bort and R Keat (eds), *The Boundaries of Understanding*, Edinburgh: Edinburgh University Press, 197-208.

"The impact of information technology on legal scholarship: commentary" (comment on paper by R Susskind), in T Coppock (ed), *Information Technology and Scholarship: Applications in the Humanities and Social Sciences*, Oxford: Oxford University Press, 186-188.

"The English constitution, the British state, and the Scottish anomaly" 101 *Proceedings of the British Academy* 289-306 (also published in *Scottish Affairs* in 1998, and with modification as ch 4 in *Questioning Sovereignty*, 1999).

"Institutions and laws again" 77(6) *Texas Law Review* 1429-1441.

"Democracy and subsidiarity" 1 *Diritto Pubblico* 49-60 (also published by *Law and Philosophy* in 1997, by Kluwer Academic Publishing in 1997, and with modification as ch 9 in *Questioning Sovereignty*, 1999).

"Editor's Preface" 18(5) *Law and Philosophy* 443-445 (special issue on "Laws, facts and values").

"Law is the New World Order. Review of *Crimes Against Humanity*, by G Robertson" *The Sunday Herald*, 15 August 1999, 9.

2000

Stands Scotland Where She Did? New Unions for Old in these Islands, presented as the 6th John Maurice Kelly Memorial Lecture, 21 October 1999, Dublin: Faculty of Law, University College Dublin, 27 pages.

"Legality without legalism", with Z Bańkowski, in W Krawietz, R S Summers, O Weinberger, and G H von Wright, *The Reasonable as Rational? On Legal Argumentation and Justification, Festschrift for Aulis Aarnio*, Berlin: Duncker & Humblot, 181-195.

"Ethical positivism and the practical force of legal rules", in T Campbell and J Goldsworthy (eds), *Judicial Power, Democracy and Legal Positivism*, Aldershot: Ashgate, 37-57.

"Wrongs and duties", in M Friedman, L May, K Parsons and J Stiff (eds), *Rights and Reason: Essays in Honour of Carl Wellman*, Dordrecht: Kluwer Academic Publishers, 139-155 (also published with modification as ch 6 in *Institutions of Law*, 2007).

"Devolved lands: 1. "Independence in Europe": a liberal road for the Scottish National Party", in J Prest (ed), *Balliol College Annual Record 2000*, Oxford: Oxuniprint (Oxford University Press), 11-14.

"Is there a constitutional path to Scottish independence?" 53(4) *Parliamentary Affairs* 721-736.

"Problems of democracy and subsidiarity" 6(4) *European Public Law* 531-542 (presented as a lecture at the University of Hull on 11 December 1999).

2001

A Special Conception of Juvenile Justice: Kilbrandon's Legacy, presented as the 5th Kilbrandon Child Care Lecture, University of Glasgow, 1 November 2001, publisher unknown, pamphlet held by Law and Europa Library, School of Law, University of Edinburgh, 27 pages.

"*De Iurisprudentia*", in J Cairns and O Robinson (eds), *Critical Studies in Ancient Law, Comparative Law and Legal History: Essays in Honour of Alan Watson*, Oxford: Hart Publishing, 79-82.

"Integration and integrity in the legal reasoning of the European Court of Justice", with J Bengotxea and L Moral Soriano, in G De Burca and J H H Weiler (eds), *The European Court of Justice*, Collected Courses of the Academy of European Law, Oxford: Oxford University Press, 43-86.

"Rhetoric and the Rule of Law", in D M Rasmussen (ed), *Proceedings of the Twentieth World Congress of Philosophy*, Charlottesville: Philosophy Documentation Center, vol 11, 51-67 (also published by Hart Publishing in 1999).

"Some observations about sovereignty", in European Law Students" Association – International (ed), *International Law as We Enter the 21st Century*, Berlin: Berlin Verlag Arno Spitz GmbH, 15-23.

"Foreword", in J Moore and K Munro, *Scottish Official Publications: An Introduction and Guide*, Edinburgh: The Stationery Office, vii-ix.

"On the very idea of a European constitution: jurisprudential reflections from the European Parliament" 3 *Juridisk Tidskrift vid Stockholms universitet* 529-541 (2001-2002) (presented as the Cassel lecture at the University of Stockholm on 1 June 2001).

2002

"Untitled", in T Devine and P Logue (eds), *Being Scottish: Personal Reflections on Scottish Identity Today*, Edinburgh: Edinburgh University Press, 152-154.

"Prólogo", with Z Bańkowski, in L Moral Soriano, *El Precedente Judicial*, Madrid: Marcial Pons, 9-10.

"On the very idea of intellectual property: an essay according to the institutionalist theory of law" 3 *Intellectual Property Quarterly* 228-239 (presented as the SCRIPT Presidential Lecture, School of Law, University of Edinburgh, 11 February 2002) (also published with modification as parts of chs 8 and 13 in *Institutions of Law*, 2007).

"EU update on legal aid; trade in services; Single Market; employment law;

company law; and a note on the Convention on the Future of Europe"
1 December, *The Journal Online: The Members" Magazine of the Law
Society of Scotland* (last accessed online at *http://www.journalonline.
co.uk/Magazine/47-12/1000357.aspx* on 25 July 2011).

*Scotland in the European Parliament: A View of Scotland's Potential in
Europe*, presented with I Hudghton, 15-minute film, Edinburgh: Picture
Perfect Production for the G/EFA Group in the European Parliament.

Why a European Parliament: A Guide to European Decision-Making,
presented with I Hudghton, 15-minute film, Edinburgh: Picture Perfect
Production for the G/EFA Group in the European Parliament.

2003

The New European Constitution: Legal and Philosophical Perspective,
Warszawa: Biuro Trybunału Konstytucyjnego (originally presented as the
Leon Petrazycki lecture, at the Polish Constitutional Tribunal, 11 June
2003, translated into Polish by W Mleczko).

Law and Legal Interpretation, with F Atria (eds), Aldershot: Ashgate.

"Introduction", with F Atria, in F Atria and N MacCormick (eds), *Law and
Legal Interpretation*, xi-xxxiii.

"Republicanism, Fletcher and Ferguson", in P H Scott (ed), *The Saltoun
Papers: Reflections on Andrew Fletcher*, Edinburgh: Saltire Society, 31-39.

"How to have a healthy constitution? Reviewing Allott's *Health of Nations*"
40(6) *Common Market Law Review* 1537-1549.

"First step on the road to ruin for Scotland" *Scotland on Sunday (Supplement)*, 8 June 2003, 8.

2004

*A Union of Its Own Kind? Reflections on the European Convention and the
Proposed Constitution of the European Union*, Edinburgh: Neil MacCormick (personal publication), 40 pages.

"Questioning post-sovereignty" 29(6) *European Law Review* 852-863.

"The European Constitutional Convention and the stateless nations" 18(3)
International Relations 331-344 (presented as the inaugural lecture
marking the establishment of the Wales in Regional Europe (WiRE)
project at the University of Wales, Aberystwyth, 3 November 2003).

"Doubts about the 'Supreme Court' and reflections on *MacCormick v Lord
Advocate*" 3 *Juridical Review* 237-250.

2005

Rhetoric and the Rule of Law, Oxford: Oxford University Press.

Translated into Portuguese by C Hübner Mendes and M P Veríssimo, as *Retórica e o Estado de Direito*, Rio de Janeiro: Elsevier, 2008.

Chapter 5, "Universals and particulars", translated into Spanish by G Moro, as "Universales y particulares" (2009) 32 *Doxa: Cuadernos de filosofía del derecho* 127-150.

Chapter 3, "On the legal syllogism", translated into Spanish by F Laporta, as "La argumentación silogística: una defensa matizada" (2007) 30 *Doxa: Cuadernos de filosofía del derecho* 321-334 (this chapter was first presented as the John Dewey Lecture, University of Minnesota, 2000).

Who's Afraid of a European Constitution?, Exeter: Imprint Academic.

"New unions for old", in W L Miller (ed), *Anglo-Scottish Relations from 1900 to Devolution and Beyond*, Proceedings of the British Academy vol 128, Oxford: Oxford University Press, 249-255.

"Legislative deliberation: notes from the European Parliament", in L Wintgens (ed), *The Theory and Practice of Legislation: Essays on Legisprudence*, Aldershot: Ashgate, 285-296.

"The sovereignty issue in the EU Constitution", in M C Specchia and S Suppa (eds), *Quaderni del Dottorato 2003*, Torino: Giappichelli Editore, 69-76 (presented at a workshop at Bari, 30 October 2003).

"The European constitutional process: a theoretical view", 39 *Anales de la Cátedra Francisco Suárez* 289-313 (special issue, "Derecho y justicia en una sociedad global", ed. by M E Castillo and M S L López) (published earlier, in a non-authoritative version for the IVR Congress, in M Scarmilla and M Saavedra (eds), *Law and Justice in a Global Society*, Spain: Anales de la Cátedra Francisco Suárez, 299-319 (and in Spanish at 275-297)).

"Adam Ferguson: how civil will future society be?", in B Shimshon (ed), *Enlightenment Lectures 2002*, Glasgow: Smith Institute, 17-24.

"The health of nations and the health of Europe" 7 *The Cambridge Yearbook of European Legal Studies* 1-16 (presented as the Mackenzie Stuart Lecture at the Faculty of Law, University of Cambridge, 11 November 2004).

"Taking responsibility seriously" 9(1) *Edinburgh Law Review* 168-175 (review essay of *Responsibility in Law and Morality* by P Cane) (also published with modification as parts of chs 6, 12 and 13 in *Institutions of Law*, 2007).

"Review of *A Life of H L A Hart: The Nightmare and the Noble Dream*, by Nicola Lacey" 14(3) *Social & Legal Studies* 433-435.

2006

The European Union and the Idea of a Perfect Commonwealth, presented as
  the 2006 Hume Lecture on 1 March 2006, Hume Occasional Paper No
  68, Edinburgh: David Hume Institute, 29 pages.
"Particulars and universals" in Z Bańkowski and J MacLean (eds), *The
  Universal and the Particular in Legal Reasoning*, Aldershot: Ashgate,
  25-40.
"An attempted response", in Z Bańkowski and J MacLean (eds), *The Universal
  and the Particular in Legal Reasoning*, Aldershot: Ashgate, 253-264.
"Does law really matter?", in M Leskiewicz (ed), *Australian Legal Philosophy
  Students Association Annual Publication*, Brisbane: UQ Vanguard, 5-23
  (presented as the inaugural lecture of the Australian Legal Philosophy
  Students Association, Brisbane, 2005) (also published with modification
  as part of ch 4 in *Institutions of Law*, 2007).
"Review of *John Smith: A Life* by M Stuart" 56 *Scottish Affairs* 142-145.
"Entrevista a Neil MacCormick", with M Atienza, translated into Spanish by
  M Atienza, 29 *Doxa: Cuadernos de filosofía del derecho* 479-489.

2007

Institutions of Law: An Essay in Legal Theory, Oxford: Oxford University
  Press.
"Why law makes no claims", in G Pavlakos (ed), *Law, Rights and Discourse:
  The Legal Philosophy of Robert Alexy*, Oxford: Hart Publishing, 59-68.
"Sir Neil MacCormick", in M E J Nielson (ed), *Legal Philosophy: 5 Questions*,
  New York: Automatic / VIP Press, 171-186.
"A common approach to crime? Observations on the European arrest
  warrant and the democratic deficit" in H Müller-Dietz, E Müller, K-L
  Kunz, H Radtke, G Britz, C Momsen and H Koriath (eds), *Festschrift für
  Heike Jung zum 65. Geburtstag am 23. April 2007*, Baden-Baden: Nomos,
  535-541.
"Judicial independence: who cares?" 151 *Proceedings of the British Academy*
  195-212 (presented as the 2006 British Academy Law Lecture).
"On public law and the law of nature and nations" 11(2) *Edinburgh Law
  Review* 149-161.
"The Law School of the University of Edinburgh: tercentenary address held
  in the McEwan Hall, February 2007" 53(2) *University of Edinburgh
  Journal* 84-87.
"Ronald Dworkin: Mr Justice. Review of *Exploring Law's Empire*, by S
  Hershovitz (ed); *Is Democracy Possible Here?*, by R Dworkin; *Justice in*

Robes, by R Dworkin; and *Ronald Dworkin*, by A Ripstein (ed)", 5462 *Times Literary Supplement*, 5 December 2007, 3-5.

"Interview about *Institutions of Law*", with M Del Mar, *Podcasts in Legal Theory Nr 1*, School of Law, University of Edinburgh, original airdate 5 June 2007, last accessed online 25 July 2011 at *http://law-srv0.law.ed.ac. uk/media/20_podcastsinlegaltheory1.mp3*.

2008

Practical Reason in Law and Morality, Oxford: Oxford University Press.

H L A Hart, 2nd ed, Stanford: Stanford University Press.

"MacCormick on MacCormick", in A J Menéndez and J E Fossum (eds), *The Post-Sovereign Constellation: Law and Democracy in Neil D* [sic] *MacCormick's Legal and Political Theory*, Report 04/08, Oslo: Arena, 11-20 (also published in 2011 by Springer).

"The Convention and its Constitution: all a great mistake?", in H Petersen, A L Kjær, H Krunke and M R Madsen (eds), *Paradoxes of European Legal Integration*, Aldershot: Ashgate, 17-27.

"Church of Scotland", in P Cane and J Conaghan (eds), *The New Oxford Companion to Law*, Oxford: Oxford University Press, 128.

"Revolution", in P Cane and J Conaghan (eds), *The New Oxford Companion to Law*, Oxford: Oxford University Press, 1020-1021.

"Scottish Parliament", in P Cane and J Conaghan (eds), *The New Oxford Companion to Law*, Oxford: Oxford University Press, 1059-1060.

"Treaty of Union", in P Cane and J Conaghan (eds), *The New Oxford Companion to Law*, Oxford: Oxford University Press, 1192.

"Introduction", in J MacCormick, *The Flag in the Wind: The Story of the National Movement in Scotland*, Edinburgh: Birlinn, ix-xvii.

"A Reply to comments on *Rhetoric and the Rule of Law*", 59(1) *Northern Ireland Legal Quarterly* 43-48.

"Review of *Our Knowledge of the Law*, by G Pavlakos and *Law as a Moral Idea*, by N Simmonds", 12(1) *Edinburgh Law Review* 150-153.

"Promises", *Interview on Philosophy Talk*, original airdate: 5 November 2008, last accessed online on 25 July 2011 at *http://philosophytalk.org/ pastShows/Promises.htm*.

"Just Law", valedictory lecture, Playfair Library, University of Edinburgh, 28 January, last accessed online on 25 July 2011 at *http://law-srv0.law.ed.ac. uk/media/42_professorneilmcormacksvalidictorylecture.mp3*.

2009

"Stair and the natural law tradition: still relevant?", in H MacQueen (ed), *Miscellany Six*, Edinburgh: The Stair Society, 1-10 (presented as a lecture at the Annual General Meeting of the Stair Society, Edinburgh, 3 November 2007).

"Concluding for institutionalism", in M Del Mar and Z Bańkowski (eds), *Law as Institutional Normative Order*, Surrey: Ashgate, 187-200.

2010

"Sovereignty and after", in H Kalmo and Q Skinner (eds), *Sovereignty in Fragments: The Past, Present and Future of a Contested Concept*, Cambridge: Cambridge University Press, 151-168.

2011

"MacCormick on MacCormick", in A J Menéndez and J E Fossum (eds), *Law and Democracy in Neil MacCormick's Legal and Political Theory: The Post-Sovereign Constellation*, Dordrecht: Springer, 17-24 (also published by Arena in 2008).

"Direito, interpretação e razoabilidade", R Porto Macedo Jr (ed), *Direito e Interpretação: Racionalidade e Instituições*, São Paulo: Editora Saraiva, 31-62.

B. A BIBLIOGRAPHICAL ESSAY ON SCOTTISH THEMES

Scottish themes are ever-present in MacCormick's work. Even when they are not explicitly discussed, a reader familiar with MacCormick's writings feels that Scottish issues or Scottish thinkers are never too far away, whether in the background or on the horizon. Certain Scottish thinkers, such as Lord Stair, David Hume and Adam Smith were lifelong intellectual companions and interlocutors for MacCormick. Arguably, though, the entire tradition of the Scottish Enlightenment was one that MacCormick not only drew on to fulfil his academic duties as Regius Professor of Public Law, and the Law of Nature and Nations, but also as inspiration for and guidance in his involvement in public affairs.

Given the breadth and depth of Scottish influences and issues in his work, what follows below is necessarily non-exhaustive. The focus is largely on publications where Scottish themes receive extended and explicit treatment, though some attention is also paid to general discussions informed by Scottish thinkers or issues. The first section focuses on Scottish thinkers, while the second focuses on Scottish issues. Each section is further sub-divided into sub-sections, which are detailed at the beginning of each section.

Full citations are omitted, providing only the title and the year – the full entry can be consulted above in the bibliography.

(1) Scottish thinkers

This section is further sub-divided into the following sub-sections: (a) Stair; (b) Hume; (c) Smith; and (d) Other figures and general remarks.

(a) Stair

The influence of James Dalrymple of Stair (known from 1661 as Lord Stair) is visible from the beginning of MacCormick's career. In some publications, the focus is on solutions to quite specific legal problems, such as in "Ius Quaesitum Tertio" (1970), where MacCormick argues that Scots law should adopt Stair's solution to the issue of the enforcement of third party rights under contracts. On other occasions, Stair is said to have provided not only "a clear expository statement of the law of Scotland" ("Law", 1993, 344), but also to have written a treatise worth pride of place in any account of general jurisprudence. Indeed, MacCormick at times bestows the highest possible praise on Stair's *Institutions of the Law of Scotland* (1681; definitive edition 1693), saying, for example, that

> for beauty and elegance of presentation, and for the lucidly systematic approach he takes to his subject, his work stands comparison with the other great works of European law in the seventeenth century ... Stair's work wins particular distinction from the philosophical originality and rigour of his approach to legal exposition. ("Law", 1993, 345)

Stair's endorsement of law as a rational order grounded in three basic principles (obedience, freedom and engagement), where positive laws are made for the convenience of imperfect practical reasoners aiming at the protection of society, property and commerce, was of central importance for MacCormick, and is particularly visible in "The rational discipline of law" (1981). Indeed, any reader of MacCormick's works should be loathe to underestimate the extent to which he subscribed to (though also often sought to qualify and soften) Stair's idea that "Law is the dictate of reason determining every rational being to that which is congruous and convenient for the nature thereof" (quoted in *Legal Reasoning and Legal Theory*, 1978/1994, 2). The most sustained analyses of Stair can be found in the following publications: "Law, obligation and consent: reflections on Stair and Locke" (1979; this also appeared as ch 4 of *Legal Right and Social Democracy*, 1982); "Stair as analytical jurist" (1981); "Spontaneous order and Rule of Law: some problems" (1986); "Autonomy and freedom", "Obedience, freedom, and engagement – or utility?", and "Society, property, and commerce" (chs 5, 6, and 7, respectively, of *Practical Reason in Law and Morality*, 2008); and "Stair and the natural law tradition: still relevant?" (2009).

(b) Hume

David Hume is perhaps the most central Scottish thinker in MacCormick's corpus. MacCormick often professed to be "an addict" of Hume's writings (see "Does law really matter?", 2006, 19), returning to them consistently throughout his career. Unlike Stair, however, Hume was for MacCormick often more of an adversary (even if an inspiring one – as was also the case for Kant) than an ally. It was Hume's "scepticism about the limits of reason in practical affairs" (*Legal Reasoning and Legal Theory*, 1978/1994, 2) that especially animated MacCormick, and many of his works (including the last book, *Practical Reason in Law and Morality*, 2008) can be considered ripostes to Hume's challenge. Of course, matters are not that simple, and MacCormick's disagreement with Hume is a nuanced one; for example, in *Legal Reasoning and Legal Theory*, MacCormick argues that although "any mode of evaluative argument must involve, depend on, or presuppose, some ultimate premises which are not themselves provable, demonstrable or confirmable in terms of further or ulterior reasons" (5; this non-cognitivism about value being a concession to Hume), he also argues that "this does not mean the same as saying that no reasons at all cannot be given for adhering to such ultimate normative premises – "principles" – as grounds for action and judgement" (although these may be reasons upon which "honest and reason-able people can and do differ", 5; see ch 10 of *Legal Reasoning and Legal Theory* for a more extended discussion). Later, in the 1994 preface to *Legal Reasoning and Legal Theory*, and again explicitly in *Rhetoric and the Rule of Law* (2005), MacCormick distanced himself from what he referred to as "the value-scepticism derived from David Hume that formed the backcloth to the argument in *Legal Reasoning and Legal Theory*" (*Rhetoric and the Rule of Law*, 1). Hume is, then, often an impetus and starting point of inquiry for MacCormick, as for instance in ch 1 of *Legal Right and Social Democracy* (1982; where a discussion of Hume on justice introduces the themes explored in the book). References to Hume are scattered throughout MacCormick's writings, and it would be impossible to list them all; some prominent examples (in chronological order) include: "Justice: an un-original position" (1976, and also ch 5 of *Legal Right and Social Democracy*, 1982, where Hume's notion of impartiality is appealed to); "What is wrong with deceit?" (1983; where Hume on trust is discussed); "Spontaneous order and the Rule of Law: some problems" (1986/1989; which includes some analysis of Hume on justice and liberty); and "Republicanism and Enlightenment thought" (1992; where "Hume on free government" is analysed, and his views are compared with those of Madison and Hamilton). MacCormick also presented a number of lectures to meetings of the David Hume Institute (of which MacCormick was an honorary vice-president), including "Commentary on 'The Future of Legal Systems' by Thijmen Koopmans" (1990); "What place for nationalism in the modern world?" (1994); and "The European Union and the idea of a perfect commonwealth" (2006), which offers an extensive discussion of the applicability of Hume's political theory to "current problems about democracy in the UK and in the European Union" (2006, 1).

(c) Smith

Like Stair and Hume, Adam Smith was a figure on whose work MacCormick drew throughout his career. Smith's moral philosophy played a central role in MacCormick's last book, *Practical Reason in Law and Morality* (2008). There, MacCormick argued that our understanding of practical reason is best served by a mixture of insights from Kant and Smith, constructing what he called "The Smithian categorical imperative" (the key discussion of Smith is in ch 3, "Right and wrong"). There were hints in earlier writings that MacCormick was positively disposed to Smith's account of the moral life (in addition to his admiration for Smith's contributions to jurisprudence). These earlier writings include: "Adam Smith on law" (1981, which later appeared, under a different title, "Law and economics: Adam Smith's analysis", as ch 6 of *Legal Right and Social Democracy*, 1982); "A moralistic case for a-moralistic law" (1985, see especially at 33-35, where duties of justice and love are discussed and compared); "What is wrong with deceit?" (1983, which includes a discussion of Smith on trust); "Reasonableness and objectivity" (1998-1999, where Smith's impartial spectator device, especially in terms of its advocacy of detached impartiality, is discussed by reference to the concept of reasonableness); "Institutions and laws again" (1999; see especially at 1439 on the inductive method); and "Universals and particulars" (ch 5 of *Rhetoric and the Rule of Law*, especially at 85-88 where the "sympathies of the impartial spectator" are discussed). Nevertheless, despite smatterings of references to Smith in earlier writings, it was arguably only in *Practical Reason in Law and Morality* that MacCormick showed just how important he felt Smith's contribution was. Other significant references to Smith, especially with respect to his *Lectures on Jurisprudence*, can be found in: "Review of A Smith, *Lectures on Jurisprudence*, ed by R L Meek, D D Raphael, P G Stein" (1978); and "Private law and civil society: law and economy" (ch 13 of *Institutions of Law*, especially at 236-7).

(d) Other figures and general remarks

Though very prominent in MacCormick's works, Stair, Hume and Smith were by no means the only Scottish thinkers that MacCormick drew on in his writings. Indeed, MacCormick was deeply influenced by the "spirit" of the Scottish Enlightenment, both in terms of the substance of his work, and in the exemplary way he was able to fulfil the Enlightenment vision of a public intellectual. His views on the importance of Enlightenment values, for instance in legal education, are clearly visible in "The Democratic Intellect and the Law" (1985). His other general writings on the Scottish Enlightenment include "Law and Enlightenment" (1982); "The idea of a free government" (1985); "Republicanism and Enlightenment thought: observations from Scotland" (1992; this and the previous paper both consider the impact of the Scottish Enlightenment on the American constitutional tradition); and "On public law and the law of nature and nations" (2007). The figures that MacCormick mentions consistently include John Erskine, Lord Bankton, Lord Kames, John Millar, Francis Hutcheson, Thomas Reid, Adam Ferguson, and Dugald Stewart (e.g. see *Legal Reasoning and Legal Theory*, 1978/1994, 4; and *Legal Right and Social Democracy*, 1982, 103). Adam Ferguson and Andrew Fletcher are singled out for discussion in "Republicanism, Fletcher and Ferguson" (2003). In addition, Ferguson is discussed in MacCormick's contribution to the 2002 Enlightenment Lectures organised by the Smith Institute in Glasgow (see "Adam Ferguson: how civil will future society be?", 2005). James Lorimer (though a figure of the nineteenth century, still considered – certainly by MacCormick – to be part of the Scottish Enlightenment tradition) is the focus of "The idea of liberty" (1984). In his "My philosophy of law" (1999), MacCormick explicitly states that in his original philosophical training at Glasgow University, "the ideas of Kant and those of the of the intuitionist moral philosophers played a great part, along with a close regard to the history of philosophy and particularly to some of the great thinkers of the Scottish Enlightenment" (141). Much remains to be done to trace the influence of Scottish thinkers, and the spirit of the Scottish Enlightenment, on MacCormick's work, but even on the basis of the references selected above, it is clear that there is plenty of evidence in support of such a task.

(2) Scottish issues

This section is sub-divided into the following five sub-sections: (a) Personal reflections on Scottish issues; (b) Internal Scottish issues; (c) Scottish relations with England; (d) The view from Europe; and (e) General reflections on constitutional matters of significance to Scotland.

(a) Personal reflections on Scottish issues

Although they are rare, there are occasions on which MacCormick delved into his and his family's history, often as a way of introducing more general themes of importance to Scottish political life. The most striking early example is his lecture to the Scottish National Party Annual National conference in Inverness in 1988 (entitled *Constitutionalism and Democracy*). Fittingly, MacCormick began that lecture with a reference to his father's (John MacCormick's) book, *The Flag in the Wind* (1955), where he noted that his "father wrote movingly, though also amusingly, of the first launching, fifty nine years ago, of the National Party in Scotland in the Highlands" (1; this launch was also held in Inverness). When invited, in 1997, by the *Times Higher Education Supplement*, to contribute to their "Speaking Volumes" series on important books, MacCormick originally thought of contributing a piece on Hume's *Treatise*, but in the end chose his father's book (see "Speaking volumes", 1997). Later, in 2008, when the second printing of his father's book appeared, MacCormick wrote a very personal, moving – and indeed amusing – introduction to it (see also "A filial look at Home Rule's founding father", *The Scotsman*, 1974). The 1988 lecture also refers to Neil Gunn as "the greatest of our modern novelists" (1), and MacCormick was later to write a tribute to Gunn in "Neil Gunn and nationalism: a memoir" (1991-1992). Another memoir of note was of the Scottish politician John Smith in 1994 ("John Smith: an appreciation"; see also "Review of *John Smith: A Life* by M Stuart" in 2006). Perhaps his most sustained personal reflection on Scottish issues was an untitled piece as part of a collection called *Being Scottish: Personal Reflections on Scottish Identity Today* (2002; edited by T Devine and P Logue), where the following quote is indicative of the value of MacCormick's personal reflections for understanding his treatment of the issue of Scottish relations with England and Europe: "In my professional life, as in the European Parliament, I move in a completely international milieu, while remaining consciously an heir of the massively significant philosophical tradition of the democratic intellect and of Scots law. I hope that means that I am very Scottish, but not narrowly so, and that my highly liberal nationalism is the other face of my internationalism" (154).

(b) Internal Scottish issues

Although his work is celebrated for its treatment of issues of importance to United Kingdom and European governance, MacCormick was also engaged with more domestic issues. Examples not directly related to Scottish independence or Scottish constitutional issues include two early pieces in *Scots Law News* ("Seabathing, sunbathing and sea coal" and "The Misrepresentation Act, 1967", both 1967); "Ius quaesitum tertio" (1970; dealing with third party rights under contracts); "Changing waterfront uses on the River Clyde, Scotland" (1987); and *A Special Conception of Juvenile Justice: Kilbrandon's Legacy* (a lecture presented in 2001 dealing with the Children's Hearing System in Scotland). MacCormick was certainly engaged with questions concerning the design of Scottish institutions, including both the judiciary and the legislature, as is evident from the following publications: "Accountability, professionalism and the Scottish judiciary" (1976); "The Scottish Parliament as law-maker: laws for an Information Age?" (1998); and "A parliament once again?" (1998). MacCormick's awareness of the importance of a proper understanding of the role of legal professionals was clear early on when he took on the task of editing *Lawyers in their Social Setting* (1976). He was also deeply interested in the history and rational quality of Scots law; see, for example: "General legal concepts" (1990; a chapter for *The Laws of Scotland: Stair Memorial Encyclopaedia*, edited by T B Smith and R Black); "Law" (1993; a chapter for a collected entitled *Scotland: A Concise History*, edited by P H Scott); and "The law is a Mongrel: how a separate legal tradition underpins Scottish nationhood. *Review of A Legal History of Scotland, Volume 2*, by D M Walker" (1996). There is no doubt, however, that MacCormick's most important contribution to domestic Scottish issues was his expertise in constitutional matters. The leading example here is "An idea for a Scottish constitution" (1991; a chapter in *Edinburgh Essays in Public Law*, edited by W Finnie, C Himsworth and N Walker), which includes not only an analysis of, but the actual text of, the Scottish National Party's policy statement on a Scottish constitution. As MacCormick explains in that chapter, he served as "Vice-Convenor ... of the policy committee which drew up the text, as well as the principal draftsman of it", taking also a "principal role in the advocacy of the proposals in the SNP's National Assembly in 1976-7 and at its Party conference in Dundee in 1977" (159).

(c) Scottish relations with England

As one would expect of a leading member of the Scottish National Party – indeed, as the son of one of its founders, John MacCormick – Neil MacCormick's works are awash with discussion of Scotland's relations with England. Discussion of those relations in MacCormick's work is often bound up with the promise of Europe as a commonwealth of post-sovereigns (see the next section on "The view from Europe"): "Scotland in Europe" was, after all, a more positive message than rupture with England (but see, "Time to tear ourselves away", *The Scotsman*, 1992; and "First step on the road to ruin for Scotland", *Scotland on Sunday (Supplement)*, 2003). A brief sub-section in a bibliographical essay is not the occasion to attempt to canvass the trajectory and shape of MacCormick's views on Scottish independence and its constitutional dimensions. MacCormick himself often said (see, for example, his interview in *Legal Philosophy: 5 Questions*, 2007, at 180) that the key starting point for his views on independence and nationalism was ch 11 of *Questioning Sovereignty*, "A kind of nationalism" (1999; this chapter overlaps, in part, with the earlier, "What place for nationalism in the modern world", 1994, and "Liberalism, nationalism and the post-sovereign state", 1996). In addition to that chapter, the following sources are important: *The Scottish Debate* (1970, a collection edited by MacCormick, which includes his "Introduction" and a chapter on "Independence and constitutional change"); "The rise of Scottish nationalism: a case of too little too late?" (1974); *Independence and Federalism After the Referendum* (1975; a lecture presented to the Andrew Fletcher Society); "Two-stranded support for legislative devolution" (*The Scotsman*, 1976); "Does the United Kingdom have a constitution? Reflections on *MacCormick v Lord Advocate*" (1978, the case referred to in the title is the famous decision of the Court of Session in 1953, where the leading petitioner was MacCormick's father); "Constitutional points" (1979); "Nation and nationalism" (1979; also published as ch 13 of *Legal Right and Social Democracy*, 1982, and then again, with some modifications, in 1999); "Constitution" (1979; this was a response by MacCormick to Lord Hailsham's lecture on "The nation and the constitution", delivered at the University of St Andrews in 1978); "Unrepentant gradualism" (1989; an important essay in a collection, edited by O D Edwards, on the *Claim of Right* (to which MacCormick was a signatory), in which MacCormick also outlined his "disagreement with the party leadership's posture of opposition to the convening of a convention on the terms proposed in the Claim", 99); "Constitutionalism and constitutions" (1989); "Sovereignty or subsidiarity? Some comments on Scottish devolution" (1998); "The English constitution, the British state,

and the Scottish anomaly" (1998; also appeared in 1999); "Does a nation
need a state? Reflections on liberal nationalism" (1999); *Stands Scotland
Where She Did? New Unions for Old in these Islands* (2000; a lecture delivered in Dublin); "Is there a constitutional path to Scottish independence?"
(2000; this being a detailed discussion of potential constitutional barriers to
independence, and solutions to them); "Doubts about the 'Supreme Court'
and reflections on *MacCormick v Lord Advocate*" (2004); "New unions for
old" (2005), and "Treaty of Union" (2008).

(d) The view from Europe

MacCormick was especially well placed to discuss Scottish, and indeed
English, relations with Europe. This was due to his experience both theoretically, as a distinguished scholar of public law and constitutional politics, but
also practically, as a Scottish public figure, Scottish politician and, from 1999
to 2004, Member of the European Parliament (including the Convention on
the Future of Europe). His contributions to the issues here can be divided
into three themes: first, his writings on sovereignty in the European context;
second, his publications on subsidiarity; and third, his work on the European
Constitution. His work on sovereignty in the European context includes:
"Beyond the sovereign state" (1993); "The *Maastricht-Urteil*: sovereignty
now" (1995); "Sovereignty: myth and reality" (1995); "Sovereignty, democracy and subsidiarity" (1995); "Liberalism, nationalism and the post-sovereign state" (1996); "After sovereignty: understanding constitutional change"
(1998); "Risking constitutional collision in Europe?" (1998); *Questioning
Sovereignty: Law, State and Nation in the European Commonwealth* (1999);
"Some observations about sovereignty" (2001); "The sovereignty issue in the
EU Constitution" (2003); "Questioning post-sovereignty" (2004); and "Sovereignty and after" (2010). His writings on subsidiarity include: "Sovereignty,
democracy and subsidiarity" (1995); "Democracy, subsidiarity and citizenship in the 'European Commonwealth'" (1997); and "Problems of democracy
and subsidiarity" (2000). In terms of the European Constitution and the work
of the Convention on the Future of Europe, the relevant publications are:
"On the very idea of a European constitution: jurisprudential reflections from
the European Parliament" (2002); "The sovereignty issue in the EU Constitution" (2003); *The New European Constitution: Legal and Philosophical
Perspective* (lecture delivered at the Polish Constitutional Tribunal, 2003);
*A Union of Its Own Kind? Reflections on the European Convention and the
Proposed Constitution of the European Union* (2004, a document published
personally by MacCormick while still a Member of the European Parliament,

which includes an account of the applicability of his theory of institutional normative order to European governance); "The European Constitutional Convention and the stateless nations" (2004); *Who's Afraid of a European Constitution?* (2005); "The European constitutional process: a theoretical view" (2005); and "The Convention and its Constitution: all a great mistake?" (2008). A number of other more wide-ranging publications on European governance are also of note here, and these include: "The European Union?" (1995; co-authored with Z Bańkowski and A Scott); "The health of nations and the health of Europe" (2005); and *The European Union and the Idea of a Perfect Commonwealth* (lecture to the David Hume Institute, 2006). MacCormick also reflected on his personal experience in the European Parliament in a number of publications; see, for example, "Legislative deliberation: notes from the European Parliament" (2005); and "Prologue: institutional theory and the lawmaker's perspective" (ch 1 of *Rhetoric and the Rule of Law*, 2005). Finally, aficionados may wish to consult two 15-minute films, presented in 2002 with I Hudghton: *Scotland in the European Parliament: A View of Scotland's Potential in Europe*; and *Why a European Parliament: A Guide to European Decision-Making*.

(e) General reflections on constitutional matters of significance to Scotland

Finally, it is relevant to list a number of other publications by MacCormick that a searching reader might wish to consider if developing a more general account of MacCormick's contribution to our understanding of Scottish issues, especially Scottish independence. Those sources already mentioned above are not listed here. These more general, but still relevant, sources include: *Enlightenment, Rights and Revolution: Essays in Legal and Social Philosophy* (1989; co-edited with Z Bańkowski); "Of self-determination and other things" (1990); "Preface" (1991; co-authored with W Twining, in the collection edited by them entitled *Issues of Self-Determination*); "Is nationalism philosophically credible?" (1991; a chapter in the just-referenced collection); "Constitutionalism and democracy" (1993); "What place for nationalism in the modern world?" (1994); "Does a nation need a state?" (1999); and "How to have a healthy constitution? Reviewing Allott's *Health of Nations*" (2003).

Enlightened Scots

3 John Millar and Slavery

John W Cairns[*]

A. INTRODUCTION
B. 1769-1771
(1) Publication of the first edition
(2) The first edition
(3) The cases
(4) The lectures
(5) The influence of Adam Smith
C. 1771-1778
(1) Critical reception
(2) Second edition
(3) The cases
(4) The lectures
(5) Smith, *Wealth of Nations*
D. 1778-1801
(1) Preparation of a third edition
(2) The third edition
(3) Further prints
(4) Lectures
E. CONCLUSION

A. INTRODUCTION

When I arrived as a first-year student in the University of Edinburgh's Faculty of Law in October 1973, the Dean who greeted the new entering class was Neil MacCormick. The next year he was to be my tutor in Jurisprudence. I only came to know him well, however, when, in January 1985, I returned to Edinburgh with an understanding that I would teach across the then Departments of Civil Law, Jurisprudence, and Scots Law. As well as tutoring for a

[*] Professor of Legal History, University of Edinburgh. I am grateful for the comments of my friends Norma Dawson, Catherine Jones, Paul du Plessis and Hector MacQueen. I also am delighted to acknowledge the permissions of the Librarians of the Mitchell Library and the University Libraries of Edinburgh and Glasgow, the Keeper of the Advocates Library, the Keeper of the Records of Scotland, and the Trustees of the National Library of Scotland for permission to cite and sometimes quote from material in their care.

while in Jurisprudence, I taught – with Neil – a class initially called Jurisprudence Honours C, later renamed History of Legal Ideas. Under both names, it dealt with legal theory in the Scottish Enlightenment. When approached about participating in this day (and volume) in honour of his memory, it therefore seemed appropriate to give a paper on the topic of the Enlightenment.

In the course, we always read parts of John Millar's work known in its third edition of 1779 as *The Origin of the Distinction of Ranks*.[1] In 1981, referring primarily to this book in a seminal essay on "Law and Enlightenment", Neil fairly described Millar as having "made his main published contributions in the vein of philosophical social history".[2] The work had first been published in London in 1771 by the famous Scots-born publisher John Murray with the title *Observations Concerning the Distinction of Ranks in Society*.[3] In it Millar applied a version of Adam Smith's theory of stages of social development to what we would now consider issues of hierarchy in a variety of social structures, including the family, political society, and the workplace. It is mainly because of this book that Millar's work has sometimes been claimed, perhaps not entirely unreasonably, as a forerunner of sociology;[4] sometimes, indeed, he has even been viewed as a type of Marxist *avant la lettre*.[5]

However we may wish to view Millar, it is notable that he served as Regius Professor of Civil Law in Neil's own University of Glasgow from 1761 to 1801. Indeed, like Neil, he was a remarkably successful and popular teacher, who broadened the curriculum from three courses on Roman law (two on Justinian's *Institutes*, the other on his *Digest*) to include classes on Scots law, Government, and even English law, while turning the second course on the *Institutes* into one on jurisprudence.[6] It has long been recognised that

---

1 J Millar, *The Origin of the Distinction of Ranks; Or, An Inquiry into the Circumstances which Give Rise to Influence and Authority, in the Different Members of Society*, 3rd edn (1779). A text is now conveniently available in the Natural Law and Enlightenment Classics series; general editor, Knud Haakonssen, edited by Aaron Garrett (2006).

2 N MacCormick, "Law and Enlightenment", in R H Campbell and A S Skinner (eds), *The Origins and Nature of the Scottish Enlightenment* (1982) 150-166 at 151.

3 W Zachs, *The First John Murray and the Late-Eighteenth-Century London Book Trade* (1998) 70, 165, 260.

4 W Sombart, "Die Anfänge der Soziologie", in M Palyi (ed), *Hauptprobleme der Soziologie: Errinerungsgabe für Max Weber* (1923: repr 1975) 3-19 at 11; W C Lehmann, "John Millar, historical sociologist: some remarkable anticipations of modern sociology" (1952) 3 *British Journal of Sociology* 30-46.

5 R Pascal, "Property and society: the Scottish Historical School of the eighteenth century"(1938) 1 *Modern Quarterly*167-179; R L Meek, *Economics and Ideology and Other Essays: Studies in the Development of Economic Thought* (1967) 34-50; J Kucyzynski, *Zur Geschichte der Wirtschafts-geschichtsschreibung* (1978) 92-93.

6 J W Cairns, "'Famous as a school for Law as Edinburgh for Medicine': The Glasgow Law School, 1761-1801", in A Hook and R B Sher (eds), *The Glasgow Enlightenment* (1995) 133-159; J W Cairns,

the themes found in Millar's published work were very evidently developed through and from his classes.[7]

The fifth chapter of the *Distinction of Ranks in Society* was entitled in the first edition "Of the condition of servants in different parts of the world".[8] It is closely related to Millar's lectures at Glasgow, and features prominently in his correspondence with his publisher, John Murray. The main focus of this chapter is on slavery, and Millar wrote and revised it through two further editions against the backdrop of litigation in Scotland and England directly dealing with the status of men of African origin held as slaves, as well as of a law suit in which an (almost certainly) enslaved African was named as a witness before the Commissary Court and the implicit recognition by a Circuit Court of Justiciary of a Bengali woman as enslaved.[9]

When Millar started his book, those who engaged to work in the coal mines and salt pans in Scotland as colliers and salters in theory became bound for life to the mine or salt works, unable to engage in other occupation or leave to work in another mine or works. They were thus in a semi-servile position. These occupations had acquired this status in 1606 by Act of Parliament in an attempt to provide labour in vital industries when manpower was scarce.[10] The position of these men was changed in 1775 and 1799. It is clear, however, that not all colliers and salters were "serfs"; and indeed, the motives behind their emancipation may also be debated as partly humanitarian and partly economic, with coal-masters wanting a more flexible work force.[11] Millar was quite aware of the status of these individuals and used it as an example in his discussions.

Millar was a well-known and acknowledged opponent of slavery and

---

"John Millar, Ivan Andreyevich Tret'yakov, and Semyon Efimovich Desnitsky: a legal education in Scotland, 1761-1767", in T Artemieva, P Jones and M Mikeshin (eds), *The Philosophical Age. Russia and Scotland in the Enlightenment: Proceedings of the International Conference 1-3 September 2000, Edinburgh* (2001 [= *The Philosophical Age*, Almanac 15]) 20-37.

7 See e.g., K Haakonssen, "John Millar and the science of a legislator" (1985) *Juridical Review* 41-68 at 43. His other work is J Millar, *An Historical View of the English Government from the Settlement of the Saxons in Britain to the Accession of the House of Stewart* (1787). There is a second edition of 1790. An edition was issued in 1803 with additional material, which has been published in the Natural Law and Enlightenment Classics series, general editor Knud Haakonssen, edited by M S Phillips and D R Smith (2006).

8 J Millar, *Observations Concerning the Distinction of Ranks in Society* (1771) 193-242.

9 See J W Cairns, "Stoicism, slavery, and law: Grotian jurisprudence and its reception", in H W Blom and L C Winkel (eds), *Grotius and the Stoa* (2004 [=(2001-2002) 22-23 *Grotiana*]) 197-231 at 222-230.

10 Act 1606, c 11.

11 See B F Duckham, "Serfdom in eighteenth century Scotland" (1979) 54 *History* 178-197; C A Whatley, "Collier serfdom in mid-eighteenth-century Scotland: new light from the Rothes MSS", (1995) 22 *Archives* 25-33; C A Whatley, "The dark side of the Enlightenment? Sorting out serfdom", in T M Devine and J R Young (eds), *Eighteenth Century Scotland: New Perspectives* (1999) 259-274.

the slave trade. Thus, he was a contact in Glasgow for the noted abolitionists William Dickson and Thomas Clarkson.[12] His nephew and biographer
John Craig described him as having taken "a most active part in the abolition of the Slave Trade, by attending all the meetings held at Glasgow for
that purpose, by drawing up the Petition to the House of Commons, and
using every exertion to interest his Towns-men in the cause of humanity and
justice".[13]

Millar thus contributed to the debates over slavery and the slave trade that
were developing in Britain in the later eighteenth century. Examination of
his lectures, chapter and letters to Murray allows us to see what concerned
Millar, and what his anxieties were in dealing with the topic. This is significant since, at all social levels, eighteenth-century Scots were either directly
implicated in slavery or indirectly benefiting from it.[14] Millar will have seen in
Glasgow enslaved men and women who had been brought to Scotland from
Africa, India and the Americas. In the later eighteenth century, despite the
economic importance of slavery to many Scots and to Scotland, a number
of individuals started to participate in movements to abolish slavery and the
slave trade; but many Scots remained supporters of both.[15] It is within this
context of conflict that Millar's views should be understood.

A pupil of Adam Smith, Millar was a rights theorist. Like his mentor, his
starting point was the judgments made by the impartial spectator of the
propriety and utility of an action. Certain actions led the spectator to approve
of punishment of the actor if they violated what the spectator saw as proper
behaviour. This meant that abstention from such actions was recognised as a
natural duty and just, and there was a corresponding natural right not to be
subject to them. Laws were intended to promote justice by protecting such
natural rights, which continued after the foundation of civil society, though
some were given up to government and others modified. Such abrogation
of natural rights was necessary and justified only in so far as the effective

---

12 See I Whyte, *Scotland and the Abolition of Black Slavery, 1756-1838* (2006) 78, 91.

13 J Craig, "Account of the life and writings of John Millar, Esq", in *The Origin of the Distinction of
    Ranks: Or, An Inquiry into the Circumstances which Give Rise to Influence and Authority, in the
    Different Members of Society*, ed A Garrett (2006) 7-80 at 68. Craig's "Life" originally appeared in
    the 4th edn (1806). Though Craig does not say, should he be correct, this presumably is a petition
    sent by the University: see Whyte, *Scotland and the Abolition of Black Slavery* (n 12) 70-71, 91.

14 For an aspect of this, see now T M Devine, "Did slavery make Scotia great?" (2011) 4 *Britain and
    the World* 40-64.

15 C Duncan Rice, *The Rise and Fall of Black Slavery* (1975) 153-185; C Duncan Rice, "Controversies
    over slavery in eighteenth- and nineteenth-century Scotland", in L Perry and M Fellman (eds),
    Antislavery Reconsidered: New Perspectives on the Abolitionists (1979) 24-48; see now generally
    Whyte, *Scotland and the Abolition of Black Slavery* (n 12) 70-106.

functioning of society required it, while historical development led to recognition of new rights and their elaboration into law.[16]

It is interesting to speculate on what Millar would have made of Neil's Kantian Smith or Smithian Kant;[17] but he would certainly have found Neil's *Institutions of Law: An Essay in Legal Theory* a sympathetic work. Indeed, in what it covers (and to some extent in its structure) it resembles Millar's classes on jurisprudence and government. In this work Neil discusses status as related to capacities;[18] Millar would have agreed, and his discussion of master and servant is about how servants – as a rank – acquire or lose capacities over the centuries, sometimes free, sometimes enslaved, and sometimes, somehow, in between.

B. 1769-1771

(1) Publication of the first edition

On 5 January 1770, Millar "gave a Discourse on the Condition of Servants in different ages and Countries" before the Glasgow Literary Society.[19] He was evidently well advanced in preparation of the relevant chapter of the *Distinction of Ranks* and was seeking reactions to his scholarship. By the summer London booksellers were interested in publishing the work.[20] Millar offered the famous publisher Thomas Cadell first refusal; but John Murray was keen to get it.[21] Millar had completed the first draft of the book by November 1770, when he sent it to some friends in Edinburgh.[22] On 9 February 1771, the manuscript finally reached Murray, who had won the rights to the book for 100 guineas.[23] By April, Millar had seen the bulk of the print and had reluctantly provided a preface at the urging of Murray, who was worried that the book was too short.[24] Millar altered the text sufficiently that a cancel leaf

16 See e.g. Haakonssen, "John Millar" (n. 7) 44-50; Cairns, "Famous as a school for Law" (n 6) 139-140.
17 N MacCormick, *Practical Reason in Law and Morality* (2008) 57-68.
18 N MacCormick, *Institutions of Law: An Essay in Legal Theory* (2007) 77-99.
19 "Minutes, Literary Society in Glasgow College, 1764-79", Glasgow University Library [hereafter GUL], MS Murray 505, 33.
20 J Murray to J Moore, 6 July 1770, National Library of Scotland [hereafter NLS], MS 41897.
21 J Murray to J Moore, 1 Sept 1770, NLS, MS 41897; see also R B Sher, *The Enlightenment and the Book: Scottish Authors and their Publishers in Eighteenth-Century Britain, Ireland, and America* (2006) 384. On Cadell, see C Dille, "Cadell, Thomas, the elder (1742–1802)", in *Oxford Dictionary of National Biography*, 2004; online edn, Jan 2008 [*http://www.oxforddnb.com/view/article/4302*, accessed 24 July 2011].
22 J Millar to J Murray, 7 Jan 1771, NLS, MS 40813.
23 J Murray to J Millar, 9 Feb 1771, NLS, MS 41897; J Millar to J Murray, 15 Feb 1771, NLS, MS 40813; J Millar to J Murray, 17 Mar 1771, NLS, MS 40813.
24 J Murray to J Millar, 7 Mar 1771, NLS, MS 41898; J Millar to J Murray, 28 April 1771, NLS, MS 40813. See Zachs, *First John Murray* (n 3) 70.

was required in the first chapter; he subsequently proposed some *errata*,
but too late for inclusion.[25] The work was published in May, Millar's friend
Gilbert Stuart having helped see it through the press.[26]

(2) The first edition

The chapter on the condition of servants may be divided into four parts (a
division made explicit in the second edition). In the first, Millar argued that,
before manners were civilised and regular government established, poor
people necessarily served the rich in servile tasks, either through voluntary
subjection or capture in war. He raised the issue of "how far" a master was
entitled "to make use of that power which fortune has put into his hands",
adding that it is "difficult to ascertain the degree of authority which, from
the principles of justice and humanity, we are ... permitted to assume over
our fellow-creatures". He commented that in those primitive times to "be a
servant ... was almost universally the same thing as to be a slave". He thus
explained how slavery had arisen among the ancient nations as well as now
existed among "those tribes of barbarians, in different parts of the world, with
which we have any correspondence". He then had to account for why "the
savages of America" had few slaves, while the Tartars many. The first were
too poor to support servants, so they killed their enemies; but the large herds
and flocks of the latter gave them a surplus to support servants, so they saved
their captives". He finally noted that "the negroes upon the coast of Guinea"
derived advantages "from sparing the lives of their enemies" because of "their
intercourse with the nations of Europe". This had also caused them to engage
in more, but less bloody, wars. But "the great demand for slaves to supply
the European market" also encouraged them "to seize the person of their
neighbours, which may excite the inhabitants of other countries to rob one
another of their property". Millar thus argued that the European slave trade
encouraged these peoples to engage in wars to supply the market.[27]

The second part of the chapter examines the effects of opulence and civili-
sation on the treatment of servants. Two issues are covered. First, Millar wrote
that as societies "become civilized" and peoples progressed "in commerce and
manufactures", one would expect that they would possess more liberal views
and be "influenced by more extensive considerations of utility". By this he

25 J Millar to J Murray, 28 April 1771, NLS, MS 40813; J Murray to J Millar, 6 May 1771, NLS, MS
    41898.
26 J Millar to J Murray, 20 May 1771, NLS, MS 40813. See W Zachs, *Without Regard to Good
    Manners: A Biography of Gilbert Stuart 1743-1786* (1992) 42-43.
27 Millar, *Distinction of Ranks* (n 8) 193-200.

meant economic calculation, and he argued that, in more advanced societies, as the development of technology made commodities better and cheaper, slavery became economically disadvantageous, as slaves lacked incentives to work and acquire skills. He gave as his example the cost of labour in the West Indies. He claimed that the yearly labour of a field-hand there was rated at no more than £9, and that of an enslaved carpenter at not more than £36, while the annual value of the labour of a free carpenter was £70.[28]

Secondly, Millar argued that in "a polished nation", acquiring slaves became very expensive. This was because, as societies become wealthier, poor individuals could come to make a living without subjecting themselves to slavery. Furthermore, peace was more cultivated so fewer slaves were acquired by capture, while the use of mercenary troops meant that captives in war were allocated to the public. The result was that in order to acquire slaves, they had to be bought or bred from slaves already owned; this made them more expensive and meant that the cost of slave labour was greater than that of free labour. But slavery was maintained, as people retained an unthinking predilection for it, while the "possession of power is too agreeable to be easily relinquished". Once established, slavery tended to be perpetuated "during all the successive improvements of society in knowledge, arts, and manufactures".[29]

Moreover, he argued that in opulent nations slaves would be less well treated, because of the increased inequality between slave and owner. Slaves would become less amenable and more obstinate, so greater discipline would be necessary to get them to work. He added:

> This is at least the pretence for that shocking barbarity to which the negroes in our colonies are so commonly exposed, and which is so often exhibited even by persons of the weaker sex, in an age distinguished by its humanity and politeness.

Millar linked the Roman love of luxury and opulence with increasing cruelty towards slaves, particularly "after the establishment of despotism". But such "enormities" eventually led to a reaction, so that under public pressure government started to ameliorate the position of slaves.[30]

The next section is devoted to the question of how and why labourers became free in Europe. Millar explained this by reference to the invasion of the "northern barbarians". They did have slaves, over whom the master "enjoyed an unlimited dominion". But their occupation of huge landed

28 Millar, *Distinction of Ranks* (n 8) 200-202.
29 Millar, *Distinction of Ranks* (n 8) 202-206.
30 Millar, *Distinction of Ranks* (n 8) 206-211.

estates in the old Roman Empire – using for possession and cultivation the enormous numbers of slaves acquired through conquest – required that their slaves lived on farms at some distance from them. This meant that the slaves were progressively transformed from slaves into villeins. This was because they were less subject to their masters' discipline and supervision, and were rewarded for good work to give encouragement, so they eventually became capable of acquiring property on their own. All over Europe the advantages of farming through encouraging peasants were perceived. This eventually meant they could offer to pay rent.[31]

Villeinage was thus progressively extinguished and the peasants emancipated from the authority of a master. Peasants also practised the "mechanical arts" to assist their masters. As they became freer, they could pursue these to their own greater benefit; the "progress of luxury and refinement" increased such specialised occupations, while also making them more profitable, thus allowing peasants to quit the land. The domestic freedom so given to those trading became "the source of great opulence", eventually raising "the people of inferior rank to political independence".[32]

Millar then turned to the other reasons given for "this remarkable change of European manners". He dismissed the argument that it was to do with the establishment of Christianity. Christianity, no doubt, encouraged compassion, he wrote, but it was not intended to "abolish the distinctions of rank, or to alter the civil rights of mankind which were already established". Slavery, in the sense of serfdom, was found in many parts of Europe, and was "still admitted, without limitation, in the colonies which belong to any of the European nations, whether in Asia, Africa, or America". Selfish motives had led the clergy to encourage the laity to free their slaves, but to discourage manumission of slaves belonging to the church.[33]

The development of civil government might be "another circumstance to which people of inferior condition have been indebted for their liberty". Sovereigns protected serfs to undermine the authority of the nobility. They also set an example by freeing their own villeins. Thus, "the interpositions of the civil power in favour of liberty were directed by general considerations of utility, more than by the private view of depressing any particular part of the inhabitants". In some countries serfdom was abolished by statutes; in others it simply went into disuse "from the natural improvement of the inhabitants", and was as completely extinguished as if abolished by statute. Colliers and

31 Millar, *Distinction of Ranks* (n 8) 211-220.
32 Millar, *Distinction of Ranks* (n 8) 220-223.
33 Millar, *Distinction of Ranks* (n 8) 223-226.

salters remained in bondage in Scotland, however, because they could be closely supervised by their masters.[34]

After "domestic liberty" had been achieved in the more agriculturally progressive European nations, America was discovered. Since the first settlers did not need to conform to European laws and customs, being far from the centres of government, they introduced slavery, initially of the original inhabitants, in order to work the gold and silver mines. These people were either exhausted by the labour or not thought robust enough, so slaves were purchased from the Portuguese settlements in Africa. The settlers then extended the practice of enslavement to the cultivation of sugar cane, employing the "negroe-slaves":

> Thus the practice of slavery was no sooner extinguished by the inhabitants in one quarter of the globe, than it was revived by the very same people in another, where it has remained ever since, without being much regarded by the public, or exciting any effectual regulations in order to suppress it.

The developments and factors that had led to freedom in Europe were not present. Close supervision was possible in the mines of the Americas. This was also the case on the plantations and in "the other occupations in our colonies, in which the negroes perform the same sort of work which in Europe is commonly performed by cattle". Further, since the slaves were kept under "the lash of their master", there was no need to ameliorate their conditions or provide them with incentives or rewards.[35]

The fourth and final section of the chapter is devoted to the consequences of slavery. Millar wrote that, even under despotic governments, people in modern Europe, because of their "laws and customs", were freer than in the republics of the ancient world, whose opulence had been in proportion to the increasing number of their slaves. He stressed that slavery suppressed industry. He argued against those who linked the alleged populousness of the ancient nations to slavery. Instead, labourers and mechanics tended to acquire as much profit as they could from their labour to promote population. Slave-owners tried to keep down the living costs of slaves: "To those who have occasion to know the extreme parsimony with which the negroe slaves in our colonies are usually maintained, any illustration of this remark will appear superfluous." He argued that slavery hurt the morals of both owners and slaves. Given "the many advantages which a country derives from the freedom of the labouring people", he regretted that "any species of slavery should still remain in the dominions of Great Britain". While the number of colliers

---

34 Millar, *Distinction of Ranks* (n 8) 227-230.
35 Millar, *Distinction of Ranks* (n 8) 230-232.

and salters in Scotland was small, and their servitude "not very grievous", he pointed out that their bondage was economically disadvantageous to their masters, but that it would need an act of Parliament to sort it out. He finished the chapter with a critique of colonial slavery both as economically inefficient and as discouraging innovation, while pointing out the contrast and contradictions between American calls for political liberty, while holding fellow men as enslaved.[36]

(3) The cases

In 1757, the Court of Session had dealt with the question of whether or not a black slave acquired in Virginia was free in Edinburgh. The case was inconclusive, as the alleged slave died before a decision was reached.[37] Despite his condemnation of colonial slavery, Millar made no reference to this or to any of the contemporary cases involving slavery in Scotland in the first edition of the work. In fact, over the period in which he and Murray were preparing the book for first publication, the Scottish courts dealt with three cases involving individuals allegedly held in Scotland as enslaved. The first was that of *Stewart Nicolson v Stewart Nicolson*, a divorce case before the Commissary Court of Edinburgh, which commenced in December 1769. An African servant or slave, known as Latchemo, was listed as a witness by the husband to prove his allegation of his wife's adultery. There was considerable debate, involving advocation to the Court of Session, over whether Latchemo was an admissible witness, first, because he was not a baptised Christian, and secondly, because he was alleged to be a slave. In the end he was not called as a witness. Among the lawyers acting in what was a relatively prolonged suit were James Montgomery, then Lord Advocate, Alexander Lockhart, and John Maclaurin for Mr Stewart Nicolson, and Henry Dundas, then Solicitor General, Ilay Campbell, and John Swinton for Mrs Stewart Nicolson. This was a distinguished group of advocates.[38]

---

36 Millar, *Distinction of Ranks* (n 8) 232-242.
37 *Sheddan v A Negro* (1757) Mor 14545; Cairns, "Stoicism, slavery, and law" (n 9) 222-224. There will be a fuller discussion in J W Cairns, "Enforced sojourners under grey skies: slaves and black apprentices in eighteenth-century Scotland" (forthcoming).
38 *Houston Stewart Nicolson v Mrs Margaret Porterfield, Register etc.*, Register of Consistorial Decreets, in National Records of Scotland [hereafter NRS], CC8/5/12; Advocates Library, Session Papers, Campbell Collection, 1770, vol 19: *Bill of Advocation Houston Stewart-Nicolson, Esq; against Mrs Margaret Porterfield* (no 61); *Answers for Mrs Stewart-Nicolson, to the Bill of Advocation for Houston Stewart-Nicolson, Esq* (no 62); *Objections for Mrs Stewart-Nicolson, to Witnesses proposed to be adduced against her by Mr Stewart-Nicolson* (no 63); *Answers for Houston Stewart-Nicolson, to the Objections for Mrs Stewart-Nicolson* (no 64); *Unto the Right Honourable the Lords Commissaries of Edinburgh, The Petition of Mrs Stewart Nicolson ...*

Early in 1770, during the dependence of *Stewart Nicolson v Stewart Nicolson*, and indeed referred to in it, the Court of Session dealt with the case of *Spens v Dalrymple*. Dalrymple, a Scots doctor in Grenada, had purchased Spens, then known as Black Tom, from Ninian Home for £30. He came home in 1768, bringing Tom with him. Dalrymple intended to send Tom back to the West Indies. On 10 September 1769, Tom was baptised in the Parish Church of East Wemyss, taking the name David Spens. Dalrymple claimed he had only done so in order to try to assert his liberty. Spens then absconded and went to live with John Henderson. In 1770, Dalrymple petitioned the Court of Session to have recognised his right to Spens as "his own proper Slave" and to have Henderson deliver Spens to him and pay damages and expenses. The Court required Spens to find caution of £30 (provided by two Edinburgh writers, William Chalmers and Walter Ferguson) pending determination of the litigation. Spens was nonetheless imprisoned in Dysart, but later released by order of the Court. The litigation was inconclusive as Dalrymple died, and the issue of Spens's status was not further pursued. Recorded as counsel in the papers are John Maclaurin for Dalrymple and William Crosbie for Spens. William Aytoun, WS, acted for Dalrymple, who was too ill to attend court.[39]

On 12 September 1771, one month after the Commissaries issued their final decreet in *Stewart-Nicholson*, "Bell alias Belinda a black Girl or Woman from Bengal in the East Indies, the Slave or Servant of John Johnston of Hangingshaw" was indicted before the Circuit Court of Perth for an offence committed under the statute on child murder. Prosecuting as Advocate Depute to James Montgomery, Lord Advocate, was Alexander Murray. On the bench were Thomas Miller, Lord Justice Clerk, and James Ferguson of Pitfour. Present was John Swinton, then Sheriff Depute of Perthshire, who "[r]epresented that the Criminal being a native of Bengal did not understand Either the Language or Laws of this Country", asking for another day

---

(no 64/1); *Answers for Houston Stewart-Nicolson to the Petition of Mrs Stewart Nicolson* (no 64/2); *Replies for Mrs Stewart-Nicolson, to the Answers for Mr Stewart-Nicolson* (no 65); *Bill of Advocation, Mrs Stewart-Nicolson against Houston Stewart-Nicolson, Esq* (no 66); *Answers for Houston Stewart-Nicolson, Esq; to the Bill of Advocation for Mrs Nicolson* (no 67); *Replies for Mrs Stewart-Nicolson, to the Answers of Mr Stewart-Nicolson* (no 68); *Memorial for Houston Stewart-Nicolson, Esq; against Mrs Stewart-Nicolson* (no 69); and *Memorial for Mrs Margaret Porterfield, spouse of Houston Stewart-Nicolson of Carnock, defender; against the said Houston Stewart-Nicolson, Pursuer* (no 70). The case is discussed in J W Cairns, "Slavery and the Roman law of evidence in eighteenth-century Scotland", in A Burrows and Lord Rodger of Earlsferry (eds), *Mapping the Law: Essays in Memory of Peter Birks* (2006) 599-618; L Leneman, *Alienated Affections: The Scottish Experience of Divorce and Separation, 1684-1830* (1998) 174-179. (Inconsistent use of hyphen as in sources.)

39 The papers can be found in NRS CS236/S/3/13 and CS236/D/4/3. See also Whyte, *Scotland and the Abolition of Black Slavery* (n 12) 8-10; A S Cunningham, *Rambles in the Parishes of Scoonie and Wemyss* ([1905]) 154-156.

to prepare letters of exculpation. The next day Bell petitioned the court, claiming she could prove her innocence under the statute by the testimony of a witness presently in London, but that she was willing to be transported to the plantations. The Advocate Depute consented to her banishment to America for life, "there to be Sold as a Slave by the Transporter, but he to be accomptable to John Johnston of Hangingshaw Esqr her master for the proceeds of the price deducing the Expence of Transporting her and to which the said John Johnston Esqr consents". The judges duly so ordered. Should she return, she was to be publicly whipped through the streets of Perth by the hangman, he whipping her upon her naked back, giving "the ordinary number of Stripes upon her naked back at the usuall places and accustomed time of day", before being transported again.[40] Both the Advocate Depute and Johnstone duly signed the Circuit's Minute Book. There can be no doubt but that, over all, this was a humanitarian gesture to prevent Bell being hanged; but the Court had in fact recognised Johnstone's claims of owner-ship and had acknowledged that she was a slave in whose person he had a pecuniary interest. This case was reported in some detail in, for example, the *Scots Magazine*, as well as the *Caledonian Mercury*.[41] In a report of *Somer-set's Case* in June 1772, the *Scots Magazine* regretted the prosecution of Bell had not been transferred to Edinburgh for a fuller debate.[42]

If it is impossible to be certain of why Millar made no mention of these cases (all litigated by prominent counsel), of which he could not have failed to have been aware, it may have had something to do with the uncertainty of the results when he actually prepared the chapter, based on material written earlier. He presumably did not wish to offer any more hostages to fortune than he needed, through any commentary he made.

(4) The lectures

Millar's analytical jurisprudence was copied from that of Adam Smith. Just law protected the rights recognised by the impartial spectator. Smith had explained in his *Lectures on Jurisprudence* that one had a right not to be injured "as a man", "as a member of a family", and as "a citizen or member of a state".[43] The last was a matter of public law. The first dealt with the rights

---

40 NRS, JC 11/28; JC 26/193. His surname is usually spelled "Johnstone". The case is brilliantly discussed and analysed in E Rothschild, *The Inner Life of Empires: An Eighteenth-Century History* (2011) 87-91, 204-206, 291-299.

41 *Scots Magazine*, 33 (1771) 498-499; *Caledonian Mercury*, 14 Sept 1771.

42 *Scots Magazine*, 34 (1772) 299.

43 A Smith, *Lectures on Jurisprudence*, ed by R L Meek, D D Raphael and P G Stein (1978; repr 1982) 7 (LJ(A) i. 10).

not to be harmed in one's person, reputation or property. The second dealt with the rights arising out of the relationships of husband and wife, parent and child, master and servant, guardian and ward.[44] Millar developed his classes to follow this analysis. His two classes on Justinian's *Institutes* and single class on Justinian's *Digest* covered the rights not to be harmed as a person and as a member of a family. Indeed, the analysis has an obvious relationship to the traditional analysis used in the Civil law found in the *Institutes* and in Millar's chosen textbook for that course, J G Heineccius' *Elementa juris civilis secundum ordinem institutionum*; but he also used it to expound the very differently structured *Digest* (again using a textbook of Heineccius).[45] He also used this analysis to teach his classes on both Scots and English law.[46] The rights as a member of a citizen or state are covered in the lectures on Government (at one time described as on the Public Law of Scotland). Indeed, it may be significant that the lectures on public law were renamed those on government in the very year he published the *Distinction of Ranks*.[47]

While a considerable number of sets of student notes of Millar's lectures survives, none has yet been identified that is as early as the first edition of the *Distinction of Ranks*.[48] This makes it difficult to know the exact extent of his prior development of the material in the lectures before publication of the book. The earliest known is a set of the lectures on Government given in 1771-1772.[49] In the first part, "Of the origin and progress of government in society", Millar is reported as picking up some of the themes found in his chapter on servants. The student recorded him as saying that hunters and fishers, when they went to war, killed "their prisoners because were they to save them their maintenance would exceed all the fruits of their labour". It was otherwise among shepherds, who had an economic surplus, so "that Servants are first introduced in this state". The weaker became "Servants or Slaves of the stronger for they can exercise all powers over them – putting to death or of restraining their property in same manner as the Romans. Thus are the Negroes upon the coast of Africa ..."[50] He explained to the class that, in the time of agriculture, the master would build cottages for his

---

44 Smith, *Lectures on Jurisprudence* (n 43) 399 (LJ(B), 6-7). The best account is K Haakonssen, *The Science of a Legislator: The Natural Jurisprudence of David Hume and Adam Smith* (1981) 99-134.
45 See Cairns, "Famous as a school for Law" (n 6) 139-142.
46 Cairns, "Famous as a school for Law" (n 60) 142-144. The structure of the lectures on English law also shows some very minor influence from Blackstone's *Commentaries on the Laws of England*.
47 Cairns, "Famous as a school for Law"(n 60) 144-146.
48 Cairns, "Millar, Tret'yakov, and Desnitsky" (n 6) 27.
49 Glasgow, Mitchell Library, MS 99. See also the printed syllabus: *A Course of Lectures on Government: Given Annually in the University* (1771).
50 Glasgow, Mitchell Library, MS 99, vol 1, fol 16.

servants near where the cattle were, so they would become progressively more independent, and eventually be given a share of the land for which they gave rent in kind, turning from slaves into villeins.[51]

The next earliest set of notes is from the first course on the *Institutes*, probably dating from the early 1770s. In discussing slavery, Millar is reported as having pointed out that domestic slaves were "in every respect dependent on the master".[52] He added, however, that in "a Rude time, when these arbitrary powers over Slaves took their Rise, they were very little felt". This was because there were few slaves and they were treated well. This changed with the introduction of luxury. More slaves were required, and because of their increased numbers they were treated more harshly. Their treatment was only ameliorated in the times of the Emperors, who restrained abuses.[53] He also discussed what were described as rural or rustic slaves. By this he meant the Roman colonate, which he clearly identified with villeinage. These he stated were more independent and were both capable of ownership and free from the master's power of life and death. This was because "slaves employed in Country work, in labouring and Reaping the fruits of an estate, were not so much under the masters [*sic*] eye" as domestic slaves, and they could "not be so easily forced to work; it was necessary to Entice them by wages, which might be increased in proportion to their Diligence". The longer one was employed on the same "Spot of Ground [he] knew more of the nature of the Soil, and was better Cut out for Labouring it, than for Labouring any other; it was therefore the Masterss [*sic*] Interest, to purchase him and the Estate together." This meant that in the long run such slaves became capable of owning property and free from the "arbitrary" powers of the master.[54]

These earliest surviving sets of lectures contain the arguments that are crucial to the chapter on servants in the *Distinction of Ranks*. Millar's later practice was certainly to revise very little the structure and content of his courses.[55] This tends to confirm that his classes on the *Institutes* and government were where he first developed his arguments about slaves and slavery. The lectures and the editions of the book continued to have a complex relationship with each other.

51 Glasgow, Mitchell Library, MS 99, vol 1, fols 21-22.
52 NLS, MS 2743, fol 31.
53 NLS, MS 2743, fols 31-34.
54 NLS, MS 2743, fols 34-35. The nature of the colonate remains controversial and raises complex scholarly questions. See e.g. C Grey, "Slavery in the late Roman world", in K Bradley and P Cartledge (eds), *The Cambridge History of World Slavery. Volume 1. The Ancient Mediterranean World* (2011) 482-509.
55 Cairns, "Famous as a school for Law" (n 6) 138.

(5) The influence of Adam Smith

Both Millar's argument against slavery on the grounds of utility and his historical account are very strongly influenced by the argument and material covered in the *Lectures on Jurisprudence* of his teacher Smith. That his thinking was so very closely developed from that of Smith tends to confirm that his lectures already contained the material used in the book. Indeed, we can be fairly certain that his second course on the *Institutes* (on jurisprudence) and that on Government were developed in part to compensate for the changes in the moral philosophy course introduced by Thomas Reid after Smith had left Glasgow in 1764.[56]

It is unnecessary here to provide a detailed comparison. One can point out that Smith treated the relationship of master and servant as an aspect of rights arising from membership of a family. He explained the grounds on which one became a slave. He explained slavery as universal in the beginnings of society, but that special circumstances had led to its abolition in western Europe. This was related to the development of feudal government. The clergy and the monarchy encouraged freedom for reasons such as Millar also gave, while nobles found their land better cultivated by free men, as free tenants had incentives to improve productivity. The position of colliers and salters showed the disadvantages of slavery. It would be cheaper for the owners of coal and salt works if the workers were completely free and engaged by contract. Slavery stopped the growth of the population. Slaves were treated better under an arbitrary government or a monarchy than in a democracy, and in a barbarous or poor country than in an opulent one.[57] The existence of slavery discouraged technical innovation in manufacture.[58]

Both men were firmly of the view that slavery was unjust and immoral; but both chose to focus on its economic aspects, while not ignoring the potential degradation slavery involved. Both also paid considerable attention to colonial slavery: Smith pointed out it had been introduced illegally by the first Spanish conquerors, while Millar stressed that the nature of work in the mines of the New World and on the plantations allowed the close supervision of the squads of slaves that facilitated its operation.[59] Both were highly critical of New World slavery in a variety of ways. Smith noted its barbarity and cruelty as well as its economic problems, though Millar tended

---

56 Cairns, "Famous as a school for Law" (n 6) 136-139.
57 Smith, *Lectures on Jurisprudence* (n 43) 175-199 (LJ(A), iii.87-147), 450-456 (LJ(B), 130-146).
58 Smith, *Lectures on Jurisprudence* (n 43) 526-527 (LJ(B), 299-301).
59 Smith, *Lectures on Jurisprudence* (n 43) 455-456 (LJ(B), 144-145); Millar, *Distinction of Ranks* 232.

to focus on its economic disadvantages.[60]

There were, however, differences of nuance. Millar's emphasis on the significance of the possibility of close supervision in maintaining slavery is not found in Smith's *Lectures*. Smith was keen to emphasise that slaves were denied the comforts of family life, and that slave women tended to be prostituted.[61] Even more than Millar, he emphasised that once slavery was established it was very difficult to abolish it, as people liked to have dominion over others, even when this was contrary to their financial interests.[62] Smith also thought that slaves were much better treated on the North American mainland than in the sugar islands. On the continental mainland the masters were not at all rich, and so the slaves were few in number and not seen as a threat; in contrast, the large number of slaves in the sugar islands caused the masters to live in fear of insurrection.[63] He emphasised that "perhaps the only advantage which attends the institution of slavery" was that it had allowed the freemen in the ancient republics to be soldiers and participate in public life.[64]

Smith stressed the universality of slavery in the world. He pointed out the Eurocentric nature of contemporary belief "that slavery is entirely abolished at this time". This was the case "in only a small part of Europe". In fact, "all over Muscovy, and all the Eastern parts of Europe, and the whole of Asia, that is from Bohemia to the Indian Ocean, all over Africa, and the greatest part of America, it is still in use".[65] He also addressed the issue of black men and women brought as slaves to Britain. In considering free servants, he told his class in 1763-1764:

A Negroe in this country is a <free> man. If you have a Negroe servant stolen from you, you can have no action for the price, but only for damages sustained by the loss of your servant. In like manner if a Negroe is killed, the person who does it is guilty of murder.[66]

60 Smith, *Lectures on Jurisprudence* (n 43) 178 (LJ(A), iii.95), 181 (LJ(A), iii.103),183-184 (LJ(A), iii.107-108), 187 (LJ(A), iii.116), 193-194 (LJ(A), iii.132-133, 451 (LJ(B), 132), 453 (LJ(B), 138), 455-456 (LJ(B), 144-145); Millar, *Distinction of Ranks* (n 8) 201-202, 208, 232.

61 Smith, *Lectures on Jurisprudence* (n 43) 178-179, 193 (LJ(A), iii.94-96, 132), 451 (LJ(B), 132).

62 Smith, *Lectures on Jurisprudence* (n 43) 192 (LJ(A), iii.130), 452 (LJ(B), 134).

63 Smith, *Lectures on Jurisprudence* (n 43) 183-184 (LJ(A), iii.107-108), 453 (LJ(B), 137).

64 Smith, *Lectures on Jurisprudence* (n 43) 231 (LJ(A), iii.81-82), 242-243 (LJ(A), iv.110).

65 Smith, *Lectures on Jurisprudence* (n 43) 181 (LJ(A), iii.101). See also 451-452 (LJ(B), 134): "We are apt to imagine that slavery is quite extirpated because we know nothing of it in this part of the world, but even at present it is almost universal. A small part of the west of Europe is the only portion of the globe that is free from it, and is nothing in comparison with the vast continents where it still prevails." Cf Millar, *Distinction of Ranks* (n 8) 224-225: "[Slavery] is still retained in Russia, in Poland, in Hungary, and in several parts of Germany; and that it is at present admitted, without limitation, in the colonies which belong to any of the European nations, whether in Asia, Africa, or America."

66 Smith, *Lectures on Jurisprudence* (n 43) 456 (LJ(B), 145). The reconstruction in the text is by the editors of the Glasgow edition.

But he added that "tho a Negroe servant is intitled to the priviledges of a freeman while here, you can oblige him to return to America and keep him as formerly". This was because it was "not from Christianity but from the laws of this country that he enjoys freedom, because there is no such thing as slavery among us".[67]

What Smith said went to the heart of debates over the issue of the freedom of slaves brought to Scotland or England from the colonies. It is interesting to see that he views such men and women as free – but not quite. Their master or mistress could still compel a return of the servant to the colonies and to full colonial slavery. This reflects his understanding of the law in the early 1760s before *Somerset's Case* in England and *Knight v Wedderburn* in Scotland.[68]

C. 1771-1778

(1) Critical reception

The first edition of Millar's book was a scholarly success.[69] It was well received in both the *Critical* and *Monthly Reviews*.[70] The former paid particular attention to what Millar had written about servants, with a lengthy quotation of his final passage about colonial slavery, while describing Millar as having shown himself "to be a lover of liberty upon the most solid principles".[71] The next year the book was translated into German.[72]

Murray, however, was understandably anxious about the finances; he thought that he had paid too much for too short a book that had appeared too late in the season.[73] He commented to Tobias Smollett that, though the book was considered to have merit, "[h]ow far it may succeed for the Bookseller is another matter".[74] To avoid the risk of a pirated Irish edition affecting the profits, Murray had sold a right to the work to Thomas Ewing, who produced a cheap Dublin edition in octavo the same year as Murray's publication.[75] By September 1771, Murray started to plan a second, cheaper edition in octavo,

---

67 Smith, *Lectures on Jurisprudence* (n 43) 456 (LJ(B), 145).
68 See the remarks of the editors in Smith, *Lectures on Jurisprudence* (n 43) 456, notes 71 and 72.
69 J Murray to J Millar, 9 Aug 1771, NLS, MS 41898; J Murray to T Smollett, 9 Aug 1771, NLS, MS 41898. See Sher, *The Enlightenment and the Book* (n 21) 91.
70 Review, *Critical Review, or Annals of Literature*, 31 (June 1771) 432-442; Review, *Monthly Review*, 45 (Sept. 1771), 188-195.
71 Review, *Critical Review* (n 70) 440-442.
72 In Germany it appeared as *Bemerkungen über den Unterschied der Stände in der bürgerlichen Gesellschaft* (1772).
73 See e.g. J Murray to Kincaid & Creech, 1 July 1771, NLS, MS 41898.
74 J Murray to T Smollett, 9 Aug 1771, NLS, MS 41898.
75 Zachs, *First John Murray* (n 3) 111-112.

and wrote to Millar asking if he had any "alterations or improvements".[76] No doubt he hoped to recoup more of his outlays.

(2) Second edition

Millar soon started work on the new edition. Following the advice of Murray, he had a copy of the first edition bound with interleaves on which he wrote his revisions. He explained that he thought it would be "improper to introduce in this new edition such alterations or additions as would give the appearance of a new book". Instead he wrote that "several small variations may be made which will pass, in some measure unobserved, at the same time that they may contribute to perspicuity".[77] Millar wrote to Murray in October, however, to say that he had found "more alterations necessary" than he had expected.[78] While this may have been reassuring to Murray because of his worry about the length of the work, it may also have raised anxieties, given the potential for delay.

Millar had sent the interleaved copy with his corrections and additions to Murray before the end of January 1772. He expressed concern about whether Murray would understand his corrections, and stressed that difficulties in interpreting the changes should be referred to him. On 2 February he sent to Murray some further small corrections, most of which (ten out of thirteen) were made in the chapter under consideration.[79] The title page of the book had also been elaborated with the addition of a couple of columns listing the contents. The second edition was described as "Greatly Enlarged". One of the most obvious changes was that, throughout the book, Millar had inserted subheadings in the chapters, which did indeed, as was claimed, "render the arrangement more obvious to the reader".[80]

Most of the alterations in the chapter – which had been renamed "Of the authority of a master over his servants" – are small, improving the style or clarifying the expression. The only substantial changes are found in the final section, now entitled "Political consequences of slavery".[81] After the paragraph on the

76 J Murray to J Millar, 7 Sept 1771, NLS, MS 41898; J Millar to J Murray, 28 Sept [1771], NLS, MS 40813.

77 J Millar to J Murray, 28 Sept [1771], NLS, MS 40813.

78 J Millar to J Murray, 9 October 1771, NLS, MS 40813. Given Millar was also trying to persuade Murray to give the work of printing to the Foulis Press, he may also have been somewhat disingenuous here.

79 J Millar to J Murray, 2 Feb 1772, NLS, MS 40813; J Millar, Observations Concerning the Distinction of Ranks in Society. Under the Following Heads … The Second Edition, Greatly Enlarged (1783) 251.

80 See Millar, *Distinction of Ranks* (2nd) (n 79) [xviii].

81 Millar, *Distinction of Ranks* (2nd) (n 79) 298.

moral harms caused by slavery, Millar added two extensive new paragraphs, arguing against the view (propounded in Scotland, for example, by Andrew Fletcher) that slavery had the advantage of providing for those too poor to maintain themselves. He agreed that in a commercial society some people will fall into penury and need support through some system such as the poors-rates. He acknowledged that in a slave-owning country such regulations were not necessary. He questioned, however, whether masters will look after old and infirm slaves, and how this would be monitored. Slavery, he suggested, would merely lead to the secret starving of slaves, and he instanced Roman history as supporting this.[82] Millar also added a very substantial footnote to his final paragraph on slavery in the colonies. In this he introduced evidence to support his Smithian argument that slavery inhibited innovation and improvement in technology, claiming that there was scarcely a spade in Jamaica, so that digging a grave could take two men a whole day.[83]

By July 1772, Millar had received the print. He sent Murray a few small corrections which he thought could be dealt with in a sheet of *errata*. He also provided the final version of the title page. There were some more major changes that he thought required cancel and reprint of a few leaves.[84] Two involved the chapter on servants. The first concerned the number of slaves in the ancient world, where he inserted material drawn from David Hume's *Essay on the Populousness of the Ancient Nations*, though questioning how Hume reached a figure he had given.[85] The other was much more substantial. Millar proposed that the note – already mentioned – on technology in the final paragraph should be extended thus:

> After the words, "in the whole Island": add as follows. "The use of the saw is also very little known. Instead of a flail, the negroes make use of a single stick in threshing the Guinea-corn, so that in this, and in winnowing, ten women are capable of doing no more work in a day than, with our instruments and machinery, two men would perform in two hours. They are unacquainted either with the sithe or the sickle, and are obliged, every night, to cut with a knife, or pull with their hands, a quantity of grass, sufficient to serve their horses, mules, and black cattle. These observations were made about the year 1765. and relate more immediately to the parishes of Vere, Hanover, and S^t. Thomas."[86]

82 Millar, *Distinction of Ranks* (2nd) 304-306; A Fletcher, "The Second Discourse concerning the affairs of Scotland: written in the year 1698", in A Fletcher of Saltoun, *Selected Political Writings and Speeches*, ed by D Daiches (1979) 46-66; M J Rozbicki, "To save them from them selves: proposals to enslave the British poor, 1698-1755" (2001) 22: 2 *Slavery and Abolition* 29-50. On the Scottish historical background to Fletcher's views, see K J Cullen, *Famine in Scotland: The "Ill Years" of the 1690s* (2010.)

83 Millar, *Distinction of Ranks* (2nd) (n 79) 310, n °.

84 J Millar to J Murray, 28 July 1772, NLS, MS 40813.

85 Millar, *Distinction of Ranks* (2nd) 299, n °.

86 J Millar to J Murray, 28 July 1772, NLS, MS 40813.

Millar's aim was to strengthen his argument about the inefficiency of slavery. Murray duly made the changes.[87]

This note continued to worry Millar, and in September he again wrote to Murray about it. He stated that in it "there are some facts that appear a little singular, and if I have committed any mistake in stating them I may expect to be severely censured". He added that he had discovered from the person from whom he had acquired the information that there was "one article improperly stated", namely that "the use of the saw is also scarce known". He proposed:

> If possible, this must either be cancelled, or mentioned among the errata. If you put it among the errata you may, after the word "known", add, "to the field negroes". [and next sentence,] for, "Instead of a flail, the negroes", read, "Instead of a flail they". If you can cancell the leaf, leave out altogether the words, "The use of the saw is also scarce known". And after the word "Island." [add as follows] Instead of a flail, the negroes use a single stick in threshing the Guinea-corn; so that in this, and in winnowing, ten women are capable of doing no more work in a day, than with our instruments and machinery, two men would perform in two hours. Instead of using a sithe or a sickle, they are accustomed, in the evening, to cut with a knife, or pull with their hands, a quantity of grass sufficient for their horses, mules, or black-cattle. These observations were made about the year 1765; and relate more immediately to the parishes of Vere, Hanover, and S^t. Thomas in the Vale."[88]

Millar did not get a response to this letter, and he wrote again to Murray on 24 December. He had obviously reflected further. This time the note was described as containing "an errour so material that there seems an absolute necessity of correcting it". He added that, should it be possible, "I must request it of you to make a cancellation, as I think the credit of the book depends upon it". He repeated the correction about the use of the saw, scythe and sickle, before explaining:

> As these facts in this note are rather new to many people in this country, any errour in stating them would undoubtedly be censured. I am sorry however to give you any farther trouble if it could be avoided. But this seems unavoidable.[89]

Millar was obviously concerned not to give any hostages to fortune. He did not wish the well-organised and powerful West-India lobby to be able to attack his critique of slavery on the grounds of his ignorance of the true conditions in the islands. Given that his main line of attack on slavery was its economic inefficiency and stifling of innovation, to get this type of thing wrong would be to weaken his whole account.

Murray was either unwilling or unable to cancel the leaf, so all that he did

---

87 Millar, *Distinction of Ranks* (2nd) (n 79) xxii, 310-311, n *.
88 J Millar to J Murray, 26 Sept [1772], NLS, MS 40813.
89 J Millar to J Murray, 24 Dec 1772, NLS, MS 40813.

was add to the list of *errata* the two small changes that Millar had indicated he wanted should Murray not cancel the leaf.[90] One suspects Murray may have taken advantage of the way Millar expressed himself in his letter of September to avoid making the cancel; the letter of December, which was rather more vehement about the need for the cancel, was probably too late given Murray's schedule. This meant that the significant change of nuance from "[t]hey are unacquainted either with the sithe or the sickle, and are obliged," to "[i]nstead of using a sithe or a sickle, they are accustomed" did not make it into the new edition, nor did the proposed deletion of the remark about the "use of the saw". The second edition appeared in the Spring of 1773. It was quickly translated into French.[91]

(3) The cases

In 1772, the Scottish newspapers had closely followed the English case of *Somerset* from the end of January through to July, reporting it with varying degrees of accuracy, their accounts drawn from the English press.[92] There was also a lengthy account in the *Scots Magazine* for June.[93] Somerset's master, Charles Steuart, was a Scotsman who had served as a high-ranking British official in North America.[94] The opinion given by Lord Mansfield, at the least, decided that a master could not compel or force his servant or slave to leave England.[95] In this, Mansfield's opinion varied for England the law stated by

---

90 Millar, *Distinction of Ranks* (2nd) (n 79) xxii.

91 J Millar, *Observations sur les commencemens de la société* (1773). This translation appeared again in 1778. I have not had an opportunity to compare copies: the 1778 version may be a reissue with a new title page.

92 *Edinburgh Advertiser*, 31 Jan 1772; *Edinburgh Evening Courant*, 1 Feb 1772; *Caledonian Mercury*, 15 Feb 1772; *Edinburgh Evening Courant*, 15 Feb 1772; *Edinburgh Advertiser*, 26 May 1772; *Caledonian Mercury*, 27 May 1772; *Edinburgh Evening Courant*, 27 May 1772; *Edinburgh Evening Courant*, 24 June 1772; *Edinburgh Advertiser*, 26 June 1772; *Caledonian Mercury*, 27 June 1772; *Edinburgh Evening Courant*, 27 June 1772; *Edinburgh Evening Courant*, 1 July 1772; *Glasgow Journal*, 2 July 1772; *Edinburgh Advertiser*, 3 July 1772.

93 "Pleadings, and a solemn judgement, on the question, Whether a slave continues to be a slave after coming into Britain?" (1772) 34 *Scots Magazine* 297-99.

94 M S Weiner, "New biographical evidence on *Somerset's Case*" (2002) 23(1) *Slavery and Abolition* 121-136.

95 The meaning of the case in law and the wording of Mansfield's judgment have been the subject of considerable dispute. See e.g. W M Wiecek, "*Somerset*: Lord Mansfield and the legitimacy of slavery in the Anglo-American world", (1974) 42 *University of Chicago Law Review*) 86-146; J Oldham, "New light on Mansfield and slavery" (1988) 27 *Journal of British Studies* 45-68; W R Cotter, "The Somerset Case and the abolition of slavery in England"(1994) 79 *History* 31-55; J Oldham, *English Common Law in the Age of Mansfield* (2004) 305-323; G van Cleve, "*Somerset's Case* and its antecedents in imperial perspective"(2006) 24 *Law and History Review* 601-645; and S M Wise, *Though the Heavens May Fall: The Landmark Trial that Led to the End of Human Slavery* (2006).

Smith in his *Lectures on Jurisprudence*.

Millar cannot have failed to note this famous case; nonetheless, he chose not to introduce discussion of it into his revisions of the *Distinction of Ranks* for the second edition. Perhaps the complexities surrounding it made it seem too difficult to incorporate discussion of it readily into his existing text, which did not consider the role of slaves brought from the colonies to Britain.[96]

In July 1772 Joseph Knight, a slave brought to Scotland from Jamaica by his master John Wedderburn, read of *Somerset's Case* in the *Edinburgh Advertiser*. He apparently interpreted it as meaning he could leave his master.[97] It was a year later, however, that he finally resolved to depart from Wedderburn's service. The Justices of the Peace of Perthshire (those sitting all being slave-owners or involved in slavery in some way) decided that he could not do so, because he was a slave or voluntary servant for life without wages. Knight managed to get his case before the Sheriff Depute of Perthshire, still the same John Swinton who had assisted with Bell or Belinda. On 20 May 1774, Swinton ruled:

> That the State of Slavery is not recognised by the Laws of this Kingdom and is inconsistent with the principles thereof and Found that the Regulations in Jamaica concerning Slaves do not extend to this Kingdom.[98]

Wedderburn sought advocation of the case to the Court of Session, where it dragged on until January 1778, when the Lords finally rejected the bill of advocation, so that Swinton's interlocutor stood. It is worth pointing out that acting for Wedderburn were James Ferguson and Robert Cullen (a relative of Millar's) and for Knight were John Maclaurin, Henry Dundas, and Allan McConnochie.

This is not the place to go further into the details of *Knight v Wedderburn*. The timing meant of course that it would have been impossible for Millar to take it into account in his second edition.

(4) The lectures

These two cases affected the development of Millar's discussion of slavery in his classes in the later 1770s. Thus, in 1775-1776, in his class on Scots law, Millar now lectured on his understanding of the impact of *Somerset's Case* in

---

96 On some of the problems, see J W Cairns, "After *Somerset*: some Scottish evidence" (forthcoming).

97 J W Cairns, "*Knight v Wedderburn*" in *The Oxford Companion to Black British History*, ed D Dabydeen, J Gilmore and C Jones (2007) 244-246.

98 (MS) Extract Process Joseph Knight against Sir John Wedderburn of Ballendean, Bart. 1774, 27-28, in NRS, CS235/K/2/2; see also Diet Book, Sheriff Court of Perthshire, 20 May 1774, NRS, SC49/1/64.

England as well as on what he considered to be the Scottish position.

He is recorded as telling the class that:

> There are different sorts of slaves – the negroe slaves in America are not at all in the same situation. In some colonies they are in a better position than in others. In all they are subjected to the powers of their master: But the power of life and death is restrained: in some colonies it is capitally punished, in others only arbitrary – what is particularly to be enquired into is the state of slaves when imported into this country …

He first dealt with England, starting out with what he believed to be the position before Mansfield's decision. He pointed out that the status of such individuals was of great consequence in England as, in *Somerset's Case*, "it appeared upon proof that there were 15,000 negroes in England". He interpreted the case in quite a complex way. He stated that by English law "a Negroe slave is a free man" who was "no longer considered as his master's property". Further, the "killing of a negroe is punished the same as killing anybody else". Nonetheless, "he owes a service to his master during life, and that without any wages, but necessaries". Millar added that the master could assign his servant's "labour by means of a fiction in the English law, that the assignment is made in America" where slaves are allowed. He summed it up: "Thus a slave coming to England acquires great privileges. He is a free man, but subject to his master for life."[99]

Turning to *Somerset*, he stated that "[t]ill of late all the privileges might have been defeated by sending the slave back to his own country where slavery is allowed". He explained:

> However by a late decision it was found that a slave cannot arbitrarily be sent abroad by his master. He must assign some sufficient cause. When a negroe slave is brought into the country, animo Remanendi his master has no right to send him abroad. By bringing him to this country where slavery is not allowed he gives up his absolute right over him; he merely emancipates his slave.

This said, he expressed the view that if slaves were brought in without the intention of them remaining, they retained their status as slaves. He stated that if the master "only brings a slave into this country occasionally without any intention of remaining, he cannot be hindered from sending him back". He gave the following example:

> [I]f a master by some or otherways should be arriven in this country with a cargoe of slaves the slaves would not by that means acquire their liberty, but might be sent to the country for which they were destined. It seems expedient that they should not remain in the condition of slaves in this country, as it might lead to revive the practice of slavery. Such is the law of England.[100]

---

99 GUL, MS Gen. 347, 59-60.
100 GUL, MS Gen. 347, 60.

He thus believed the effect of *Somerset's Case* to be quite limited. He may also have given a somewhat wider scope to the authority of the master than Adam Smith had.

He next stated that Scots law was not settled on the point as the issue had never been decided here, adding, however, that "the same reasons which take place in England, take place also in Scotland". Because there was "the same court of last resort in both countries ... whatever is the law in England on this point will in time be the law of Scotland". He alluded to the earlier, inconclusive Scottish case of *Sheddan v Montgomery*, and, referring to *Knight v Wedderburn*, commented that "[a]t present there is a question of this kind depending before the Court of Session, which when it is decided will determine this point".[101]

At the same time as these detailed considerations of the law in England and Scotland, Millar's account of slavery in his second course on the *Institutes*, that sometimes described as on jurisprudence, had come to reflect closely what was said in the chapter in the *Distinction of Ranks*. Thus, the same explanation was given of the rise of domestic slavery and its ending in Europe, while the same emphasis was placed on its economic disutility as regards productivity and population, using again the examples of colliers and salters in Scotland as well as Caribbean slavery. Fletcher's views of the institution as a way of maintaining the poor were also dismissed.[102]

(5) Smith, *Wealth of Nations*

Smith finally published the *Wealth of Nations* in 1776. As in his *Lectures on Jurisprudence*, he emphasised that "the work done by freemen comes cheaper in the end than that done by slaves".[103] In his chapter "Of the discouragement of agriculture in the antient state of Europe after the fall of the Roman Empire", he described the position of serfs or bondmen, whom he described as "slaves", but whose "slavery was of a milder kind than that known amongst the antient Greeks and Romans, or even in our West Indian colonies". He again made the point that slavery, at least of this type, was still found over much of Europe, other than the west and south-west. Once more he stated his belief that work done by slaves was "in the end the dearest of any"; but human love of domination and the mortification of having "to condescend to persuade his inferiors" meant that where "the law allows it,

---

101 GUL, MS Gen. 347, 60-61; *Sheddan v Montgomery* (1757) Mor 14545; Cairns, "Stoicism, slavery, and law" (n 9) 222-224.

102 NLS, Adv. MS 28.6.8, fols 122-139.

103 A Smith, *An Inquiry into the Nature and Causes of the Wealth of Nations*, 2 vols (1979; repr 1981) vol 1, 99 (I.viii.41).

and the nature of the work can afford it" a man "will generally prefer the services of slaves to that of freemen". He claimed that the raising of sugar in particular and to a lesser extent tobacco was sufficiently profitable to afford slave labour, but that of corn was not. This explained the proportionally differing numbers of negroes in the sugar and tobacco colonies and why the Quakers of Pennsylvania had resolved to free their slaves. He gave the same explanation as in the *Lectures* of how the serfs or villeins came to become free, leading ultimately to modern tenancies.[104] Again, Smith emphasised that the position of a slave was better under an arbitrary than a free government, instancing Roman history, though pointing out once more that slaves were rarely innovatory in manufacture.[105]

D. 1778-1801

(1) Preparation of a third edition

Towards the end of 1778, the print-run of the second edition was nearly exhausted. Murray accordingly wrote to Millar asking him if he had "looked over [his] observations with a view to a new edition".[106] Millar replied on 22 December in an encouraging way, setting out the changes he wished to make and mentioning that he thought a change of title appropriate as the current one was "not sufficiently explicit". He also indicated that he wanted the book to be published the next winter, that is in 1779, presumably to allow adequate time for carrying out the revisions. Murray agreed.[107] He also agreed that the alterations should be made on an interleaved copy, and advised Millar to have the interleaves in quarto to give plenty of room for revision. He also thought that Millar should provide a short advertisement to explain his reasons for changing the title.[108]

Millar intended to do the bulk of the work after the end of his classes, advising Murray that he would be finished by the end of June. Since Millar also wanted to correct the proof sheets, Murray proposed that the printing be done in Glasgow by the Foulis Press.[109] Murray agreed the new title and the cancellation of the old preface, which Millar had so reluctantly produced.[110] It was replaced with a related introduction.

104 Smith, *Wealth of Nations* (n 103) vol 1, 386-391 (III.II.8-13); see also Smith, *Wealth of Nations* (n 103) vol 2, 557 (IV.vii.a.3).
105 Smith, *Wealth of Nations* (n 103) vol 2, 683-684 (IV.ix.47).
106 J Murray to J Millar, 12 Nov 1778, NLS, MS 41902, 202.
107 J Murray to J Millar, 31 Dec 1778, NLS, MS 41902, 251-252.
108 J Murray to J Millar, 26 Feb 1779, NLS, MS 41902, 286-287.
109 J Murray to J Millar, 6 July 1779, NLS, MS 49103, 9-10.
110 J Murray to J Millar, 24 July 1779, NLS, MS 49103, 24-26.

The Foulis Press had now passed into the hands of Andrew Foulis the younger.[111] Murray found the relationship with Foulis difficult.[112] Initially he thought Foulis was charging too much;[113] Millar intervened and the two men came to an agreement.[114] Murray wished to see the first sheet printed by Foulis before the book "was worked off". By September, he was wondering why he had not yet received it.[115] It had still not arrived by mid-October, and Murray wrote to Millar expressing his anxiety and suggesting in exasperation that if Foulis continued like this, the book would not be published until January 1781.[116] The first sheet was received soon after and approved by Murray, who wrote to Foulis urging him to make haste, so that he did not lose opportunities for sales, as "the Parliament is near meeting and the India Ships near sailing".[117] The quarrel then extended to money, and Millar weighed in on Foulis' side.[118] It was no doubt exasperation with this that led Murray to write to Professor William Richardson, Millar's colleague, in July 1780, requesting that he "Be pleased to tell Professor Millar that the new edition of his book arrived only 3 days ago, & the summer being so far advanced I mean to delay the formal publication till next winter".[119]

The third edition was nonetheless dated 1779. Foulis was later to fall out with the University of Glasgow over the delays in printing the catalogue of the University's Library;[120] but it is also possible that some of the delay was caused by Millar's wish to alter the text in the course of production. He certainly changed his mind about the text of the first two editions during printing. He also tended to be dilatory. Because the printing took place in Glasgow, there is no detailed correspondence from Millar about its production; but it is a plausible suggestion that he revised the third edition after or during the printing, creating further delay. We may note that the third edition, in contrast to the first two, has no list of *errata*. Rather than reflecting Foulis'qualities

---

111   Most of the literature focuses on the glory days of his father and uncle: see e.g. R D Macleod, "The Foulis Press" (1910) *The Library* 172-189; D Murray, *Robert and Andrew Foulis and the Glasgow Press, With Some account of the Glasgow Academy of Fine Arts* (1913).

112   See Zachs, *First John Murray* (n 3) 105-106.

113   J Murray to J Millar, 24 July 1779 NLS, MS 49103, 24-26.

114   J Murray to J Millar, 5 Aug 1779, NLS, MS 49103, 29; J Murray to A Foulis, 5 Aug 1779, NLS, MS 49103, 30.

115   J Murray to A Foulis, 5 Aug 1779, NLS, MS 49103, 30; J Murray to A Foulis, 18 Sept 1779, NLS, MS 49103, 60.

116   J Murray to J Millar, 15 Oct 1779 NLS, MS 49103, 93.

117   J Murray to A Foulis, 19 Oct 1779 NLS, MS 49103, 93.

118   J Murray to J Millar, 10 Jan 1780 NLS, MS 49103, 132-135; J Murray to J Millar, 14 Feb 1780, NLS, MS 49103, 140-141.

119   J Murray to W Richardson, 13 July 1780, NLS, MS 49103, 185-186.

120   R Ovenden, "Foulis, Robert (1707–1776)", in *Oxford Dictionary of National Biography*, 2004 [*http://www.oxforddnb.com/view/article/9991*, accessed 24 July 2011].

as a printer or Millar's satisfaction with the work, this is probably simply the result of Millar being at hand when the book was being printed, able to influence Foulis to make changes during the printing.

Murray can seem quite testy. He was also prone to quarrels and disputes.[121] But it is a testimony to him that he continued to work with Millar, collaborating in publication of his *Historical View of the English Government* in 1787;[122] he was even to associate again with Foulis.[123]

(2) The third edition

Millar's book had now acquired its familiar title – *The Origin of the Distinction of Ranks: Or, An Inquiry into the Circumstances which gave Rise to Influence and Authority, in the Different Members of Society* – and was described as "The Third Edition, Corrected and Enlarged". The changes we can identify in the chapter on master and servant again reflect those made in the second.[124] Millar still had the same anxieties and concerns.

First, the language was tidied up. Some notes were moved into the main text as new paragraphs and expanded. In the first section, Millar now pointed out that there were three ways of acquiring slaves, now adding into the main text that the third was by the sentence of a judge, which had been in a note in earlier editions.[125] In the second section, to the remarks on the value of the labour of a "field-negro" and of free and enslaved carpenters, he added a lengthy footnote presenting further figures and evidence.[126] In the third section, citing the work of Anthony Benezet, the Philadelphian abolitionist, he now commented on slavery in the colonies of the European nations, that the "Quakers of Pennsylvania" were the first men to have scruples about slavery and to think its abolition "a duty they owe to religion and humanity".[127] In the final section, towards the beginning, he added a new paragraph on the proportion of slaves to free people in the West Indies.[128] He also noted the recent (1775) Act of Parliament on Scottish colliers and salters, which, in a series of complex provisions, basically prevented the

---

121 Zachs, *First John Murray* (n 3) 184-199.
122 J Millar, *An Historical View of the English Government, From the Settlement of the Saxons in Britain to the Accession of the House of Stewart* (1787); Zachs, *First John Murray* (n 3) 343.
123 Zachs, *First John Murray* (n 3) 107.
124 The title was trivially altered by the deletion of "Of" at the beginning.
125 Millar, *Distinction of Ranks* (3rd) (n 1) 299-300.
126 Millar, *Distinction of Ranks* (3rd) (n 1) 306-307, n °.
127 Millar, *Distinction of Ranks* (3rd) (n 1) 334. On Benezet, see now M Jackson, *Let This Voice Be Heard: Anthony Benezet, Father of Atlantic Abolitionism* (2009).
128 Millar, *Distinction of Ranks* (3rd) (n 1) 346.

bondage of new recruits, and allowed existing miners and salters to petition for freedom.[129]

The footnote at the end of the penultimate paragraph that had given Millar so much trouble in the second edition was now taken into the text and once more revised, mainly by deleting the sentence on the "use of the saw" being little known. Instead Millar now wrote that: "In procuring firewood for boiling sugar, &c. a work that takes up about five or six weeks yearly, no use is made of the saw, but the trees are cut with an ax into logs of about 30 inches in length." Instead of being "unacquainted with" the scythe or sickle, it is "want of" these tools that requires the slaves to pull grass by hand.[130]

Next, what had been the final paragraph of the chapter was split into two and edited, with the first part expanded to suggest the owners of sugar and tobacco plantations might benefit from allowing the workers a share of the produce. He stressed that, "the interest of our colonies seems to demand that the negroes should be better treated, and even that they should be raised to a better condition".[131]

Millar finally added four new paragraphs at the very end of the chapter. In the first, he suggested that in those provinces of North America where there had always been few slaves, and where the type of production did not suit the use of slave labour, that the "pernicious effects upon industry" of slavery would soon be felt, and the practice abandoned. Indeed he added that there already were moves in some of them to forbid or to discourage the importation of "negroes".[132] In the second additional paragraph, after remarking on how the "advancement of commerce and the arts, together with the diffusion of knowledge, in the present age" has led to the removal of many prejudices, he commented that in Britain it had "long been held … that a negro-slave, imported into this country, obtained thereby many of the privileges of a free man". He referred to *Somerset's Case* of 1772, in which "it was found that the master could not recover his power over the servant by sending him abroad at his pleasure".[133] In the third paragraph, he stated that, in Scotland, it had recently been decided in *Knight v Wedderburn*:

---

129 Millar, *Distinction of Ranks* (3rd) (n 1) 356; An Act for Altering, Explaining, and Amending Several Acts of the Parliament of Scotland, Respecting Colliers, Coal-Bearers, and Salters, 15 Geo. III, c. 28. Complete lifting of the restrictions on colliers finally came in 1799 with the Act to Explain and Amend the Laws Relative to Colliers in that Part of Great Britain called Scotland, 39 Geo. III, c. 56.

130 Millar, *Distinction of Ranks* (3rd) (n 1) 357-358.

131 Millar, *Distinction of Ranks* (3rd) (n 1) 358-359.

132 Millar, *Distinction of Ranks* (3rd) (n 1) 360.

133 Millar, *Distinction of Ranks* (3rd) (n 1) 360-361, and 361, n °.

That the dominion assumed over this negro, under the law of Jamaica, being unjust, could not be supported in this country to any extent: that therefore the defender had no right to the negro's service for any space of time; nor to send him out of the country against his consent.

This is a purported quotation from the decision.[134] The final paragraph concluded:

This last decision, which was given in 1778, is the more worthy of attention, as it condemns the slavery of the negroes in explicit terms, and, being the first opinion of that nature delivered by any court in the island, may be accounted an authentic testimony of the liberal sentiments entertained in the latter part of the eighteenth century.[135]

The revisions, including the somewhat self-satisfied final paragraph, are once more geared to emphasising the economic inefficiency of slavery, pointing out that both justice and utility demanded its abolition. It is important to note that Millar remained of the view that black slaves landing in England still owed some duties towards their masters. They only acquired many – not all – of the privileges of freedom. It was now otherwise in Scotland.

(3) Further prints

Murray reissued the third edition in 1781 with the old title page cancelled and a new title page affixed.[136] The third edition was also published in English in Basel in 1793.[137] A "fourth edition" was posthumously published in 1806, with a biography of Millar by his nephew John Craig.[138] The text is that of the third edition with occasional variations in spelling or punctuation and correction of occasional errors.[139]

(4) Lectures

The account of slavery that Millar gave in his lectures was also now basically fixed. What is essentially the same discussion is still found in his second course on the *Institutes*, or in his lectures on Scots law, with variations to support the

---

134 Millar, *Distinction of Ranks* (3rd) (n 1) 361.
135 Millar, *Distinction of Ranks* (3rd) (n 1) 361-362.
136 Zachs, *First John Murray* (n 3) 297.
137 J Millar, *The Origin of the Distinction of Rank; Or, An Inquiry into the Circumstances which give Rise to Influence and Authority in the Different Members of Society* (1793).
138 J Millar, *The Origin of the Distinction of Ranks: Or, An Inquiry into the Circumstances which give Rise to Influence and Authority, in the Different Members of Society ... To which is prefixed, An Account of the Life and Writings of the Author, by John Craig, Esq.* (1806).
139 See e.g. Millar, *Distinction of Ranks* (4th) (n 138) 284, where a textual indicator for a footnote is inserted after "number" in line 2, correcting an omission in Millar, *Distinction of Ranks* (3rd) (n 1) 346 line 13, where "°" has been omitted.

nature of the lectures.[140] When in the later 1790s Millar introduced lectures on English law, his now standard account was given.[141] Student lecture notes survive from this course from Millar's last year of teaching, 1800-1801, shortly before his death. In these we find a condensed account of the explanation in the *Distinction of Ranks* of why all servants or labourers were once slaves, and how they came to be free in western Europe. He again explained that this was because after the barbarian invasions huge estates were managed at a distance, so that the serfs or villeins needed inducements to work, and the "state of the Bondmen grew daily better, till they were at last advanced to a state of compleat emancipation from slavery, and to the condition of free men".[142]

Millar next pointed out that when "slavery was wore out in Europe, it came from various causes to be introduced into America". He noted that it "might happen, that Colonists returning to the mother country, might bring their slaves along with them". It was "the condition of these imported Negroes" he wanted to consider. He claimed that, "in England, and Holland, and several other European countries, that a negro upon his arrival, obtains certain priviledges, and is reputed a free man". He gave as examples of these that "he is held to be protected in his person, and in his property, and not recoverable, like a chattel, by an action of trover". This said, Millar added that the "imported Negro" was "liable in England to perpetual service to his master". Moreover, his labour could "be assigned from one person to another". This was done "by a fiction – it being feigned, that the assignment took place in the West Indies". Whereas once he could have been sent back by his master to the colonies, which, "in a manner did away all his other priviledges", now, because of the case of Somerset in 1772, "masters could not send their negro servants abroad at their pleasure". He noted that:

> If we examine this opinion of Lord Mansfield, we will find that it is expressed with a good deal of delicacy, probably from the fear of giving an explicit opinion upon a matter of such importance. His Lordship only gave it as his opinion, that in this particular instance there were not sufficient causes for sending the Negro abroad, and that therefore Somerset ought to be discharged.

He summed up the state of "Negroes" in England thus: "They owe their masters perpetual service, and their service can be assigned from one person to another; but they cannot be sent abroad at their masters [*sic*] pleasure." He drew a contrast with Scotland, stating that, in the decision in 1778:

---

140 See e.g Edinburgh University Library, MS Dc.2.45, 56-74 (second course on the *Institutes*, 1794); GUL, MS Gen 1078, fols 23-25 (lectures on Scots law, 1792).
141 See Cairns, "Famous as a school for Law" (n 6) 139, 144.
142 GUL, MS Gen. 243, 60.

The judges were clearly and decidedly of opinion, that slavery was contrary both to the law of nature, and the municipal law of this country; that the laws of Jamaica could here have no force; that the master had no right to the negro's service for any space of time, and could not send him abroad without his consent ...[143]

To the end, therefore, Millar still saw the impact of *Somerset's Case* as limited, in this contrary to the decision in *Knight v Wedderburn*. It would not have been obvious, however, to the readers of the third edition of his *Distinction of Ranks* just how extensive Millar still thought were the duties in England imported black slaves continued to owe to their former owners. Perhaps he preferred to leave the matter ambiguous in print; but the lectures make his views clear.

E. CONCLUSION

Adam Smith was explicit in his abhorrence of slavery and firm conviction of the immorality of its presence in the New World. In the midst of a discussion of the effect of custom on the moral sentiments, in a passage on how "savages and barbarians" were accustomed to self-denial because of their need to cope with a harsh and strenuous way of life, he wrote:

> The same contempt of death and torture prevails among all other savage nations. There is not a negro from the coast of Africa who does not, in this respect, possess a degree of magnanimity which the soul of his sordid master is too often scarce capable of conceiving. Fortune never exerted more cruelly her empire over mankind, than when she subjected those nations of heroes to the refuse of the jails of Europe, to wretches who possess the virtues neither of the countries which they came from, nor of those which they go to, and whose levity, brutality, and baseness, so justly expose them to the contempt of the vanquished.[144]

The imagery of noble African savages and decadent Europeans is undoubtedly too strong. Like much hyperbole it weakened his point and made an easy target.[145] But Smith was certain of his view. In 1790, he added a passage to the sixth edition of his *Moral Sentiments* to the effect that it was not less cruel than extirpating one's enemies "to reduce them into the vilest of all states, that of domestic slavery, and to sell them, man, woman, and child, like so many herds of cattle, to the highest bidder in the market".[146]

His pupil never wrote anything quite so strong; but Millar's opposition to slavery and condemnation of it as a denial of natural freedom are also clear.

---

143 GUL, MS Gen. 243, 60-62.
144 A Smith, *The Theory of Moral Sentiments*, ed by A L Macfie and D D Raphael (1976; repr 1982) 206-207 (V.2.9).
145 C L Brown, *Moral Capital: Foundations of British Abolitionism* (2006) 115-116.
146 Smith, *Moral Sentiments* (n 144) 282 (VII.ii.1.28).

Slavery deprived an individual of a natural right; there had to be a very good reason for a natural right to be abrogated. There was none for slavery. Slavery degraded the slave, and perhaps made "him worthy of that contempt with which he is treated"; but it was also hurtful to the morals of the master, and could lead to his contracting "vicious habits … unrestrained by the laws".[147] It was thus socially harmful, particularly in opulent societies.

Millar nonetheless focused much of his attack on slavery on its economic inutility. It stifled innovation and repressed production. Much of his argument on this account developed from his claims about the state of colliers and salters in Scotland. There is indeed a good argument that the "emancipation" of the colliers and salters was sought by the coal-masters in particular to create a free market in labour without possibility of combinations by the workers in order to reduce wages and promote the economic efficiency of the mines.[148] Millar had then to fit this to New World slavery. This was where his problems arose. It was far from obvious that slavery was holding back economic growth in the West Indies or North America. Indeed many people must have appeared to be making huge profits from enslaved labour. Millar seems to have had no access to statistics about the economics of the slave plantations. He thus attacked them on the grounds that slavery discouraged innovation: hence his material on saws, spades, scythes and sickles. Money could be made, but only by driving the slaves hard, with close supervision and discipline under "the lash of their master".[149]

Millar must have been conscious of just how many Scots were involved in slavery and the slave trade and how many owned or had worked on or were working on plantations and in the sugar trade and the tobacco trade, as well as serving in the Americas as soldiers, artisans, doctors and the like. He will have been at least acquainted with many Glasgow merchants and fellow landowners in Lanarkshire and nearby who knew the West Indies, the Chesapeake, and the Carolinas very well indeed.[150] In Antigua in 1774, Janet Schaw described herself as being among "a whole company of Scotch people, our language, our manners, our circle of friends and connections, all

147   Millar, *Distinction of Ranks* (3rd) (n 1) 349-350.
148   C A Whatley, "'The fettering bonds of brotherhood': combination and labour relations in the Scottish coal-mining industry, ca 1690-1775" (1987) 12 *Social History* 139-154.
149   Millar, *Distinction of Ranks* (1st) (n 8) 230-232.
150   See e.g. R B Sheridan, "The rise of a colonial gentry: a case study of Antigua, 1730-1775" (1961) 13 *Economic History Review* 342-357; R B Sheridan, "The role of the Scots in the economy and society of the West Indies" (1977) 292 (1) *Annals of the New York Academy of Sciences* 94-106; A L Karras, *Sojourners in the Sun: Scottish Migrants in Jamaica and the Chesapeake, 1740-1800* (1992); D J Hamilton, *Scotland, the Caribbean and the Atlantic World, 1750-1820* (2005). For a fuller discussion see Cairns, "Enforced sojourners" (forthcoming).

the same";[151] but she could have said the same in many parts of the British Caribbean or North America. This explains Millar's anxieties about his claims of conditions in the West Indies. Were he wrong, many could contradict him. Not only would this have threatened the value of his claims about slavery in the British dominions; it potentially challenged his economic analysis of slavery in general. This was why he wanted to revise the text of the second edition before publication; as he explained to Murray "the credit of the book depends upon it".[152] While Murray must have been frustrated by Millar's desire for changes; Millar must likewise have been disappointed when the cancellations he wanted did not take place.

Millar's influence in the developing movement to end the slave trade and his opposition to slavery have long been recognised. Forty-five years ago, David Brion Davis, in the chapter on natural law and utility in his classic study, *The Problem of Slavery in Western Culture*, described the *Distinction of Ranks* as "a sociological study which must be rated as one of the most imaginative products of the Scottish Enlightenment". He indicated some of the problems with Millar's utilitarian opposition to slavery, and suggested that what influenced Millar's attitude was the fact that he had just lived through a decade of tremendous technological innovation in Great Britain. This had coloured his views.[153] A decade later, C Duncan Rice placed the *Distinction of Ranks* in the context of the Scottish Enlightenment, and noted that Millar's chapter "was an elaboration of his [i.e. Smith's] essential though briefly expressed point on the inutility of slave labour".[154]

Both these scholars are correct in their analysis. But I hope it is now clear just how aware Millar was of the weakness in his economic argument about slavery when applied to colonial slavery. His was an essentially rhetorical extrapolation from his claims about the Scottish miners and salters to the plantations.[155] But it was not without value. Plantation slavery remained economically viable; but Millar's emphasis on how it could only be so through violence was perceptive and convincing. His – and Smith's – pessimistic view that slavery was powerful because humans liked to dominate others and would only be ended when its economic disadvantages became progressively

---

151 J Schaw, *Journal of a Lady of Quality: Being the Narrative of a Journey from Scotland to the West Indies, North Carolina, and Portugal, in the Years 1774 to 1776*, ed by E Walker Andrews in collaboration with C McLean Andrews (2005) 81.
152 J Millar to J Murray, 24 Dec 1772, NLS, MS 40813.
153 D B Davis, *The Problem of Slavery in Western Culture* (1966) 435-437.
154 Rice, *Rise and Fall of Black Slavery* (n 15) 172.
155 See S Drescher, *Capitalism and Antislavery: British Mobilization in Comparative Perspective* (1987) 133-134.

clear was countered by their arguments on the cruelty and inhumanity of slavery. Sympathetic imagination allowed impartial spectators to experience at some level being in the place of a slave – subject to the lash, to the arbitrary whim of masters, with the women prostituted – and thus provided a powerful motivation to action.

Though there may have been some differences of nuance, Millar simply expounded an elaborated version of what Smith was to write in the *Wealth of Nations* and had already delivered to the moral philosophy class in Glasgow in his *Lectures on Jurisprudence*. But he did so not just through his book, but also in his lectures to generations of students in Glasgow. It must be remembered that he was one of the most successful teachers of the age, and many future leaders of the legal profession in Scotland and indeed statesmen studied with him.[156] Millar's Smithian account of slavery's injustice and economic inutility had in this way an incalculable influence among influential sectors of British society. The importance and influence of an inspired teacher and scholar is something of which Sir Neil MacCormick's life can also remind us all.

---

156 See W C Lehmann, *John Millar of Glasgow, 1735-1801* (1960) 30-42; Cairns, "Famous as a school for Law" (n 6) 134, 148-150.

4 Adam Ferguson, Classical Republicanism and the Imperative of Modernity

Alexander Broadie[*]

A. INTRODUCTION

B. WHAT DOES "SCOTTISH ENLIGHTENMENT" MEAN?

C. ADAM FERGUSON'S SCIENTIFIC APPROACH

D. ADAM FERGUSON'S REPUBLICANISM

E. ADAM FERGUSON: MAGISTRATES AND MILITIAS

F. THE SCOTTISH ENLIGHTENMENT AS AN ONGOING PROJECT

> We would do well to remind ourselves of the arguments of Adam Ferguson, not the least enlightened member of our Enlightenment, from whose *Essay on the History of Civil Society* spring many of the ideas essential to a discussion of civil liberties and the law. (N MacCormick, *Legal Right and Social Democracy* (1982) 59)

A. INTRODUCTION

Among the Scottish Enlightenment thinkers, none was more overtly republican than Adam Ferguson. This essay considers Ferguson's republicanism both in its relation to the modernity of his day and in relation to the modernity of ours. The concept of modernity that I shall be deploying is one that I believe to be an inseparable and major element within the broader concept of Enlightenment. Such a concept of modernity is well represented in the Scotland of our era by Neil MacCormick who, I shall argue, may fairly be seen as a literatus in the Fergusonian mould. This perception of the relation between the two men prompts a question on the relation between the Scottish Enlightenment and present-day Scotland, for both men were *philosophes engagés* whose engagement with the world was deeply informed by their Scottish context.

[*] Honorary Professorial Research Fellow and Emeritus Professor of Logic and Rhetoric, University of Glasgow.

My starting point will be the concept of "Scottish Enlightenment", which I shall unpack in order to have a firm base for making a comparison with our own day; the concept requires an account both of what it is that makes something an Enlightenment and also of what it is that makes an Enlightenment Scottish.

B. WHAT DOES "SCOTTISH ENLIGHTENMENT" MEAN?

My point of departure is Immanuel Kant's short essay "What is Enlightenment?" in which he identifies two features of Enlightenment.[1] The first is people's use of their own faculty of reason as a means of reaching conclusions, as contrasted with people's turning to authorities for guidance on what to think, and the second is the tolerance that those in authority show to those with ideas. If it is not safe for people to put their ideas into the public domain without fear of being silenced by authorities who do not like the ideas that have been published, an Enlightenment is less likely to arise and may even be impossible. I should like to add a third feature, which depends on the two just mentioned, namely the presence of robust public debate. The Age of Enlightenment was marked by the fact that people thinking for themselves disputed, all motivated by the thought that public debate enhances the prospects for progress across the whole range both of intellectual disciplines and also of civic practices. For we cannot be sure of the quality of our ideas if we do not pass them to others who will criticise them or defend them and thereby help us to decide whether our ideas should be retained, abandoned or modified. Hence, and deploying the most distinctive term in Kant's technical vocabulary, it may be said that central to Enlightenment is "critique" or "critical analysis" carried out in the public domain. The most prominent examples of critique that Kant himself offers in his seminal essay are a pastor's critique of his church's theology, a soldier's critique of strategic thinking by his military leaders, and a citizen's critique of the tax system. If the critiques are in each case hostile, motivated by a wish to see improvements in thinking and in practice, and if, despite being criticised, the religious, military and political leaders tolerate the fact that the critiques have been published, their toleration is a sign of Enlightenment.

The role of authorities in this narrative is crucial. People must be able to publish their ideas without fear of the reaction of those in authority. This central fact about Enlightenment prompts the question as to why authorities

---

1 See I Kant, "What is Enlightenment?", in H Reiss (ed), *Kant: Political Writings*, ed Hans Reiss (1996) 54-60.

should be minded to move against those with whom they disagree, and one obvious answer is that they judge their authority to be under threat. Public discussion in which someone presents and defends ideas critical of the political, social and religious authorities will naturally test the tolerance levels of those authorities, and these areas, which tended to be organised on a hierarchal basis, with power concentrated in the hands of particular groups, therefore have a special relation to Enlightenment.

In light of all this, there can be no doubt that Scotland during the eighteenth century was living through an age of Enlightenment. Things were, as always and everywhere, far from perfect, but the country had come a considerable distance over a period of a few decades. There were certainly many people in Scotland who were thinking for themselves, enjoying a significant measure of free speech, and engaged in vigorous public debate on a wide range of matters, theoretical and practical. There is also good reason to think that there were features or aspects of the Enlightenment in Scotland that were distinctive of the movement's manifestation in Scotland. Such distinctiveness was in fact inevitable for, overwhelmingly, enlightened activity in Scotland was conducted by members of three great, and distinctively Scottish, institutions, namely the universities, the Kirk and the law, three institutions that were granted privileged status under the Acts of Union in 1707. Professors, ministers of the Kirk and lawyers, all of them educated in the values of their Scottish vocation, could not write about matters philosophical, religious, legal, and so on, as if they were not deeply informed by those same values.

I said above that modernity was inseparable from Enlightenment and I shall here offer grounds for this claim. Modernity is a distinct kind of attitude to the modern – not just our attitude to the modern of our day but any person's attitude to his or her modern. What makes the attitude modernist is that the agent observes in a creative way, thinking for him or herself, and seeing the world as open to change to which he can and should contribute. In that sense, modernity implies an attitude of engagement with the world, and a recognition that such engagement is not a moral option but is instead a demand that morality makes on us. As such, modernism implies critique of the present for the sake of a better future. Its target can be anything that is in the agent's presence: he or she can critique institutions, whether of law (as when it is argued that a legal decision constitutes undue encroachment on civil liberties), or of politics (as when a voting system is demonstrated to be unjust), or of religion, of education or of industry, and so on, and he or she seeks change in response to a moral demand that arises from the critique. Because moral demands flow from these critiques, I speak of the "imperative of modernity", the demand that we make improvements wherever they are within our reach. Modernity, as so understood, is a reflective and also active participation in reality, by which the agent seeks to inform the future through his or her present reflections. Such acts are obstructed by effective intolerance, and it is hard to think of an imperative more pressing than that which demands a tolerant society in which people with ideas can safely put their ideas into the public domain. It is plain that modernity is very close to Enlightenment and arguably modernity is what Kant had in mind when he defined Enlightenment in and for his own day.[2]

As regards Scotland in the eighteenth century, no one better represents the Enlightenment of that day or was more manifestly a modernist than Adam Ferguson. In the next three sections I shall discuss his Enlightenment and modernist credentials, with particular reference to his promotion of classical republican ideals, and I shall then argue that the Scottish Enlightenment, far from being long dead, is an ongoing project.

C. ADAM FERGUSON'S SCIENTIFIC APPROACH

Adam Ferguson articulated his republicanism both in his writings and also in his conduct, and the extent to which his theory and his practice were in harmony will be demonstrated here. From the beginning he was open to influences that were to leave a lasting mark both on his writings and on his behaviour. He was born in Logierait, a Perthshire village on the Highland-Lowland line, and he was thus a native speaker of Gaelic, a rare quality among the literati.[3] His Logierait origins also meant that he had close contact with Highland culture, with its clans, its system of mutual support and its respect for military virtues. A further crucial influence on him was his father, a minister of the Kirk, who introduced his young son not only to Calvinist presbyterianism but also to the languages and literatures of ancient Greece and Rome. From these beginnings to Ferguson's ordination into the ministry and his acceptance of a post as chaplain in the Black Watch regiment, to which he delivered sermons in Gaelic, and from there to his professorship at Edinburgh University and his scholarly work on the Roman Republic, for which he would quickly gain a Europe-wide reputation – all this seems a natural progression, and on inspection it emerges that Ferguson's republicanism is a principle of unity in this progression.

---

2 For a concept of "modernity" in line with the one I offer, see M Foucault, "Qu'est-ce que les lumières?", in *Dits et écrits vol 2* (2001) 1381-1397. English translation "What is Enlightenment?", in P Rabinow (ed), *The Foucault Reader* (1984) 39-42.

3 Colin Maclaurin was perhaps the only other significant literatus who spoke Gaelic.

Ferguson attends to the historical question of the stages by which our society came to be as it is. This historical question has to be asked, for to understand a given state of society it is necessary to know how it reached its present state. Societies have a dynamic that is part of their nature, and insight into that dynamic requires knowledge of their history, knowledge of the forces of change in them as well as the forces of resistance to change. Ferguson was interested not only in recent and contemporary states of society but also in states in the distant past. We have noted his work on the Roman Republic, but in fact he wrote about much earlier states than that, and wanted to go back as far as possible in his investigations of human society. This prompts a question about the methodology appropriate to such an investigation, and Ferguson's response is that the question of the origins of human society is an empirical question, which can therefore be answered only by the deployment of empirical evidence. This answer draws him to a criticism of two influential narratives.

The doctrine of Thomas Hobbes and Jean-Jacques Rousseau, that antecedent to living in society human beings lived in a state of nature, was criticised by Ferguson on the grounds that there was no empirical evidence to support it. It is not at issue that Hobbes' doctrine concerning a state of nature and Rousseau's are unlike each other in almost all respects; Ferguson's criticism is that on one point, and this the most important, they are identical: both affirm that there was indeed a state of nature, one out of which people emerged, by means of a contract, into a state of society. Ferguson, in the spirit of the Enlightenment, asks how Hobbes and Rousseau can know this, and replies that both philosophers have mistaken the nature of their question concerning the origin of human society, and therefore have failed to see what counts as relevant evidence. He believes the question to be one of natural history, the natural history of human beings, and the method that has to be deployed en route to the answer to be of the same kind as that deployed by natural historians in other areas of science, namely the derivation of general tenets from particular observations and experiments, and attention to empirical historical records. When the natural historian investigates any particular species of animals: "he supposes, that their present dispositions and instincts are the same they originally had, and that their present manner of life is a continuance of their first destination".[4] On this basis, Ferguson concludes that Hobbes and Rousseau show by their conjectures that they have mistaken imagination and poetry for reason and science. For all the evidence that is

4 A Ferguson, *An Essay on the History of Civil Society*, ed by F Oz-Salzberger (1995) 8.

to hand conflicts with their conjecture about a social contract that removes
people from a state of nature:

> If both the earliest and the latest accounts collected from every quarter of the
> earth, represent mankind as assembled in troops and companies; and the individual
> always joined by affection to one party, while he is possibly opposed to another;
> employed in the exercise of recollection and foresight; inclined to communicate
> his own sentiments, and to be made acquainted with those of others; these facts
> must be admitted as the foundation of all our reasoning relative to man.[5]

Ferguson here advises those researching human nature to draw their
evidence from as wide a data base as possible, one not confined to information
about the researcher's own century or his own country. Ferguson, who shows
himself familiar with the anthropological writings of contemporary explorers
such as Cadwallader Colden[6] and Pierre-François Xavier de Charlevoix,[7] and
perhaps also of Joseph-François Lafitau,[8] as well as with the literature of
Greece and Rome, and indeed with the Bible, had an exceptionally rich data
base on which to draw, and he concluded that all reports indicate humans
living in society while none furnish evidence that man's nature is non-social.
In short, to be social is natural to humankind. The state of nature is not
something antecedent to the state of society, but on the contrary is what the
state of society is. This is plainly not to reject the claim made by Hobbes and
Rousseau that human beings lived in a state of nature. It is, quite the contrary,
to accept that all the available evidence points to humankind as having always
and everywhere lived in a state of nature, as doing so to this day, and as doing
so in the future. The error is in the doctrine that the state of nature was
historically antecedent to the social state. As Ferguson puts the point:

> If we are asked therefore, Where the state of nature is to be found? we may
> answer, It is here; and it matters not whether we are understood to speak in the
> island of Great Britain, at the Cape of Good Hope, or the Straits of Magellan.
> While this active being [the human being] is in the train of employing his talents,
> and of operating on the subjects around him, all situations are equally natural.[9]

The places here named are carefully chosen; their inhabitants are, in
his judgment, the most highly civilised and the least civilised on earth. It is
crucial to note therefore that while Ferguson has a great deal to say about

---

5 Ferguson, *Essay* 9.
6 C Colden, *The History of the Five Indian Nations of Canada, which are Dependent on the
Province of New-York in America* (1744).
7 P-F Xavier de Charlevoix, *Histoire et description générale de la Nouvelle-France* (1744); translated
as *Journal of a Voyage to North America, Undertaken by Order of the French King* (1761).
8 J-F Lafitau, *Moeurs des sauvages Américains, comparées aux moeurs des premiers temps* (1724).
9 Ferguson, *Essay* (n 4) 14.

humankind's progress or development, he has in mind a movement not from the pre-social state to the social, but from the rude state to the civilised. The progress from rude to civilised will soon take centre-stage in our discussion.

D. ADAM FERGUSON'S REPUBLICANISM

Ferguson's stadial theory is about human progress. He thought us capable of progress, both as individuals and as societies, and capable of it to a degree far beyond anything achievable by the rest of the animal kingdom, for we can learn from experience, make improvements in light of what we have learned and can then pass on these improved ways of living to the next generation. So practices, and whole institutions, can come into being and be improved upon, all this in contrast to animals, for in their own lifetime they can achieve their full perfection as members of their species. Yet Ferguson thinks both that human progress does not happen by necessity, and also that where progress is made, the more advanced state may not be maintained and is unlikely to be maintained without a holding operation. Even with such an operation it might fall back, and the very title of his *History of the Progress and Termination of the Roman Republic* (1783) reminds us of this fact. Ferguson is well aware that often, perhaps almost always, what actually happens in human history is a product as much of chance as of planning, but he has a good deal to say about principles in the human mind and in human society that militate strongly against progress, and he holds in particular that even those who are dedicated to progress can, through something intrinsic in them or in society, be an obstacle to it. Of course to call something "progress" is to assign a value to it, and we need therefore to know what things have a special place within Ferguson's system of values. To this question I now turn.

Ferguson's *History of the Progress and Termination of the Roman Republic* is systematically related to his other writings on matters moral, political and social, for in all of these there is, either on or just below the surface, a concern both theoretical and practical with the concept and the promotion of republicanism. The Roman Republic embodied the virtue of active or participatory citizenship whereby citizens engage in the political processes. To this virtue Ferguson attached a special significance, in that he judged it central to the explanation of the rise of the Republic and also thought the undermining or destruction of the virtue as central to the explanation both of the Republic's fall, and of its replacement by a worse political-cum-social setup.

Aristotle's definition of man as "a political animal" struck a chord with Ferguson. Where there are people there is politics, because it is our nature to be political, in the sense of being engaged in political activity. Not to be political is therefore to be living contrary to nature, and if this contrary state is habitual or dispositional then the person's nature is corrupt. But there are also forms of corruption specific to the political life and these are a matter of lively interest to Ferguson. Above all he promotes the idea of the due watchfulness of citizens, who scrutinise the acts of the political leaders, who are willing to engage in public debate on the merits of those acts, and who are also willing publicly to criticise the political leaders if they are perceived to act not out of the spirit of society but out of a spirit of self-interest.

The republican imperative is therefore that every citizen be a politician, not leaving a distinct political class to practise the art of politics while everyone else gets on with their lives. Quite the contrary, all citizens should see themselves as forming a vigilante society in a broad sense of that phrase, watchful of *res publicae*, debating and disputing about what should be done on behalf of society as a whole, and ready to call to account a political leadership that fails to listen to and act on citizenly advice. The danger and vice in relation to this imperative is political quietism, where we leave others to do the political thinking and acting for us, and we slide into what Ferguson terms "languor and listless indifference",[10] through which civil liberties are lost because those who should be fighting for them have opted for a quiet life.

There is a parallel here, that Ferguson notes, with the academic, or more broadly the intellectual world, where again the vice is that of intellectual quietism, where we leave others to do the thinking for us and again slide into an intellectual languor and listless indifference. As Ferguson puts the point:

> When we only mean to learn what others have taught, it is probable, that even our knowledge will be less than that of our masters … We become students and admirers, instead of rivals; and substitute the knowledge of books, instead of the inquisitive or animated spirit in which they were written.[11]

The issue here is the virtue of unanimity in the academic or more generally the intellectual world. Some might think unanimity a good thing, but it can occur for all sorts of reasons that do not promote confidence in the thesis agreed on, and Ferguson is sensitive to the fact that agreement might be voiced because those who would otherwise speak out in opposition have either felt it safer to remain silent or have been silenced. And without a vigorous public discussion, debate and dispute about what is at issue, it cannot be determined whether the contradicting party would have won the argument if they had decided, or been allowed, to speak out.

10 Ferguson, *Essay* 204.
11 Ferguson, *Essay* 206.

The political analogue of this situation is plain, and points to a feature of Ferguson's discussion that needs emphasis, namely that for the sake of civil liberty it is no bad thing if the body politic is composed of argumentative, obstreperous and sometimes turbulent factions, in which everyone is a vigilante, scrutinising everyone else's position, and especially the position of those exercising leadership in the state. We observed above that in his discussion of the corruption of the intellectual life, Ferguson spoke of the unhealthy relation in which people stand to their masters: "We become students and admirers, instead of rivals". This is no less appropriate a figure for the political life; it is also important for the health of the body politic that citizens are perceived by the state's political leaders to be not their admirers but their ever-vigilant rivals. Factions are a solution to the problem of how to ensure the maintenance of civil liberties, and if factions did not exist they, or something like them, would have to be invented. Plainly a good deal of perceptive argumentation lies behind Ferguson's conclusion: "our very praise of unanimity, therefore, is to be considered as a danger to liberty".[12] Granted that the concept of robust public debate is central to the concept of Enlightenment, it is hard to not to read the *Essay on the History of Civil Society* as a theorising, on specifically republican lines, of the virtue of Enlightenment.

E. ADAM FERGUSON: MAGISTRATES AND MILITIAS

Robust public debate, as a barrier to governmental encroachment on civil liberties, can become tumultuous for many reasons, one being a perception that despite the asseverations of those in power, they are acting, or intending to act, without regard to the wishes of those over whom they exercise power. There is however a paradox in this state of affairs. For on the one hand the law is perceived to be a safeguard, perhaps the great safeguard, of our civil liberties; on the other hand a commotion by a group of citizens might itself be judged a breach of the peace and contrary to the law even if people are protesting against a threat to or withdrawal of their civil liberties. This paradox brings us within reach of a major Fergusonian insight, concerning the fragility of our civil liberty where the threat to it is due to forces within, and not outwith, the state. The forces he has in mind are those engaged in the processes of legislation and law enforcement, and the mechanism that underlies them is the systematic application of the principle of division of labour, to which I must now turn.

---

12 Ferguson, *Essay* 252.

This latter principle, around which a substantial body of thought had grown by the time Ferguson wrote his *Essay on the History of Civil Society*, was given its classic formulation by his friend Adam Smith. Smith noted that if the manufacture of an artefact requires *n* stages, more copies will be made in a given time if the total labour is divided up so that each stage is handled by a different worker. His famous illustration of the benefits of the division of labour is that the manufacture of a pin involves eighteen stages, and one person working by himself takes about a day to make a single pin, but, as witness the production rate at a pin factory, he knew that ten workers, with some of them engaged in perhaps two or three stages, can make 48,000 in a day. The case for division of labour as a means of enhancing economic productivity is thus demonstrated by Smith to be overwhelming. He believes the principle to have a role in all aspects of economic activity, and accordingly he attaches special weight to it in his *Wealth of Nations*.

However, for all the principle's economic credentials, Smith is worried about it on grounds both moral and economic, and his worry should be noted since there is an instructive contrast between Smith and Ferguson on this matter, where the Fergusonian dimension essentially concerns his republican stance. Systematic application of the principle results in each worker performing a minute task, hour by hour, for days, even years, and this must have a crippling effect on his intellect, spirit and morale:

> The torpor of his mind renders him, not only incapable of relishing or bearing a part in any rational conversation, but of conceiving any generous, noble, or tender sentiment, and consequently of forming any just judgment concerning many even of the ordinary duties of private life.[13]

One has to sympathise with workers reduced to this sad state, and one would also sympathise with their resentment at those who have brought them so low. Plainly, this effect of the principle of division of labour on the workers is morally unacceptable and Smith, who always takes his moral philosophy with him in his researches into political economy, sees that it needs to be addressed. He is equally conscious that the economic implications also must be noted; a workforce crippled in intellect, spirit and morale is bound to be less efficient, in respect of economic productivity, than one spared that same fate. Smith's response is to promote the idea of education for the workers. They will be taught "the most essential parts of education ... to read, write, and account". They will also learn the "elementary parts of geometry

13 A Smith, *An Inquiry into the Nature and Causes of the Wealth of Nations*, ed by R H Campbell and A S Skinner (1976) 782.

and mechanicks", all this to be paid for by the government, not by private philanthropy, since the source of funding has to be assured.[14]

This response is a reminder that Smith's economic thinking operates entirely within the framework of a moral philosophy, and that the moral dimension has primacy in the sense that if the systematic application of an economic principle has a morally unacceptable outcome, then an adjustment has to be made in the interest of morality. I believe that Ferguson would be in full agreement with Smith's account of the relation between morality and economics, and that he would probably endorse Smith's solution to the particular problem that arises from systematic application of the principle of division of labour. But there are large differences of principle between the two men. One, which I shall merely mention here as being of serious concern to Ferguson, relates to the fact, as he perceives it to be, that: "in its termination, and ultimate effects, [division of labour] serves, in some measure, to break the bands of society ... and to withdraw individuals from the common scene of occupation, on which the sentiments of the heart, and the mind, are most happily employed".[15] This is a point that is important to Ferguson because he is bound to see it as implying that human nature accords well with a society organised on classical republican lines.

However, the difference between Ferguson and Smith on which I wish to concentrate here relates to the reach or coverage of the principle of the division of labour. In brief, Ferguson thinks that the principle cannot properly be made to cover as many tasks as Smith thinks it can. One issue is that of political action and the political life. Smith is relaxed about the fact that there is a political class, that is, a class of professional politicians, people who spend their time being political and who have therefore become efficient at it, as workers are likely to in any role for which they have an aptitude if they spend a long time honing the skills appropriate to the role. Ferguson, on the other hand, is not at all relaxed about the fact that there is a political class, a point to which I now turn.

Earlier I emphasised Ferguson's promotion of the republican idea of a vigilant citizenry examining the government's activities, engaging in public debate about those activities and, especially, criticising political leaders who are acting out of a spirit of self-interest or of class interest and not out of a spirit of society – hence what I termed the "republican imperative", that every citizen should be a politician. A corollary of this is that there should not be a political class except in so far as all the citizens belong to it, which

14 Smith, *Wealth of Nations* 785.
15 Ferguson, *Essay* 206-207.

means in effect that there should not be a political class *tout court*. But to rule out such a class as inappropriate is implicitly to set a limit to the principle of the division of labour. There can be a class of bakers, a class of brewers, of carpenters, of journalists, and so on, each class fulfilling a valuable role in society, each one saving other citizens having to carry out those relevant tasks, and thus leaving them free to get on with their own jobs. This kind of thing happens in a well-functioning state. But a political class is not like the other classes; it has a special dangerousness, in that it poses a permanent threat to our civil liberties. This is the heart of Ferguson's critique.

In "Of corruption, as it tends to political slavery"[16] Ferguson discusses the relation between law and civil liberty, focusing on the role of legislators and law officers in the process of the systematic corruption of civil society, a process that ends in a hoodwinked citizenry discovering too late that it has lost liberties that it had not perceived to be under threat. Ferguson affirms:

> Liberty results, we say, from the government of laws; and we are apt to consider statutes, not merely as the resolutions and maxims of a people determined to be free, not as the writings by which their rights are kept on record; but as a power erected to guard them, and as a barrier which the caprice of man cannot transgress.[17]

Laws might have been formulated by legislators intent on protecting the civil liberties. If they were, then how do they cease to protect us? The question leads Ferguson to a disturbing comparison between pashas and Enlightenment magistrates. From whom do we receive a better quality of justice? The magistrate is constrained by the positive law published in law books which set out the law in all its detail. If the law is formulated by politicians with a will to protect and enhance the citizenry's civil liberties, then the magistrate can surely not be an agent in a corruptive process. On the other hand, the pasha, who has no law books that he need consult, is not constrained by positive law, but instead judges on the basis of his sense of natural justice, natural fairness or equity. From which it surely follows that he is more likely to be in error in his conclusions than is the Enlightenment magistrate, given that the pasha lacks the detailed guidance provided by a multitude of well-intentioned legislators who collectively have decided what the law should be. Suppose that the pasha has a corrupt nature. In that case the considerable room he has for the exercise of discretion implies that he is more likely to act corruptly than is the magistrate, even if the latter is corrupt, for the magistrate is bound by the mass of positive law.

16 Ferguson, *Essay* part 6, sect 5.
17 Ferguson, *Essay* 249.

Yet Ferguson does not take this view of the relation between the pasha and the magistrate, and this because he is more distrustful of the relation between the magistrate and his law books than of the relation between a pasha and his faculty of reason. The party to the pasha's judicial proceeding is assured a significant measure of just treatment since, as Ferguson puts the point: "his rights are discussed, on the foundation of a rule that is open to the understandings of mankind". We all have access to the rules of natural equity, and in that sense there is a significant transparency in the pasha's proceedings.

This may be contrasted with the magistrate's proceedings, for he bases himself on his own interpretation of written laws, which form "an intricate system, which it has become the object of a separate profession to study and to explain".[18] Two potential obstacles to fairness are in play here. One, which concerns transparency, is that positive law is a system of such intricacy that it requires the employment of a whole class of workers, lawyers, to find out what the law means. A proper grasp of the law, far from being accessible to all, is accessible to very few. The second obstacle is of a different order. Ferguson asks: "When a judge in Europe is left to decide, *according to his own interpretation of written laws*, is he in any sense more restrained than the [pasha]?"[19] His answer is negative, and the reason, though not spelled out, is plain. It is that the judge or magistrate reaches a decision that is based not only on what the law says, but also on what he takes to be the law's meaning. Mediating between the law in the statute books and the judgment delivered by the judge is the judge's interpretation, something that he and he alone can provide, and his interpretation may arise not only from sources clear to all, but also from deeply hidden sources which others could hardly guess at. It is within this opaque space in the judicial process that the work of corruption can be wrought.

One kind of scenario that Ferguson has in mind is a magistrate's response to an alleged breach of the peace, or public disorder, committed by people who are being disorderly, tumultuous, even riotous, from outrage at some act of great injustice. There are a number of possible responses by the magistrate. The one that disturbs Ferguson is a product of the magistrate's inclination to act from the spirit of his class and not from the spirit of society. He lives comfortably and relatively securely, and sees public disorder as a potential threat to his way of life. The disorderly conduct must therefore be dealt with in a suitably tough manner. In so responding, the magistrate may think that he is the true embodiment of Enlightenment values, protecting the

18 Ferguson, *Essay* 249.
19 Ferguson, *Essay* 249 (my italics).

civitas, and thereby allowing polite society to maintain its standards. And yet it is in fact those disturbing the civic peace, those who are thereby taking risks with their freedom and even with their lives in order to secure justice, who are the true embodiments of Enlightenment values. It is they, as Ferguson would say, who embody the classical republican spirit, the spirit of participatory citizenship, acting vigorously in the spirit of society, and not for the sake of the dear self.

Neil MacCormick, referring to the passage I have just discussed, describes Ferguson's position as "a striking antinomianism, an outspoken mistrust of laws as alone sufficient (if even necessary) to the preservation of liberty".[20] I am not sure I want to go quite so far as to call Ferguson's position antinomian for two reasons, the first of which, however, would cut little ice with MacCormick. The first reason is this: the pasha is represented as passing judgment on the basis of natural law; he deploys what Ferguson terms "the rules of natural equity" and reasons, as Ferguson adds, "on the foundation of a rule that is open to the understandings of mankind". It seems therefore a step too far to say that Ferguson displays a preference for antinomianism in his approval of the pasha's performance; and here we should recall both that the European natural law tradition was deeply embedded in the Scottish Enlightenment and also that Ferguson was fully committed to that same tradition.

Ferguson's respect for the pasha, however, could not have impressed MacCormick who rejects natural law theory on the grounds that it makes what he terms "unsustainable ontological assumptions about the existence of objective and rationally discoverable principles of right".[21] MacCormick himself supported a sophisticated form of positivism; for him laws are purely institutional facts. That being the case, I need a second reason for rejecting the claim that Ferguson displays an antinomian inclination. And it is that Ferguson does not at all disparage positive law – how could he? He is very clear that, without it, civil society, civil liberty and civic virtue would be impossible. His point is that our laws form one part of the system that defends our liberties. Other parts also are required, and in particular the law must be administered by law officers motivated by the spirit of society and not the spirit of class:

> And the influence of laws, where they have any real effect in the preservation of liberty, is not any magic power descending from shelves that are loaded with

20 N MacCormick, "Republicanism, Fletcher and Ferguson", in *The Saltoun Papers: Reflections on Andrew Fletcher*, ed by P Henderson Scott (2003) 37.
21 See the essay "Civil liberties and the law", in N MacCormick, *Legal Right and Social Democracy: Essays in Legal and Political Philosophy* (1982) 54.

books, but is, in reality, the influence of men resolved to be free; of men, who, having adjusted in writing the terms on which they are to live with the state, and with their fellow-subjects, are determined, by their vigilance and spirit, to make these terms be observed.[22]

This is surely not an antinomian position. Elsewhere, but with this same passage in mind, MacCormick does say: "it is true that laws alone do not guarantee either liberty or social justice. There must also be an attitude among citizens of vigilance for their own and others' liberty."[23] This position seems to me an endorsement of Ferguson's position.

Ferguson's line of attack on magistrates is very closely related to his attack on the class of politicians, a class prone to the same kind of corruption as the magistrates. In a fine piece of rhetoric Ferguson outlines his concern:

> We have reason to dread the political refinements of ordinary men, when we consider, that repose, or inaction itself, is in a great measure their object; and that they would frequently model their governments, not merely to prevent injustice and error, but to prevent agitation and bustle; and by the barriers they raise against the evil actions of men, would prevent them from acting at all. Every dispute of a free people, in the opinion of such politicians, amounts to disorder, and a breach of the national peace ... Men of superior genius sometimes seem to imagine, that the vulgar have no title to act, or to think.[24]

Laws are passed, therefore, to diminish the range of political activities in which the citizens can engage.

On this analysis, full-blooded participatory citizenship is incompatible with the existence of a political class, for such a class will naturally move to limit the ways in which citizens can participate in the political processes. Politicians would no doubt say in their own defence that their motive for moving to prevent participatory citizenship arises not at all from any desire to protect the well-being of the political class, except to the extent that the class, unlike the mass of citizens, is clear-sighted about where the interests of society lie, and therefore must not be obstructed in its virtuous and selfless labours. It should now be clear why Ferguson believed that there should not be a political class.

I should now like to dig deeper into Ferguson's republicanism by devoting space to the fact that he gives us a second example of a case in which application of the principle of the division of labour is inappropriate. He holds that responsibility for national defence, no less than for political decision-making, should be in the hands of the citizenry as a whole and not of a class

22 Ferguson, *Essay*, 249.
23 MacCormick, "Civil liberties and the law" (n 21) at 59.
24 Ferguson, *Essay* 209.

within the state. His first significant discussion of the issue is in a pamphlet *Reflections Previous to the Establishment of a Militia*,[25] which he wrote as a contribution to the animated debate, then in full swing, on the best means to defend the country in the event of an invasion by the French. Many more insights on the merits of militias as compared to standing armies are added in his *Essay on the History of Civil Society*. Two years before publishing *Reflections*, Ferguson had resigned from his post as principal chaplain to the Black Watch after nine years' service in the regiment. So at the time of the penning of the *Reflections*, he wrote on the base of lengthy personal experience of life in a standing army.

The Seven Years War broke out in 1756, when Britain had 35,000 regular soldiers stationed on home soil plus 15,000 German troops brought to Britain to supplement the country's otherwise rather meagre defensive strength. This state of affairs prompted a debate as to whether the citizens themselves should be given military training, so that militias would be available in the event of a French invasion. Some of Ferguson's anxieties about standing armies are parallel to anxieties he felt about politicians. Wherein lies the guarantee that soldiers will be animated by the spirit of society and not by the spirit of their class? And if the army is not animated by the spirit of society, how is society to defend itself from its own army? To which latter worry Ferguson adds the thought that if the army is called elsewhere and meantime a new enemy appears, then, as he puts the point, the citizens, if not trained in warfare, would stand with "hopeless amazement and terror" at the sight of the enemy.[26] This would not arise if the state were defended by militias – not a class of professional soldiery but the citizens themselves trained, equipped and highly motivated to defend the state, an army deep within the population. As Ferguson later pointed out, this was the situation as regards the army of the American rebels who in the 1770s finally overcame the British professional armies sent out to quell the rebellion.[27] Ferguson's classical republicanism is again visible in this discussion of the limits of the

---

25 (1756).

26 Ferguson, *Essay* 216.

27 An interesting rejoinder to this line of Ferguson's came from Adam Smith, who was familiar with Ferguson's views. While not hostile to the idea of a Scottish militia as such, Smith thought militias "must always be much inferior to a well disciplined and well exercised standing army" (Smith, *Wealth of Nations* (n 13) 700. To which he adds: "A militia of any kind, it must be observed, however, which has served for several successive campaigns in the field, becomes in every respect a standing army ... Should the war in America drag out through another campaign, the American militia may become in every respect a match for the [British] standing army" (Smith, *Wealth of Nations* 701). For Ferguson on the militia see J Robertson, *The Scottish Enlightenment and the Militia Issue* (1985) passim.

applicability of the doctrine of the division of labour. The discussion promotes the concept of a citizen who can feed and clothe himself, who is energetic in the field of politics and when necessary knows how to acquit himself as a warrior on the field of battle. Ferguson here extols the vita activa, though vita hyper-activa might be thought a more apt description.

For Ferguson, whose experiences in the Black Watch are never far from the surface of the *Essay on the History of Civil Society*, war and civil society could hardly be more tightly bound up with each other:

> Without the rivalship of nations, and the practice of war, civil society itself could scarcely have found an object, or a form … To overawe, or intimidate, or, when we cannot persuade with reason, to resist with fortitude, are the occupations which give its most animating exercise, and its greatest triumphs, to a vigorous mind; and he who has never struggled with his fellow-creatures, is a stranger to half the sentiments of mankind.[28]

Commentators have paid but slight attention to these words, but they seem to me to bear an impressive message; for they imply that anyone seeking to write a treatise on human nature, the topic of central interest to the luminaries of the Scottish Enlightenment, would do well to experience a soldier's life; not merely to put on a uniform but to be where the fighting is. Without such experience half the sentiments of mankind, and therefore much of what a philosopher of human nature would wish to expound, would remain unknown territory to the author. If Ferguson is correct about this, then he was better placed than most of the literati to write about what was their favourite topic.

It should be added that Ferguson's interest in the militia issue had a Scottish national dimension. Ferguson deeply resented the fact that, though by the Militia Act of 1757 England and Wales had militias, the Scotch Militia Bill was defeated at Westminster, almost certainly because of English distrust of Scottish intentions after the 1745 Jacobite uprising. Famously one of Ferguson's responses to the defeat at Westminster was to found the Poker Club, whose purpose, as the name suggests, was to stir things up, in this case on behalf of the claim that Scotland had no less a right to a militia than did England and Wales. It is true that he had a variety of reasons other than patriotic ones for promoting the idea of a Scottish militia, and in particular there were moral, social and national defence arguments in his formidable armoury, all of them underpinned by his commitment to the virtues of republicanism. But his love of his native country was a major element in his motivation.

28 Ferguson, *Essay* 28.

F. THE SCOTTISH ENLIGHTENMENT AS AN ONGOING PROJECT

Part B of this chapter was dedicated to an analysis of the concept of "Scottish Enlightenment". In that analysis, a prominent role was assigned to the concepts of autonomous reason, toleration and robust public debate. The narrative, which was philosophical in character, prompted a question, which was historical, concerning whether there had ever been something that fell under the concept of "Scottish Enlightenment" and, in light of an array of activities and achievements in eighteenth-century Scotland, the answer given was, of course, affirmative. Historians speak about *the* Scottish Enlightenment as if there was only ever one, the great cultural flowering of the eighteenth century, but there is nothing in the concept to exclude the possibility that there might yet be another, a second. However, I think that if the concept of a Scottish Enlightenment is understood in the way that I suggest, then we may have to wait a long time for a second Enlightenment, because the criteria that I presented in Part B fit Scotland not only in the eighteenth century, but in the nineteenth as well, and in the twentieth too. I have argued this thesis at length elsewhere,[29] and here shall only say that there has been in Scotland over the past few centuries an immense amount of activity by people thinking for themselves, and engaging in robust public debate in conditions of sufficient tolerance to allow people with ideas to put them into the public domain without fear of reprisal by those in authority. Since the nineteenth century, Scotland has even produced thinkers of world status, thinkers whose achievements are a match for those of David Hume, Adam Smith, Joseph Black and James Hutton. What happened to the Scottish Enlightenment at the end of the eighteenth century is that it neither stopped nor even slowed down, but instead just kept marching on, and I think it demonstrable that it has not yet stopped. We are still living through *the* Scottish Enlightenment, and talk about a second Scottish Enlightenment is therefore premature.

These considerations suggest that the Scottish Enlightenment is an open-ended performance, a project still unfolding. Speaking of his own era, Kant affirms: "If it is now asked whether we at present live in an *enlightened* age, the answer is: No, but we do live in an age of *enlightenment*." The distinction at issue is immediately elucidated:

As things are at present, we still have a long way to go before men as a whole can be in a position (or can even be put into a position) of using their own under-

---

29 A Broadie, "The rise (and fall?) of the Scottish Enlightenment", in T Devine and J Wormald (eds), *The Oxford Handbook of Modern Scottish History* (forthcoming, 2012).

standing confidently and well in religious matters, without outside guidance. But we do have distinct indications that the way is now being cleared for them to work freely in this direction, and that the obstacles to universal enlightenment, to man's emergence from his self-incurred immaturity, are gradually becoming fewer. In this respect our age is the age of enlightenment, the century of Frederick.[30]

"Enlightenment", therefore, as Kant intends the term, and as I use it here, refers to a process, a dawning, not the static brilliance of high noon. In the sense here at issue, the Scottish Enlightenment is an ongoing project.

During the last two centuries the project has been carried forward by a large number of thinkers, who were the literati of their day no less than Adam Ferguson, David Hume and Adam Smith and a host of others were the literati of the eighteenth century.[31] During the past half century no one has more suited the title "literatus of the Scottish Enlightenment" than Neil MacCormick, who wrote the sentence that sits as a motto at the head of this chapter. When he and I first met up at Balliol College in the 1960s we had both already developed an interest in the Scottish Enlightenment, and our subsequent conversations reflected this interest. I began the chapter by indicating in the motto an aspect of the relation in which Neil stood to Adam Ferguson, and I should like to end by looking further at the relation. Four points in particular.

First, Adam Ferguson was a patriotic Scot, a fact about him that is not diminished by his also being a unionist. For many years principal chaplain of the Black Watch Regiment, a position to which he was called partly because he was a native Gaelic speaker, the insights that he gained as a member of the Black Watch did not in the least undermine his enthusiasm for the idea of the reintroduction into Scotland of militias. His decades-long campaign on behalf of the idea of a Scottish militia was waged with a vigour and tenacity that bespeaks a Scottish patriotism with which Neil would have felt entirely at home.

Secondly, the concept of Europe played a major role in Ferguson's thinking on matters moral, political and social; a Europe-directedness encouraged his long-standing interest in the Roman Republic, that great unifying principle of Europe. And it is to be remembered that in his own day Ferguson was perhaps best known in Britain and America as the author of *The History of the Progress and Termination of the Roman Republic*, a work that marked him out as one of the two or three leading Roman historians of Europe.

---

30 Kant, "What is Enlightenment?" (n 1) at 58. Frederick is of course Frederick the Great.
31 See A Broadie, *A History of Scottish Philosophy* (2010) 301-364 for discussion of many whom I regard as literati of the period 1800-1960.

Ferguson's study of the Roman Republic went hand in hand with his classical republican enthusiasm for the idea that all citizens should be both competent to bear arms and also entitled to use them in defence of the state, a point of course lying on the surface of his campaign for a Scottish militia. Furthermore Ferguson travelled widely in Europe, and was a member of the great academies of Europe, in Berlin, Rome and Florence. He took a close interest in political events in Europe and was a supporter of the French Revolution. Again, his Europe-directedness articulates closely with the values of Neil MacCormick MEP.

Thirdly, Ferguson wrote of the virtues of the vita activa, a life embodying the sense of duty and also of privilege that all citizens should feel at the prospect of defending and enhancing the civitas. It may be added that, on this matter, Ferguson practised what he preached. His nine years in the Black Watch bear witness to this fact, as also does his role as secretary to the Carlisle Commission that was in America in 1778 to negotiate with the leaders of the American rebellion. Neil likewise believed in a vita activa dedicated to the well-being of the civitas and, in his tireless activities, political, academic and otherwise, he practised the precepts that he commended to others.

Fourthly and finally in this list of similarities, I want to turn to the chief source of Ferguson's present-day reputation, his *Essay on the History of Civil Society*, in which close attention is paid to the relations between liberty and the law, and to note that that same topic surfaces repeatedly in Neil's writings. The starting point is the familiar idea that our liberty is constrained by means factual and normative and that, though the law is commonly represented as a condition of our liberty, in reality it encroaches on our liberty no less than does imprisonment or paralysis, even if in a different way. Nevertheless Ferguson is as clear as anyone could be that law is necessary if we are to be able to embody in our lives what we think of as civilised values, whether by our open disagreement with political or religious authorities, or by our watching the plays of our choice or by attending the house of prayer of our choice, and so on. The law is the principal means of defence of these liberties that enable us to flourish as human beings. Neil fully accepted this characterisation of the role of the law, and in line with this insight argued forcefully for such things as the ending of the privileged position that English law conferred on Christianity in respect of acts of blasphemy, and for the right of extremist political parties, such as the National Front, to hold meetings and processions.[32] Furthermore, as we have seen, both Adam Ferguson and Neil

32 See N MacCormick, *Legal Right and Social Democracy* (1982) 48-49.

MacCormick agree that law by itself cannot be a sufficient means of defence of our civil liberties, and that in addition citizens themselves must be resolved to be free and must be determined, by their vigilance and spirit, to ensure that the terms of the law are observed. We see in all this a formidable unity of values and of philosophy between these prominent literati as they respond in their various ways to the imperative of modernity.

What's in a Legal System?

5 The Many Conceptions of a Legal System

Gerry Maher°

A. INTRODUCTION
B. TEACHING "SCOTTISH LEGAL SYSTEM"
C. LEGAL SYSTEMS AND LEGAL STRUCTURES
D. A SOCIOLOGICAL CONCEPTION OF LEGAL SYSTEM
E. LEGAL SYSTEMS AND LEGAL DOCTRINE
F. LEGAL SYSTEM AND IDENTITY: IS THERE A SCOTTISH LEGAL SYSTEM?
G. LEGAL SYSTEM AS "COUNTRY": THE SCOTTISH LEGAL SYSTEM AND INTERNATIONAL PRIVATE LAW

A. INTRODUCTION

Joseph Raz once wrote a book called *The Concept of a Legal System*, a work intended as an introduction to a general theory of legal system, and as seeking to elucidate the concept of a legal system.[1] However, it is not at all obvious that there is such a thing as *the* concept of legal system. Certainly, in legal discourse the term "legal system" is used in a variety of contrasting ways. Different perspectives may give emphasis or priority to one or more of these different senses of legal system, but it is wrong to assume that there is, or can be, only one concept involved. This paper will sketch of some of the ways in which lawyers talk about legal systems. Whether or not there is a core aspect (or aspects) common to these different conceptions can be determined only once we are clear what each different conception involves. My argument is that there are clearly overlapping elements between some of these conceptions but there is no single common or unifying element; nor is there any

---

° Professor of Criminal Law, University of Edinburgh. Most of this paper was written in Scotland but parts were also drafted in Hong Kong; two places, each a part of a larger state but each with its own legal system.

1 J Raz, *The Concept of a Legal System*, 1st edn (1970), 2nd edn (1980). At page 1 he states that the work involves the "examination of the presuppositions and implications underlying the fact that every law necessarily belongs to a legal system (the English, or German, or Roman, or Canon Law, or some other legal system)".

good reason for privileging one conception as embodying the sole concept of a legal system.[2] That is, with one notable exception, personal rather than conceptual in nature. For what all, or at least most, of these conceptions share in common is that they attracted the attention of Neil MacCormick.[3]

B. TEACHING "SCOTTISH LEGAL SYSTEM"

In Scottish law schools most teachers, and all students who study Scots law, are familiar with a course called Scottish Legal System or some very similar variant.[4] The same sorts of academic course are to be found elsewhere, English Legal System or Irish Legal System, and the like. The content of these courses is typically the same, covering such matters as:

(1) the sources of law (statute, judicial precedent, custom, works of authority)
(2) the institutions of law (parliaments, government executive bodies, courts)
(3) the legal professions (advocates, solicitors, lay advisers)
(4) legal procedure (civil actions, criminal trial, tribunal hearings).

Many also deal with issues of legal reasoning; provision and funding of legal services; legal history; law reform.

One topic that has perhaps fallen out of fashion is the structure and branches of (1) law and (2) legal study. The first deals with such matters as the distinctions between international and municipal law, and public and private law, and the subdivisions in each category (for example, public law as consisting of constitutional law, administrative law, criminal law;[5] private law as made up of law of persons, obligations, property, and adjective law). There are also subjects that cut across these divisions, such as commercial law and EU law. The second area is concerned with the branches and subjects of legal study itself, for example legal history, comparative legal studies, legal philosophy, sociology of law.

---

2 Famously Wittgenstein, in describing the idea of family resemblances, wrote that "Consider for example the proceedings that we call 'games'. I mean board-games, card-games, ball-games, Olympic games, and so on. What is common to them all? – Don't say: 'There *must* be something common, or they would not be called "games"' – but *look and see* whether there is anything in common to all" (L Wittgenstein, *Philosophical Investigations* (1953), section 66 (emphases in original))

3 In particular, N MacCormick, *Rhetoric and the Rule of Law: A Theory of Legal Reasoning* (2005); *Institutions of Law: An Essay in Legal Theory* (2007); "Law as institutional fact" (1974) 90 *Law Quarterly Review* 102; N MacCormick and O Weinberger, *An Institutional Theory of Law: New Approaches to Legal Positivism* (1986).

4 At present (2011) in Edinburgh Law School, this class is called "Legal Reasoning and Legal System", with no indication that either element is Scottish in focus.

5 Many academics, and virtually all students, forget that on any definition of public law, criminal law is *par excellence* part of that law.

This subject is in many ways different from all others in a (undergraduate) law degree. It is almost always taken at the very beginning of a student's course of study. But the subject is odd in that it does not replicate any subject or branch of the law used in legal practice, at least in the sense of comprising a legal category that may be the focus of legal argument or judicial decision.[6] As expressed in one of the first books on the Scottish Legal System, the subject (and the book):[7]

> is intended not as a first or general introductory course on Scots Law itself, but as an attempt to tackle the problem of teaching the novice law student how to go about the study of law and an attempt to equip him [*sic*] to do so. It is an introduction to the *study*, not to the law itself.

So why are such academic courses generally named Legal System and why also "Scottish"? These are issues generally not considered by the standard texts on the subject.[8] Yet again, the exception is Walker's *Scottish Legal System*. In an Introduction, missing from the first three editions, a legal system is described as a general name for the complex of institutions, ideas, techniques and methods, covered in the book.[9] It is Scottish in the sense that it "exists in relation to the people living in Scotland". What is more, the Scottish legal system coexists and interacts with social, political, economic and other systems in the community.

This definition is far from ideal. It fails to explain the nature of the academic subject as involving a "legal system" but it does usefully suggest that what is taught in that course uses a range of conceptions of legal system (some of which will be examined below). Perhaps that is as far as this conception of Legal System can be taken. Law teachers group together diverse topics, some of which are, or involve, legal systems in other senses, which are seen as necessary or useful in introducing students to the study of law. The systematic or systemic nature lies precisely in that grouping together.

---

6   There are, of course, statutes and judicial decisions on the topics covered by Legal System courses, such as the provisions of the Constitutional Reform Act 2005 which established the Supreme Court of the United Kingdom but such laws are usually characterised as belonging to Constitutional Law rather Legal System. Likewise with case law. The case of *Jessop v Stevenson* 1988 JC 17, which involved an important issue of judicial precedent, is reported under the general headings of "administration of justice" and "procedure".

7   D M Walker, *The Scottish Legal System*, 1st edn (1959) v (emphasis in original). The passage is repeated in the preface to all subsequent editions, the last (8th) of which was published in 2001.

8   The issue is not mentioned in A A Paterson, T StJ N Bates & M Poustie, *The Legal System of Scotland*, 4th edn (1999) who begin their book (vii) by noting that a "legal system is the product of its time", but do not explain what conception or conceptions of legal system is being talked about.

9   4th edn (1976) 1.

C. LEGAL SYSTEMS AND LEGAL STRUCTURES

A second sense of legal system has its home in analytical jurisprudence, in for example the writings of Kelsen, Hart and Raz.[10] What is important about laws, at least in their paradigmatic sense, is that they are related to each other in certain structural ways. Two issues are involved in this approach. What is the individual unit making up a single law (the form of the norm)? And secondly, what is the exact nature of the relationship between different norms? Legal theorists present quite different answers to these questions, but the conception of legal system remains much the same.

For Kelsen, each legal norm has a fixed form, which rarely if ever corresponds to the form of laws enacted by legislatures or established by courts. Rather the point of legal science is to show the logical structure of every norm, which for Kelsen is an authorisation of a legal sanction to be applied whenever a certain form of conduct has taken place. But legal norms have other characteristics, the most important of which is their validity. A norm is valid if it is authorised by some other norm; that other norm in turn depends for its validity on yet another norm. This point is important for it stresses that every legal unit is linked in some way to others, and ultimately to a set of basic constitutional norms. To provide order and meaning to this multiplicity of laws, legal science uses various logical principles; this can be summed up as the theorem of the basic norm. In a narrower sense the basic norm is a logical presupposition of any theorist trying to understand legal units as having validity, but in a wider sense it also incorporates other principles such as that of non-contradiction, and *lex posterior derogat priori*.[11] Kelsen is clear on one point at least: to know and understand law we must interpret it as a meaningful ordering of legal norms.

A similar but looser conception of legal system is used by Hart. But one immediate point of difference is Hart's insistence that there need not be any one form of a law unit. Hart insists that rules can serve distinct social functions, such as those conferring powers and those imposing duties, and there is no theoretical gain in insisting that these distinctions should be collapsed into one form of law. Indeed, Hart's work combines a number of contrasting perspectives, some of which are focused on a sociological account of how law operates and the language used to capture its functions.[12] For example, in his discussion of secondary rules such as rules of change and rules

10 Especially, H Kelsen, *General Theory of Law and State* (1945); H Kelsen, *The Pure Theory of Law* (1967); H L A Hart, *The Concept of Law*, 2nd edn (1994); Raz, *Concept of a Legal System* (n 1).
11 This approach to the basic norm is most evident in the *Pure Theory of Law*, 201-208.
12 Hart himself described *The Concept of Law* (at page v) as "an essay in descriptive sociology".

of adjudication, he can be seen as focusing on social-legal institutions such as legislatures and courts.[13]

But it is equally the case that Hart also deploys a conception of legal system very much like Kelsen's. For Hart argues that a necessary feature of any legal system is a rule of recognition which sets out the criteria for the validity of all rules in a system and as such constitutes the unity and coherence of the system in question.

A more detailed version of a structural conception of a legal system is to be found in the writings of Joseph Raz. One key point in Raz's analysis is the presentation of a much richer model of the basic legal unit (what he calls the individuation of laws).[14] For example, he argues that individuated laws should make clear important connections between various parts of a legal system. A perhaps even more fundamental insight into the nature of a legal system is that not every legal unit in a legal system is necessarily a legal norm.[15] Raz argues that there are laws that are not themselves norms but concern the existence or application of legal norms. This "internal" relationship brings out the systemic nature of law. The structure of a legal system is based on the relationship between different types of legal unit.

What is the point of conceptualising a legal system in this way? For a start, it offers logical insight into a deeper structure of law. However, its value lies not just in clearer thinking in analytical jurisprudence. Many of the writers who have explored this conception of legal system have also argued that it connects to wider inquiries about law. Even Kelsen, who insisted on the purity of legal science, pointed out that the value of seeing law as part of a legal science is that this perspective presents law as a meaningful system of basic legal units. The function of the "pure" legal scientist is to give law a specific form of interpretation.

This approach is even more evident in other writers in the analytical tradition. Hart, of course, is renowned for his use of the internal perspective as a way of locating meaning in law.[16] Significantly, Raz, whose version of the analytical conception of legal system is highly sophisticated, linked his work in this area to the topics of his own later interest in the relationship of law and practical reasoning.[17]

13 Hart, *Concept of Law* 94-96.
14 Raz, *Concept of a Legal System* (n 1) 140-147.
15 See especially *Concept of a Legal System* 169-170.
16 In *The Concept of Law* (n 10), Hart adopts the writings of Peter Winch (*The Idea of a Social Science* (1958)). Winch's work in turn derives much from Wittgenstein. However there is an argument that Hart's approach was influenced as much by Weberian notions of *Verstehen*. See further N Lacey, *A Life of H L A Hart* (2004) 229-231.
17 Raz, *Concept of a Legal System*, 2nd edn 210-216.

Note must also be made of a much more refined approach to this conception of legal system to be found in the writings of Neil MacCormick.[18] He argues for a version of the analytical approach, but one that uses an "institutional" sense of legal system. MacCormick accepted the idea of basic legal units as constituent parts of a legal system but argued that approaches such as those of Kelsen or Raz fail to locate what is truly systematic about law. Rather, legal rules are grouped into certain forms or institutions, which have a subject-matter unity; examples are ownership, promises, delicts, trusts, theft. Each such legal institution is itself made up of rules with different logical functions, namely rules that indicate how specific instances of each concept are brought into being, rules indicating the legal consequences of each instance of the concept, and rules on how any specific instance comes to an end. For MacCormick such organising concepts are crucial to knowing the law and understanding its functions:

> The whole point of postulating the existence of instances of such concepts is that it enables us to achieve two potentially conflicting goals in the exposition of law. On the one hand, we can break down complex bodies of legal material into comparatively simple sets of interrelated rules; and yet on the other hand we can treat large bodies of law in an organised and generalised way, not just as a mass of bits and pieces.[19]

What is to be noted about this institutional approach to law is that it uses the same general idea of legal system as, for example, in Kelsen, that is, an ordered relationship between components of each system. The radical difference is that for MacCormick the individual parts are to be seen as much more complicated in nature. But this difference is not simply one of identifying the appropriate analytical units. Rather, for MacCormick, there is a major theoretical significance in using units of institutional fact as the building blocks of a legal system, namely that doing so captures a social reality about the significance of law as normative, that is as guiding social action.

D. A SOCIOLOGICAL CONCEPTION OF LEGAL SYSTEM

The works of Hart and MacCormick indicate a further sense of legal system. For Kelsen and Raz, a legal system is essentially a logical concept, used in explaining the structural properties of laws and legal units.

18 MacCormick once wrote that it "is one objective, perhaps the objective, of analytical legal philosophy to explain the structure of legal systems" ("Law as institutional fact" (n 3) at 121).
19 MacCormick, "Law as institutional fact" at 108.

But a quite different idea is the sociological sense of legal system. In this sense the term "legal system" refers to the operations of a number of social institutions that perform various roles and practices in relation to the making and application of standards that function as guides to general social behaviour. In other words, a sociological sense of legal system is concerned with special types of social action (institutionalised action) that have a certain subject-matter, namely law.

This sense can be called "sociological" because it is concerned with the conditions for the existence of a particular mode of social action and social control. But this is a familiar conception of legal system for academic lawyers. When, in the Legal System class, we teach about the courts or the legal profession, our concern is not only (or primarily) with the legal rules about how these institutions are constituted but more with how they actually operate and with the social and political dynamics of their operation.

Moreover, this sense of legal system is also a central one in legal theory and used not only by writers who are dealing with the social-legal studies (the sociology of the legal profession and the like), but also by jurists concerned with more theoretical aspects of law.

For example, much of Hart's writings on legal system combine both the analytical-logical sense with the sociological sense. In a celebrated passage in *The Concept of Law* Hart poses the question of what a society would be like that lacked "a legislature, courts or officials of any kind".[20] The purpose of constructing this model is to show those features of a modern legal system that distinguish it from a simple regime of social rules. In such a regime there would be no easy way of introducing new rules or interpreting and enforcing existing ones. The remedy is the introduction of institutions with precisely those functions. What he seems to be saying is that the characteristic mark of law (or a legal system) is the existence of such specialised institutions. The problem in reading Hart is that he tends to talk about rules (secondary rules)[21] rather than institutions. The outcome is that it is far from clear whether Hart has in mind a sociological notion of legal system or an analytical-logical one.

Hart seems to be putting forward two separate claims. One is that what constitutes a (or the) step from the pre-legal to the legal world is the development of these secondary rules, the existence of which indicates the existence of specialised institutions. The other is that in every legal system there is always one fundamental rule that is the ultimate reason for the validity of all other rules of the system. But there is no necessary connection between these

20 Hart, *The Concept of Law* (n 10) 89.
21 He mentions rules of change, rules of adjudication and the rule of recognition.

two claims. The importance of this point is that the two claims use different conceptions of legal system. Indeed one can argue without absurdity that legal standards are not "systematic" or "systemic", in that it is simply not possible to arrange them in an ordered pattern, without at the same time having to deny that "legal systems" exist where we are referring to particular types of social rules and social action.[22]

A similar, though perhaps clearer, approach was taken by Neil MacCormick, who had always noted a distinction between the logical (or juristic) and the sociological senses of institutions.[23] In addition to the analytical idea of legal institutions, which is used to explain structural properties of a legal system, there is a wide variety of social systems or institutions, a sub-category of which are legal institutions such as courts, police forces, the Faculty of Advocates and the like (what in total might be called a "legal system"). But the ambiguity of the term "legal institution" is purely a linguistic one; the two ideas are conceptually distinct. He makes the point that social, or informal, rules (such as those involved with the practice of forming a queue) provide a way in which people can order their actions and interactions. A crucial aspect of these rules is that they provide reasons for assessing the correctness or appropriateness of how everyone acts, a situation MacCormick calls "normative order". But law is a special form of normative order, an institutional order. This sense of institution refers not to the rule-based categories necessary for understanding the structure of legal systems but to the existence of institutional agencies such as legislatures or courts, each with specialised roles within a legal system.[24]

It must be said, however, that, as with Hart, MacCormick is never entirely clear whether he sees these agencies as in themselves forming something that could be conceptualised as a legal system, that is, in its sociological sense, or

22 That Hart has moved in his discussion of the rule of recognition from a sociological to a structural perspective is evidenced by the fact that there is no social-legal institution that corresponds to the rule of recognition in the way that legislatures and courts correspond respectively to rules of change and rules of adjudication.

23 In talking of institutions and institutional facts he wrote: "there are two quite distinct points to be made by the use of such words in relation to law, a philosophical and a sociological one; they depend upon different senses of the terms involved, which I suspect have often been more or less confused in discourse about law." ("Law as institutional fact" (n 3) at 108) Elsewhere he noted a further sense of institution, namely that used to describe a particular manner of exposition of the law (see *Institutions of Law* 12-13). See further the discussion at section E below.

24 "There are distinct public institutions – 'institutional-agencies' let us call them – charged with legislative functions, with adjudicative functions, with executive-administrative functions, and law-enforcement functions. Crucial to the coherent unity of the state [*sic*] to which these institutions belong is their effective co-ordination and balanced interaction in performing their functions" (*Institutions of Law* 35). There is an irony that MacCormick refers to a state rather than a legal system. See the discussion of the identity of legal systems at section F below.

whether they are simply a subset of the special legal institutions that make up a logical sense of legal system.[25]

E. LEGAL SYSTEMS AND LEGAL DOCTRINE

A further conception of legal order or legal system is concerned with the activity of legal exposition. The actual content of the law of any legal system is made up of rules derived from legal sources, usually at different levels such as statute, case law and so on. Moreover, these rules will develop and multiply over time. An important and specific task of the jurist is to describe these rules intelligibly, by presenting them in an ordered and coherent way.[26] Examples of this approach to legal ordering are legion, ranging from the work of the Roman law jurists to modern academic writings.

Indeed, the approach taken by Roman lawyers, as exemplified in the Institutes of Gaius and Justinian, created a tradition of legal exposition that had a profound influence on legal writing in many parts of Europe, including England and Scotland. The major characteristic of such institutional writings was the division of law into broad organising categories, most significantly those of persons, things and actions. This tripartite division had a profound historical influence and was reproduced as the general organising categories of works such as Stair's *Institutions of the Law of Scotland* and Blackstone's *Commentaries on the Laws of England* and of codifications such as the French *Code Civil* of 1804 and the German *Bürgerliches Gesetzbuch* of 1900, both of which in turn influenced the development of legal codes throughout the world.

Stair's book deserves a special mention for the use made of a nuanced approach to the classical distinctions. In particular, Stair advanced a further refinement whereby the focal element within each of the three broad branches of law of Scotland was the idea of rights.[27]

25 He does accept that there are legal "institutions" which are primarily of concern to the sociology of law ("Law as Institutional Fact" 110; 129) but he also analyses these institutions in term of the triadic structure (as consisting of institutive, consequential and terminative rules) used in the analytical sense (see *Institutions of Law* (n 3) 36-37).

26 In this discussion of legal system as legal ordering, the focus is on juristic writings but a similar idea also applies to law making (especially codification) and to law reform. By statute the duty of the Law Commissions in the United Kingdom is "to take and keep under review all the law with which they are respectively concerned with a view to its *systematic* development and reform" (Law Commissions Act 1965 s 3(1)) (emphasis added).

27 An analysis advanced by A H Campbell, *The Structure of Stair's Institutions* (1954), a writing which influenced certain themes in Hart's *The Concept of Law*. For further discussion of Stair's use of the classical division of law, see D M Walker, "Introduction" in Stair, *The Institutions of the Law of Scotland*, ed by D M Walker (1981), 17-20.

Furthermore the task of ordering and systematising laws has applied not only to general bodies of law but also to more specific subjects. At times this work is truly revolutionary, revealing a deep structure to a mass of seemingly unrelated rules which can now be seen as forming part of one subject. For example, *The Law of Restitution* by Lord Goff of Chieveley and Gareth Jones[28] introduced a general concept of unjustified enrichment into English law.

Two further examples can be seen in the writings of two of Neil MacCormick's colleagues at Edinburgh Law School. Prior to the publication of Gerald Gordon's book on *The Criminal Law of Scotland*,[29] Scots criminal law had lost any sense of structure or cohesion. But this book changed the subject. It drew upon philosophical writings (such as those of Ryle and Wittgenstein) and re-interpreted existing Scottish rules from the perspective of Anglo-American writings on concepts such as *mens rea* and causation. A similar tale can be told of property law in Scotland. The rules governing such matters as rights in land or in corporeal and incorporeal moveables were generally known, but the rules were seen as disparate and lacking any unifying element. All this was changed by the publication of the work of Kenneth Reid, who pointed out that there is a unitary law of property, based on the fundamental distinction between real rights and personal rights.[30]

There may be some connections between this sense of legal system and others. Indeed, MacCormick and Weinberger once claimed that a "structural theory furnishes legal dogmatics with schemata for the exposition of the substance of the laws".[31] However, for this conception of legal system, a key aspect of order and system is making sense of what legal rules and principles say, and something more than attention to structure alone is required. What gives order to a body of legal rules is substantive coherence. But here again this requirement is not too far removed from Neil MacCormick's legal theorising, for a key concept in his writings on legal reasoning is that of coherence.[32] For laws to guide conduct they must be ordered, and for them to be ordered they must be expressed in terms of values. Although MacCormick's main concern was with judicial reasoning, his approach to coherence applies equally to the

---

28 1st edn (1966).

29 1st edn (1967).

30 "Property", in *The Laws of Scotland: Stair Memorial Encyclopaedia* vol 18 (1993). Reid was the principal author of Part I of that title on General Law and wrote the introductory sections that set out the arguments for the internal coherence of the subject.

31 MacCormick and Weinberger, *An Institutional Theory of Law* 17.

32 *Legal Reasoning and Legal Theory* (1978) ch 7; *Rhetoric and the Rule of Law* ch 10, where he develops in some detail the idea of "normative" coherence, as contrasted with "narrative" coherence which is concerned with reasoning in fact-finding.

task of legal dogmatics. To revert to one of the examples mentioned earlier, Gerald Gordon could make sense of, and impose order on, Scottish rules of criminal responsibility by presenting them in terms of a mainly (though not entirely) subjective approach to *mens rea*.

F. LEGAL SYSTEM AND IDENTITY: IS THERE A SCOTTISH LEGAL SYSTEM?

It may seem obvious that there is such a thing as the Scottish legal system. After all, as noted earlier, many law schools teach a course which has that name. Moreover, it is even more obvious that in Scotland there are legal institutions such as a parliament, courts, police forces and so on; and there are legal rules on all manner of topics, such as property, family law, criminal law and the like. But what does it mean to say that there is a Scottish legal system, which has its own distinctive identity? The existence of legal institutions and of legal norms is not enough, for the same could be said about Glasgow or the Highlands, yet it does not make sense to talk about the legal system of Glasgow or the Highlands, at least in the sense of it having a distinct identity.

For a long time these questions were given a short and simple answer: the identity of a legal system derived from the identity of a state, an approach that was buttressed by analytical jurisprudence such as Kelsen and Hart. But analytical jurisprudence gives rise to paradoxes when dealing with issues of the identity of legal systems. A key aspect of the analytical conception of legal system is that each rule of a system receives its ultimate validity from a fundamental rule or norm, which is (or concerns) a rule or set of rules of a constitution. So a theory of identity can be based on the premise that for each distinct basic norm or rule of recognition; there is a separate and distinct legal system made up of all the rules that derive from that norm or rule.[33] But in certain contexts this conclusion gives odd results. Assuming that there is a fundamental rule about the constitution of the United Kingdom means that there is a UK (British) legal system. But if that is so, then it would not make sense to talk about a Scottish (or indeed an English) legal system. This approach is unattractive for we, intuitively at least, want to be able to talk of both a UK and a Scottish legal system.[34]

---

33 See on this form of argument, N MacCormick, "Does the United Kingdom have a constitution? Reflections on *MacCormick v Lord Advocate*" (1978) *Northern Ireland Legal Quarterly* 1 at 15-18.

34 Indeed the legislation setting up the Supreme Court of the United Kingdom states that "Nothing is this Part is to affect the distinctions between the separate legal systems of the parts of the United Kingdom" (Constitutional Reform Act 2005 s 41(1)).

But if it is the case that the analytical jurisprudence conception of legal system does not allow for the combined existence of a British legal system and a Scottish legal system, then the solution is to use a different sense of legal system in discussing identity. One possible candidate is a legal system in terms of its substantive (i.e. content-based) distinctiveness. Scots law, it is said, is distinctive and different from, for example, English law because of its adherence to principle (as opposed to rigid case law) and historical-conceptual links to Roman law. Certainly these characteristics of Scots law have for a long time been used in arguments about the distinctiveness of the Scottish legal system. But other systems also use or were historically influenced by Roman law, so some other criterion must provide the clue to identity. If anything, substantive similarities in the law point to the demarcation of different legal families or cultures but not to specific units or legal systems within these categories.

A more fruitful approach is to look to the sociological sense of legal system. If it is the case that courts or the legal profession see themselves as having a distinct identity, and this was true of much of the history of Scotland from the eighteenth century onwards, then this argues for a distinct identity of a Scottish legal system in that sense. The effect is to locate issues of the identity of the Scottish legal system in more general questions of Scottish identity and involves consideration of the "Scottishness" of Scotland's political, educational, economic and cultural systems.[35]

G. LEGAL SYSTEM AS "COUNTRY": THE SCOTTISH LEGAL SYSTEM AND INTERNATIONAL PRIVATE LAW

A final sense of legal system is to be found in international private law (IPL). In that subject, rules are laid down that, for example, specify which legal system's courts have jurisdiction to try a case, or which legal system's laws are to be applied in resolving a legal dispute. But IPL uses a distinctive conception of legal system. The IPL world is divided not into states in the sense of public international law but into units known as legal systems or countries. But there is no obvious basis for the rules as to the identity of these countries. Thus for most IPL purposes,[36] there is no such thing as Britain or a British

---

35 For a rudimentary statement of this argument, see G Maher, "The identity of the Scottish legal system" (1977) *Juridical Review* 21. For a detailed discussion of the distinctiveness of the Scottish political system as an aspect of a more general Scottish culture, see Neil MacCormick, *Questioning Sovereignty* (1999), chs 11 & 12. See also W J M Mackenzie, *Political Identity* (1978), especially 15-16; 170-172.

36 There are occasional exceptions where for certain very specific issues the appropriate legal unit

legal system; rather there are the separate countries of Scotland, England and Wales, and Northern Ireland. Likewise the USA is divided into the fifty "countries" of New York, Maryland and so on. A similar approach applies to the constituent parts of Canada and Australia. Yet Germany is one country for IPL purposes, as is Spain or Brazil.

Certainly this sense of legal system is recognised in IPL sources and instruments. For example, the Civil Jurisdiction and Judgments Act 1982 applied a modified version of the 1968 EC Brussels Judgments Convention to allocation of jurisdiction between the different "parts" of the United Kingdom, which are defined as meaning England and Wales, Scotland and Northern Ireland.[37]

Furthermore many IPL conventions and EU regulations contain provisions like the following:

Non-unified legal systems

(1) In relation to a Contracting State in which two or more systems of law apply in different territorial units with regard to any matter dealt with in this Convention -

a) any reference to the law or procedure of a State shall be construed as referring, where appropriate, to the law or procedure in force in the relevant territorial unit;

b) any reference to residence in a State shall be construed as referring, where appropriate, to residence in the relevant territorial unit;

c) any reference to the court or courts of a State shall be construed as referring, where appropriate, to the court or courts in the relevant territorial unit;

d) any reference to a connection with a State shall be construed as referring, where appropriate, to a connection with the relevant territorial unit.[38]

The problem with these provisions is that they do not provide any criteria for determining which states have different countries in an IPL sense, but seem to take for granted that this phenomenon exists. Some versions hint more strongly at a content-based difference. For example the (EU) Rome I Regulation on contractual obligations states that:

---

is the United Kingdom, Australia or Canada. See L Collins, A V Dicey, C G J Morse, D McClean et al, *Dicey, Morris & Collins on The Conflict of Laws*, 14th edn (2006) 30.

37 1982 Act section 16 and Schedule 4 as read with section 50. Many instruments that recognise that some states may have more than one IPL country provide that the state does not have to apply the provisions of the instrument in case involving conflicts only between those different countries. See, for example, Regulation on the law applicable to contractual obligations (Rome I) (Commission Regulation 593/2008 OJ 2008 L177/6) art 22(2): "A Member State where different territorial units have their own rules in respect of contractual obligations shall not be required to apply this Regulation to conflicts solely between the laws of such units."

38 Hague Convention on Choice of Court Agreements (2005) art 25. Provisions of this sort are to be found in most of the conventions made under the auspices of the Hague Conference on Private International Law. See, for example, the 1980 Hague Convention on the Civil Aspects of International Child Abduction arts 31 and 32.

Where a State comprises several territorial units, each of which has its own rules of law in respect of contractual obligations, each territorial unit shall be considered as a country for the purposes of identifying the law applicable under this Regulation. [39]

But this provision cannot mean that there are different countries within one state only where the law of contract differs. Contract law in Northern Ireland is much the same as that in England and Wales, but these remain different IPL countries.

A further aspect of the analysis of this idea of a country is that some states (for example, Spain and China) are themselves countries in the IPL sense, and have rules that deal with "internal" conflict of laws. These provisions are usually referred to as involving "inter-regional" conflict of laws and apply the same or a modified version of international IPL rules to issues between different autonomous areas within the state.[40] Although such areas are legal systems of sorts, for international IPL purposes they are not full countries in the way that Scotland or the state of New York is. Their exact characterisation remains problematic.

Clearly, there is work still to be done on the conception of legal system used in IPL.[41] What may be surmised at this stage is that none of the other notions of legal system considered earlier in this paper is likely to be dispositive (or even perhaps of any use at all) in clarifying the meaning of a country for IPL purposes. But this should be no surprise. The subject of IPL has its own distinctive issues and problems, and uses a range of special concepts and principles in dealing with them. There is accordingly no theoretical or practical need for the conception of legal system that is appropriate to that subject to be identical to any other sense of the term.

---

39 Rome I Regulation (n 37) art 22(1). See also Regulation on the law applicable to non-contractual obligations (Rome II) (Commission Regulation 864/2007 OJ 2007 L199/40) art 25. The provision in the Rome I Regulation was based on an earlier version of that instrument (The Rome Convention (1980)). An official report on that Convention simply explains the provision with an example: "If, for example, in the case of Article 4, the party who is to effect the performance which is characteristic of the contract has his habitual residence in Scotland, it is with Scottish law that the contract will be deemed to be most closely connected" (M Giuliano and P Lagarde, Report on the Convention on the law applicable to contractual obligations OJ 1980 C282/1 at 38).

40 This has long been a feature of Spanish law and predates the more modern development of autonomous regions. See L Neville Brown, "The sources of Spanish civil law" (1956) 5 *International and Comparative Law Quarterly* 364-377 at 372-377. For a discussion of the approach in China, see G Zhu, "Inter-regional conflict of laws under 'one country, two systems'" (2002) 32 *Hong Kong Law Journal* 615-676.

41 The pity is that IPL, despite the range of conceptual puzzles to which the subject gives rise, was an area of the law which Neil MacCormick does not appear to have much noted or discussed. For a brief treatment, see N MacCormick, "The Maastricht-Urteil: sovereignty now" (1995) 1(3) *European Law Journal* 259-266 at 262-263.

6 The Idea of a Legal System: Between the Real and the Ideal

Julie Dickson[*]

A. INTRODUCTION
B. LEGAL SYSTEMS: THEIR SOCIAL FACT OR INSTITUTIONAL
   REALITY SENSE
C. LEGAL SYSTEMS AS IDEAS, AND AS ASPIRING TO IDEALS
D. UNDERSTANDING LAW: BETWEEN THE REAL AND THE IDEAL

A. INTRODUCTION

In common with the other contributors to this volume, and with countless others from various walks of life and parts of the world, I have very fond memories of Neil, who was extremely generous and kind to me in my professional life. I could mention many examples but will confine myself to just two here. The first is when Neil was the external examiner for my DPhil thesis. Above all, he was kind to me on that occasion in actually passing me! But he was also kind in giving me much useful advice on taking my work forward, which I still try to heed today. The second occasion was in respect of a colloquium on Neil's book, *Institutions of Law*, held at Edinburgh University in 2007. I was due to give a paper at the colloquium, but ill-health prevented me from attending. Not only was Neil extremely gracious about that, and very encouraging that I should still submit my paper to the book which emerged from that colloquium, but he even asked me to send him the draft paper I was due to present, and then he presented it himself, on my behalf, at the colloquium, no doubt with considerably more panache than I could have managed myself. As well as his immense intellectual strengths, that sort of well-judged kindness was, to me, the mark of the man, so I was honoured to be a speaker at the "MacCormick's Scotland" event which took place at Edinburgh University in June 2010, and to be asked to contribute to this volume which was inspired by it.

---

[*] Fellow and Senior Law Tutor at Somerville College and CUF Lecturer in the Faculty of Law, University of Oxford. As regards my interest in the themes in this paper, I am indebted in various ways to Dr Laurence Sullivan.

The title of this chapter is "The Idea of a Legal System: Between the Real and the Ideal", and the main point which I seek to convey is that the key to comprehending legal systems lies in understanding them not only as consisting of social facts and institutions having a practical effect on our legal lives, but also as *ideas*: as things that people have attitudes towards, beliefs about, hopes for, that they can identify with or indeed become alienated from, and that they regard as supposed to realise certain values. In a sense, then, it is the "dualistic" character of legal systems that I am interested in: that they have an existence in social practice, in the existence and activities of courts and legislatures and legal officials, but that they are also what Neil MacCormick once referred to as "thought-objects".[1] and have an existence as ideas, and indeed as ideals.

The discussion is divided into three parts. First of all I consider legal systems in their social fact or institutional reality sense. I then move on to discuss legal systems as ideas, and indeed as ideals. The chapter concludes with a claim that legal phenomena in general, and legal systems in particular, have to be understood in both these senses in our theories of law in order for those theories to be successful. Throughout, I will try to use the Scottish legal system to illustrate various of the points I make, although I do not pretend to offer anything resembling a fully-fledged theory of the sense in which it is rightly viewed as a distinct legal system (as I believe it is). Rather, I use the example of the Scottish legal system to indicate the kinds of avenues our theories must explore in order to be capable of embracing, and properly explaining, both the real and the ideal of legal systems.

Much of what follows is somewhat schematic in character, and draws on and refers to other work of mine on the concept of a legal system which is, in terms of my interest in this topic as a whole, very much work in progress. I hope, however, that the discussion will give a flavour of what I regard as the important themes in approaching the idea of a legal system, and of how those themes relate to, and were illuminated by, the work of Professor Sir Neil MacCormick.

B. LEGAL SYSTEMS: THEIR SOCIAL FACT OR INSTITUTIONAL REALITY SENSE

Those caught breaking the law are quickly aware of one important feature of legal systems, namely, the sense in which they really are "out there": they have a social reality to them, and are comprised of social practices and social facts

---

1 N MacCormick, *Questioning Sovereignty* (1999) 113.

of various kinds. For example, were A to be caught in the act of assaulting B, it is likely that certain things would happen: someone might call the police, who would come to question A, perhaps arrest her, charge her with an offence, she might have to make a court appearance before a legal official, be convicted, receive a sentence, etc. All this tells us that, although legal systems may *also* be ideas or, as MacCormick put it, "thought-objects",[2] they are not *merely* ideas or thought-objects – they have a social reality of a certain kind, and it is a reality that is often manifest in the practices of social *institutions* of various sorts, such as law enforcement agencies, legislatures and courts.

The trickier matter for many legal theorists has been to explain the precise sense in which legal systems are "out there" and have a reality to them – clearly they are not out there in the same sense as the desk in front of me is out there, so in what terms should we explain their social reality? And, in particular, for legal theorists interested in questions of identity and continuity of legal systems – questions such as where does one legal system end and another begin, or what criteria indicate that one legal system has divided into two, or two come together into one – the trickier matter has been to identify which aspects of law's social and institutional reality give us reason to say that we have a distinct legal system on our hands, and which aspects of that social and institutional reality delineate one legal system from another. So, for example, if we think of the Scottish legal system, these issues would play out in questions such as: which institutions does the Scottish legal system need to possess in order to for us to be correct in accounting it as a distinct legal system? Does it need to have its own courts? Its own legislature? Its own legal profession? Its own law enforcement agencies? And so on.

Two approaches have tended to predominate amongst legal theorists interested in the identity conditions of legal systems. For some theorists, such as John Austin,[3] the key to the identity of legal systems lay in law-*creating* institutions such as sovereigns or legislatures. According to such theorists, legal systems must possess such law-creating institutions in order to exist, and the key to the identity of the legal system in question lies in identifying all those norms that can be traced back to that system's law-creating insti-tutions. For other legal theorists, however, such as Salmond – that is John William, not Alex – or Joseph Raz,[4] it is not law-*creating* institutions such as legislatures, but law-*recognising* or law-*applying* institutions such as courts

---

2 MacCormick, *Questioning Sovereignty* 113.

3 J Austin, *The Province of Jurisprudence Determined*, ed by W E Rumble (1995).

4 J W Salmond, *Salmond on Jurisprudence*, ed by G Williams (1957) c 41; J Raz, *The Concept of a Legal System*, 1st edn (1970), 2nd edn (1980) ch VIII.

and tribunals that unify legal systems, and that hold the key to the identity of legal systems.

I believe that this second approach has the better of the argument, and that it is to the existence and activities of law-recognising and applying institutions such as courts that we must look in order to determine when a separate, distinct legal system exists and what norms are properly regarded as belonging to it. The reasons for taking this approach include the fact that not all law in legal systems is created by legislatures – there is also judge-made law and possibly law from other sources, so that the only way to identify all the norms of a given legal system is to look not to law-creating but to law-recognising bodies, and to all the sources of law they recognise. They also include the fact that some legal systems do not have "their own" dedicated law-creating institution; for example the legal system of England and Wales, which, although I cannot argue the point here, I regard as a distinct legal system, does not have "its own" legislature; rather it has the Westminster parliament of the United Kingdom; and the Scottish legal system does not possess "its own" legislature as regards reserved matters, and did not have its own legislature at all between the Acts of Union and the creation of the present Scottish Parliament by virtue of the Scotland Act 1998. Moreover, many legal systems recognise multiple law-making bodies, not all of which are located in the legal system in question, such as the legal systems of the EU's member states, which recognise law emanating from EU legislative institutions while, I believe, remaining distinct legal systems.[5] It follows that we cannot identify those legal systems and their norms by looking only to norms that "their own" legislatures make. For all these reasons, in order to ascertain what is properly to be regarded as one distinct legal system, and which norms belong to it, I believe we are better advised to look to law-recognising and law-applying institutions such as courts, not law-creating institutions such as legislatures.

A theoretically adequate investigation of the Scottish legal system, and of the sense in which it is properly regarded as a distinct legal system, would thus need to consider the institutional autonomy of the Scottish legal system in terms of it possessing "its own" law-recognising-and-applying institutions, i.e. its own courts and recognising "its own" law for reasons grounded in the distinctive law-recognition practices of those courts.[6]

---

5 I discuss this point more fully in J Dickson, "How many legal systems? Some puzzles regarding the identity conditions of, and relations between, legal systems in the European Union" (2008) 2 *Problema* 9-50, available at *http://www.juridicas.unam.mx/publica/librev/rev/filotder/cont/2/pr/ pr4.pdf* (accessed 24 July 2011) and in J Dickson, "Directives in European Union legal systems: whose norms are they anyway?" (2011) 17 *European Law Journal* 190-212.

6 This latter point is discussed further at the close of this section.

Any such investigation would, in my view, find that there is a strong case for Scotland possessing a distinct legal system according to these criteria. Not only does it have "its own" court system, but certain of its institutions, namely the Court of Session and High Court of Justiciary, have their continued existence guaranteed in the Treaty of Union, and by virtue of the Scottish and English Acts of Union which gave the articles of that Treaty legal force.[7] Moreover, that Scotland has "its own" court system – recognising norms as norms of Scots law for reasons grounded in the practices of the institutions of the Scottish legal system – is not called into question by the fact that, in civil cases, final appeal lies from the Court of Session to the UK Supreme Court (formerly House of Lords),[8] nor that the Supreme Court has assumed the jurisdiction of the former Judicial Committee of the Privy Council over devolution issues under the terms of the Scotland Act.[9]

As regards the former – the right of final appeal in civil cases – the Constitutional Reform Act s41(2) plainly states that, when acting in this capacity, the Supreme Court is to be regarded as rendering judgment as a Scottish court, hence maintaining the idea of Scotland having "its own" system of law-applying institutions. As Neil Walker observes in his recent report on final appellate jurisdiction in the Scottish legal system:

> Indeed, in formal terms, even the Supreme Court itself, like the predecessor House of Lords, is not one court but many, its umbrella status speaking not only to its functional versatility but to its variety of formal identities as an English, Scottish and Northern Irish court.[10]

That same Act, moreover, contains provisions indicating that the state of which Scotland is one constituent part also views Scotland as possessing its own legal system as regards aspects of its institutional arrangements, providing that, in the transfer of jurisdiction from the Appellate Committee of the House of Lords to the Supreme Court, "Nothing in this Part is to affect the distinctions between the separate legal systems of the parts of the United Kingdom".[11]

As regards devolution jurisdiction, things may be a little more complicated because the principle in s 41(2) of the Constitutional Reform Act, that the Supreme Court sits as a court of whichever part of the UK it is hearing an

---

7 Treaty of Union art XIX; Union with England Act 1707; Union with Scotland Act 1706.
8 Constitutional Reform Act 2005 s 40(3).
9 Constitutional Reform Act 2005 s 40(4)(b) and Sch 9.
10 N Walker, "Report on Final Appellate Jurisdiction in the Scottish Legal System", published on the Scottish Government website, 22 January 2010, at *http://www.scotland.gov.uk/Resource/Doc/299388/0093334.pdf* (accessed 24 July 2011) ch 2 at 19.
11 Constitutional Reform Act 2005 s 41(1).

appeal from, does not apply to devolution issues according to that same subsection. This raises the question of exactly which jurisdiction the Supreme Court *does* sit as a court of in cases raising devolution issues – for surely it does not sit as a court of the England and Wales legal system or of the Northern Irish legal system, and it is a commonly held view, apparently endorsed by s 41(2) of the Constitutional Reform Act itself, that there is no "UK legal system" but only the separate legal systems of those jurisdictions just mentioned. This being so, as the Supreme Court does not seem to be sitting as a court of some other legal system, in relation to which the Scottish legal system could then be viewed as a mere sub-system, its devolution jurisdiction does not *prima facie* seem a threat to the existence of a distinct Scottish legal system.[12] A fully-fledged theory of the distinctness of the Scottish legal system would require further explanation of the exact capacity in which the Supreme Court does sit as regards its devolution issues jurisdiction, and, more broadly, of how we should understand its institutional position. Although this cannot be addressed further here, I believe that an adequate account of the Scottish legal system can show that, the Supreme Court's civil appeals and devolution jurisdictions notwithstanding, it does possess the requisite institutional and normative self-determination, as regards its courts, and the norms of Scots law whose existence, force and effect those institutions determine, in order for us to affirm in our theories of law the commonly held view that there exists a distinct Scottish legal system.

Much more would need to be said fully to substantiate these points. My goal here, however, is not to provide a decisive account of why the Scottish legal system is to be regarded as a separate legal system. Rather, I am trying to indicate and begin to open up the kind of issues that need to be addressed in order to understand legal systems adequately, and to claim that one vital aspect of legal systems that such theories must address is their "social factness" or institutional reality. My point here is thus more a methodological one, to try to explain what aspects of law's existence need to be addressed in order to delineate legal systems and understand their important features, and

---

12 Although as regards the distinctive *content* of Scots law, it should be noted that the Lord Advocate has recently warned of the potential for a loss of identity in light of the Supreme Court's decision in cases such as *Cadder* [2010] UKSC 43, which, as a matter of criminal law, could not have been heard by a London court until 1998, and the introduction of a human rights dimension to the devolution jurisdiction: see *http://www.bbc.co.uk/news/uk-scotland-12399287*, accessed 24 July 2011. Further controversy followed in the spring of 2011, including public criticism of judges by the Scottish First Minister, Alex Salmond, in the wake of subsequent decisions by the Supreme Court that took issue with the High Court of Justiciary's interpretation of Scots criminal law. See *Scotsman* 15 June 2011; *http://business.scotsman.com/legalissues/Alex-Salmond-launches-scathing-attack.6785206.jp*, accessed 24 July 2011.

why those kinds of issues matter. It is important to consider issues such as the distinctness of a putative legal system's institutions, especially its law-recognising and applying institutions, because those institutions, and their activities, form a significant part of law's distinctive social reality.

The contribution made by Neil MacCormick's work to understanding the "social fact-ness" or institutional reality of legal systems is considerable. His work on law as institutional fact and as institutional normative order supplies a subtle explanation of the distinctive character of the social reality or "out there-ness" of legal systems,[13] and although he used the term "institutions of law" in a broader sense than I have done here, he gave a central place to law's institutional reality as expressed through what he called "institution-agencies"[14] such as legislatures, courts and police forces. MacCormick's work hence does not only recognise, but does much to improve our understanding of the precise sense in which legal systems form a distinctive kind of social reality.

Moreover, MacCormick has also made a notable contribution to the consideration of the institutional autonomy of the Scottish legal system in terms of it possessing "its own" law-recognising-and-applying institutions, i.e. its own courts and recognising "its own" law for reasons grounded in the distinctive law-recognition practices of those courts. In "Does the United Kingdom have a constitution? Reflections on *MacCormick v Lord Advocate*",[15] he discusses various of the Treaty of Union cases, including *MacCormick v Lord Advocate*[16] itself – a case with which he was, of course, intimately familiar, his father being the lead petitioner – and *Gibson v Lord Advocate*.[17] Although the petitioners in both cases were unsuccessful in their attempts to have legislative provisions set aside on the grounds that they conflicted with articles of the Treaty of Union, MacCormick regards it as important to note Lord Cooper's (in *MacCormick*) and Lord Keith's (in *Gibson*) respective views of the sense in which the Treaty of Union constitutes fundamental constitutional law. He observes that both judges reserved judgment as to whether, and in what manner, the courts would intervene as regards, "the validity of any legislation concerning the Scottish courts or matters of 'private right' which might be found to contravene fundamental and unalterable articles of the Treaty".[18] MacCormick infers from this

---

13 Much of this work is brought together in N MacCormick, *Institutions of Law: An Essay in Legal Theory* (2007).
14 MacCormick, *Institutions of Law* 34-37, 50, 243-245.
15 N MacCormick, "Does the United Kingdom have a constitution? Reflections on *MacCormick v Lord Advocate*" (1978) 29 *NILQ* 1-20.
16 1953 SC 396.
17 1975 SLT 134.
18 MacCormick, "Does the United Kingdom have a constitution?" (n 15) 4.

dictum that the Scottish courts accept a different rule of recognition than is accepted by the courts of England and Wales. The rule of recognition is, of course, a central feature of legal theorist H L A Hart's work, and is the ultimate rule accepted by legal officials in order to identify what is to count as law in a given jurisdiction.[19] In MacCormick's view, given opinions expressed by the Scottish courts on the potential force and effect of unalterable articles of the Treaty of Union:

> the Scottish courts' view of the ultimate rule of recognition appears to be that "Whatever the Queen in Parliament enacts, unless in derogation from the justiciable limits set by the Articles of Union, is law".[20]

In the discussion earlier in this section, I claimed that a theoretically adequate investigation of the sense in which the Scottish legal system is properly regarded as a distinct legal system would need to consider the institutional autonomy of that system in terms of it possessing "its own" law-recognising-and-applying institutions, i.e. its own courts, and recognising "its own" law for reasons grounded in the distinctive law-recognition practices of those courts. MacCormick's discussion of the Treaty of Union cases illustrates more fully what I mean by the second part of this claim. In my view, it would count as evidence in favour of there being a distinct Scottish legal system that the Scottish courts adopt distinctive law-recognition practices which are differentiated in some ways from those of other legal systems. In the article referred to above, MacCormick makes a convincing case, based on his reading of the Treaty of Union cases, that the Scottish courts do indeed take such a view, and accept a different and distinctive recognition rule from that which is accepted in other legal systems, even within the same state. Such work of MacCormick's hence again assists us in considering the social and institutional reality of legal systems, and the way in which their distinctive recognition practices may represent one important element in delineating them from one another.

C. LEGAL SYSTEMS AS IDEAS, AND AS ASPIRING TO IDEALS

Questions regarding the identity and limits of legal systems, and indeed questions concerning the role of the concept of a legal system itself, cannot be addressed solely by considering social facts such as which institutions a given entity possesses, how autonomous those institutions are, and which

---

19 See H L A Hart, *The Concept of Law* 2nd edn, with a postscript ed by P A Bulloch and J Raz (1994), *passim* but especially ch 6.
20 MacCormick, "Does the United Kingdom have a constitution?" (n 15) 11 (internal footnote omitted).

norms are recognised by them and for what reasons. This is because of the point I raised at the beginning – that legal systems are *ideas* as well as social facts – and because the concept of a legal system plays a particular role in our thinking as citizens of law-governed polities.[21]

What do I mean by this? The answer has to do with my view of the task of legal theory. In my work on jurisprudential methodology, I contend that a theory of law, in order to be successful, must take to heart the point that the concept of law, and other legal concepts such as the concept of a legal system, are concepts already used by those living in societies to understand and navigate the course of their lives under law. People living in societies governed by law are aware of law's importance in their lives, and have views about its character and purpose, whether and when they ought to obey it, which law is the law of their society and which is to be viewed as foreign law, and so on. The concept of a legal system, like other legal concepts, is not some esoteric theoretical tool introduced anew by legal philosophers in order to further their research projects; it is an idea, and a concept, which is already "out there" in people's discourse and thinking about law, and is already part of the conceptual currency used by individuals to understand themselves and their social and political world. This being so, a theoretical account of law, if it is to advance our understanding of society, must do adequate justice to the *idea* of a legal system and to participants' attitudes towards, beliefs about and self-understandings in terms of the concept of a legal system, because those attitudes, beliefs and self-understandings form part of the data to be explained.[22]

Moreover, it is not merely that citizens of law-governed polities *do* make use of the concept of a legal system, but that we do so in the service of drawing distinctions which are of importance and which matter to us, such as where "our own" legal system ends and another begins. In referring to "our own" legal system, I have in mind the notion that legal systems can become the focus of attitudes of identification and attachment (as well as of alienation and disaffection), and that the concept of a legal system is used to demarcate that which is the object of those attitudes, and to differentiate it from other instances of legal phenomena in the world.

---

21 Parts of the following section draw on J Dickson, "Towards a theory of European Union legal systems", in J Dickson and P Eleftheriadis (eds), *Philosophical Foundations of European Union Law* (forthcoming). Thanks are due to Oxford University Press for allowing me to draw on this material here.

22 For further discussion, see J Dickson, *Evaluation and Legal Theory* (2001). Many legal philosophers have been committed to this view of the task of legal philosophy, for examples see H L A Hart, *The Concept of Law* (n 19); J M Finnis, *Natural Law and Natural Rights* (1980) ch 1; J Raz, "Authority, law and morality", in J Raz, *Ethics in the Public Domain* (1994) 210-237.

In my view, this is frequently the case with the Scottish legal system. To take but one example: on the Scottish Government's website can be found a factsheet entitled "Legal System",[23] in which the Scottish legal system is referred to as "proudly independent", and "a cornerstone of Scottish life for centuries".[24] The document goes on to elaborate on that legal system's "integrity and independence"[25] in terms of its historical roots, legal sources and institutional structure,[26] which distinguish it from other legal systems including (and perhaps especially) the legal system of England and Wales. An appreciation of Scottish legal, political and academic culture readily reveals that such views concerning the distinctive character of the Scottish legal system, and the role it plays in both shaping and expressing Scottish national identity, including political identity, are no mere passing fancy of the Scottish Government, but are rather a distillation of themes which echo down loudly through the media, political debate, legal academic thinking and teaching in law schools in Scotland, and which have done so for many years, not merely in the post-devolution era.[27] Those living in law-governed polities can come to hold such attitudes of attachment to, identification with and even pride in their own law, and in order to be able to say which law is "their law" and to

23 "Legal System", factsheet produced by the Scottish Executive (now rebranded as the Scottish Government) (2004) 2, available online: *http://www.scotland.gov.uk/Resource/Doc/925/0000078. pdf*, accessed 24 July 2011.
24 Scottish Executive, "Legal system" 1.
25 Scottish Executive, "Legal System" 2.
26 Scottish Executive, "Legal System" passim.
27 See e.g. "MPs warn UK reform must protect Scottish legal tradition", *Edinburgh Evening News*, online edition, 10 Feb 2004, *http://edinburghnews.scotsman.com/uksupremecourt/MPs-warn-UK-reform-must.2502230.jp*, accessed 24 July 2011; "Scotland is proud of, and jealously guards, its separate legal system", from "Fighting fraud", *The Herald*, online edition 20 February 2009, *http://www.theherald.co.uk/features/editorial/display.var.2487857.0.fighting_fraud.php*, accessed 24 July 2011. Of significance in this regard is the existence and proceedings of the Stair Society, instituted in 1934 to encourage the study and to advance the knowledge of the history of Scots law, *http://www.stairsociety.org/home.htm*, accessed 24 July 2011. Legal and academic discourse more generally on the topic is voluminous: for but a tiny sample, see T B Smith, "Scottish nationalism, law and self-government", in N MacCormick (ed), *The Scottish Debate* (1970); G Maher, "The identity of the Scottish legal system" (1977) *Juridical Review* 21-37; N MacCormick, "Does the United Kingdom have a constitution? Reflections on *MacCormick v Lord Advocate*" (n 15) 1-20; N Walker and C M G Himsworth, "The Poll Tax and fundamental law", (1991) *Juridical Review* 45; D J Edwards, "The Treaty of Union: more hints of constitutionalism" (1992) 12 *Legal Studies* 34-41; and for discussion of the challenges faced by the Scottish legal system in the post-devolution era, see e.g. C M G Himsworth, "Devolution and its jurisdictional asymmetries" (2007) 70 *MLR* 31-58; Neil Walker, "Report on Final Appellate Jurisdiction in the Scottish Legal System" (n 10); H L MacQueen (ed), *Scots Law into the 21st Century: Essays in Honour of W A Wilson* (1996); E Attwooll, *The Tapestry of Law: Scotland, Legal Culture and Legal Theory* (1997); and P Maharg, "Imagined communities, imaginary conversations: failure and the construction of legal identities" and L Farmer, "Under the shadow of Parliament House: the strange case of legal nationalism", both in L Farmer and S Veitch (eds), *The State of Scots Law* (2001).

begin identifying its distinctive characteristics they need to, and do, make use of the concept of a legal system. So the concept of a legal system is not merely an idea that we happen to have recourse to in navigating our way around our societies and their law. It is also a concept used to draw distinctions of vital importance to us in terms of the way we think about those societies and their law: their boundaries, distinctiveness, their relation to other societies, our relation to them, and the values to which they do and ought to aspire.

My point here is simple. Because the concept of a legal system is an important idea used by those living in law-governed polities to express aspects of national identity, and to demarcate that which is legally distinctive about their societies, and the values to which they aspire, then legal theorists must turn their attention to these beliefs about, attitudes towards and self-understandings in terms of the concept of a legal system in constructing their theories, and in determining questions such as what constitutes a distinct and autonomous legal system, and how do legal systems relate to one another. In other words, people's attitudes towards and beliefs about legal systems and the values to which they aspire are going to be relevant factors in determining many important questions regarding the existence, identity and continuity of legal systems, the relations between legal systems, and between legal systems and other normative systems.

As I mentioned in the Introduction to this chapter, in referring to legal systems as "thought-objects, products of particular discourses",[28] MacCormick signalled his awareness of the importance of the concept of a legal system as idea. Although this theme can be found throughout his later work, it is in his earlier work on legal philosophy that we find its genesis, in particular in his masterful study of H L A Hart, first published in 1981,[29] and in his earlier work of 1978, *Legal Reasoning and Legal Theory*.[30] In these works, MacCormick did more than any other legal theorist at the time to bring out the importance of the "hermeneutic" character of legal philosophy, namely that the data of legal theory is constituted to a considerable extent by the attitudes, beliefs, self-understandings and evaluative judgements of those living under law, and that legal theorists, in order to be worth their salt, must strive in their theories to do adequate justice to those attitudes, beliefs and evaluations. In so doing, MacCormick greatly improved our understanding of the work of H L A Hart, but, more importantly, of the character and tasks of legal philosophy in general.

28 MacCormick, *Questioning Sovereignty* (n 1) 113.
29 N MacCormick, *H L A Hart*, 1st edn (1981), 2nd edn (2008).
30 N MacCormick, *Legal Reasoning and Legal Theory* (original edn 1978, new edn 1994).

D. UNDERSTANDING LAW: BETWEEN THE REAL
AND THE IDEAL

Law, and legal systems, then, must be understood *both* as social facts and institutions *and* as ideas, and, as regards the latter, part of understanding legal systems as ideas involves understanding them in terms of the ideals or values to which they aspire and which citizens living under law expect them to realise. In his later work, especially in the chapters on jurisprudential methodology in *Institutions of Law*, Neil MacCormick acutely appreciated the need to do adequate justice to both of these facets of legal systems. His realisation that legal theorists must pay adequate attention to both the "ideal" and the "real" of law forms yet another invaluable part of his intellectual legacy in terms of our understanding of the character of legal systems.

MacCormick's appreciation that any theory of law worth its salt must do adequate justice to the values and ideals to which legal systems aspire, is evidenced in statements such as:

> Our understanding of [law as institutional normative order] has to be in terms of its functionality towards certain values.[31]

> It is hardly disputable that a conceptually satisfactory understanding of law ... must take fully into account the values to which legal activity is essentially oriented.[32]

> The methodology of the kind of explanation offered here has to be interpretive or hermeneutic. That is, it must seek to understand the practices and institutions of human beings in terms of what makes them intelligible and worthwhile ... to their human participants.[33]

However, although clearly appreciating the need to understand legal systems in terms of the values and ideals to which they aspire, because that is part of their character as purposive human enterprises, MacCormick never lost sight of the need *also* to do adequate justice to the social reality of law, including to the fact that "real law", as it actually exists and is implemented in human social institutions, often falls short of those ideals and values, and remains law nonetheless.

To illustrate this point further, we can briefly consider a legal theorist whom I regard as taking a contrasting position to MacCormick on this issue. As I have argued elsewhere,[34] for John Finnis, when law starts to fall short of

---

31 MacCormick, *Institutions of Law* (n 13) 297.
32 MacCormick, *Institutions of Law* 299.
33 MacCormick, *Institutions of Law* 295.
34 J Dickson, "Is bad law still law? Is bad law really law?", in M Del Mar and Z Bankowski (eds), *Law as Institutional Normative Order* (2009); J Dickson, "Legal positivism: contemporary debates", in A Marmor (ed), *Routledge Companion to the Philosophy of Law* (forthcoming). The current section draws on both of these pieces.

those ideals and values it ought to realise, it becomes less than fully law, or law only in a secondary sense, or law but not "really" law in its focal meaning, or not law at all.[35] Finnis himself would likely deny this, as he has claimed that it is important and useful in legal philosophy to focus on law's positivity,[36] and on social fact based tests for the intra-systemic validity of law.[37] Finnis has also contended that law's dependence on social facts is an important element in enabling law to carry out the moral task which he claims it has: to reasonably resolve the co-ordination problems of a political society and so allow its members to participate in the basic goods and pursue valuable lives.[38] But Finnis' deeper commitments as regards the importance or otherwise of law's social facticity – the "real" of law – come to the surface when he discusses how we should understand instances of law that are legally valid according to the relevant social facts tests in a given jurisdiction, but that fail to carry out law's moral task of reasonably resolving co-ordination problems for societal common good.

According to Finnis, although there is still a certain sense – a social fact sense, or a possessing technical legal validity sense – in which such unjust laws can be referred to as law,[39] they are also regarded – depending on the stridency of Finnis' turn of phrase – as not really law,[40] less than fully law,[41] law only in a secondary, watered-down or distorted sense,[42] or, simply, not law.[43] Moreover, and more importantly in terms of Finnis' demotion of, and lack of adequate attention to, the "real" of law, it is this second set of understandings that he regards as being explanatorily more significant, as is evident from his response to a challenge by Joseph Raz as to why law should be regarded as not really or fully law when it is bad, whereas novels or paintings or people still remain novels or paintings or people even when they are bad.[44] Finnis responds to Raz as follows: "like argument, medicines, and contracts, law has

---

35 See e.g. J Finnis, *Natural Law and Natural Rights* (1980) ch I; 266-70; 276-81; ch XII; J Finnis, "Natural law theories", in E N Zalta (ed), *The Stanford Encyclopaedia of Philosophy* (Spring 2007 edition), *http://plato.stanford.edu/archives/spr2007/entries/natural-law-theories/*, accessed 24 July 2011, section 4; J Finnis, "Law and what I truly should decide" (2003) 48 *American Journal of Jurisprudence* 107-129 at 114.

36 J Finnis, "The truth in legal positivism", in R George (ed), *The Autonomy of Law, Essays on Legal Positivism* (1996) 195-214.

37 J Finnis, "Law and what I truly should decide" (n 35) 107.

38 J Finnis, "Natural law theories" (n 35) section 1.

39 See e.g. Finnis, *Natural Law and Natural Rights* (n 35) ch XII.4.

40 Finnis, *Natural Law and Natural Rights* 277-278.

41 Finnis, *Natural Law and Natural Rights* 279.

42 Finnis, "Natural law theories" (n 35) section 4.

43 Finnis, "Law and what I truly should decide" (n 35) at 114.

44 For the relevant exchange, see Finnis, "Law and what I truly should decide" at 114-115 and especially note 9.

a focused and normative point to which everything else about it is properly to be regarded as subordinate". People, on the other hand, "exist in the natural order as living substances even if they are not functioning adequately or at all in the orders of logic and thought".[45] In the case of law, then, its "focused and normative point" or, to put it another way, its ideal – i.e. its moral task of reasonably resolving co-ordination problems for the common good – is hence what is regarded as most important about it, and law's other qualities, such as its social nature, and the fact that its existence and content can be ascertained ultimately by reference to social facts, are to be regarded as "subordinate". This being so, although Finnis states that natural law thinking is interested both in law's social facticity and in its moral purpose and propensity to generate reasons for action,[46] the reality is that he regards the latter, and the explanation of the latter, as primarily important. Aspects of law's social facticity – the "real" of law – are demoted by Finnis to being subordinate qualities of law, and law that exhibits those qualities, but that does not fulfil law's moral task is seen as a watered-down or secondary kind of law (when it is seen as law at all).

This Finnisian approach, of smoothing away or regarding as less than fully law any actually existing instances of legal phenomena that do not realise the values and ideals to which law aspires, fails to do justice to the sense in which, whether or not it lives up to those values and ideals, law is "out there" and has a social reality to it, and an institutional manifestation. Law that is not as it ought to be still exists in our social and political lives, and can have important consequences for us, hence we should not ignore or discount it. This point is also recognised by MacCormick:

> Law ought to be just and ought to serve the common good for all within the jurisdiction. But law frequently fails to be as it ought to be.[47]

> … the high likelihood that any real system will have serious blemishes judged in light of the very values which are the final causes of institutional normative order.[48]

And, crucially:

> There can indeed be unjust laws, and what is alarming about this *is that they are perfectly genuine laws*, upheld and enforced through the coercive power of the state. "An unjust law is a corruption of law" – yes, but it is real law that is thus corrupted.[49]

45 Finnis, "Law and what I truly should decide" at 114, note 9.
46 Finnis, "Natural law theories" (n 35) Introduction.
47 MacCormick, *Institutions of Law* (n 13) 264.
48 MacCormick, *Institutions of Law* 297.
49 MacCormick, *Institutions of Law* 271 (my emphasis; internal footnote reference (to St Thomas Aquinas, *Summa Theologiae*) omitted).

All of this evidences MacCormick's dual commitment to doing adequate justice in his theory of law as institutional normative order *both* to the values and ideals that legal systems ought to realise, and to their social and institutional reality. He did not wish to smooth away or claim as not law any law that fails to be as it ought to be. Instead, legal systems as they ought to be, and legal systems as they are, are both vitally important matters to explore, and it is in the combined investigation of both these facets of legal systems that we work towards a successful explanation of their character, purpose and value.

To conclude, I would like to suggest that this dual commitment to the ideal and the real of legal systems ties in with something else that I regard as vitally important about MacCormick's work: that he sought to end fruitless divisions between schools of thought in legal theory. He explicitly claimed in *Institutions of Law* that his work drew from the legal positivist (which might be thought more rooted in the "real" of legal systems), natural law, (which might be thought to be more concerned with the "ideal" of legal systems) and Dworkinian interpretive traditions, and that allying oneself with a legal philosophical school of thought in opposition to another such school might obscure as much as clarify the issues being addressed:

> In truth, such dichotomies [between legal positivism and natural law] are rarely revealing of any important truth.[50]

> It is better to reject the aforesaid dichotomy as based on a misleading account of the history of ideas ...[51]

> It is perhaps most sensible to say this book presents an institutional theory of law, and that this theory draws inspiration both from some strands of thought previously advanced by self-proclaimed "legal positivists" and from others derived from "natural law" theorizing. It is post-positivist, if not anti-positivist.[52]

So much ink has been spilt and time wasted in legal theory in delineating legal philosophical "teams" and in deciding who gets to play for them, rather than in trying to improve our understanding of the puzzles about law that concern us all, that I cannot but firmly agree with these statements. In his desire to overcome misleading theoretical dichotomies, and in his commitment to explain both the real and the ideal of legal systems (and in so much else), Neil MacCormick's contribution to our philosophical understanding of law has been immeasurable.

---

50 MacCormick, *Institutions of Law* 278.
51 MacCormick, *Institutions of Law* 279.
52 MacCormick, *Institutions of Law* 279.

Sovereignty and Beyond

7 Scottish Nationalism For and Against the Union State

Neil Walker[°]

A. INTRODUCTION
B. LIBERALISM, POST-SOVEREIGNTY AND NATIONALISM
(1) Liberal nationalism
(2) Post-sovereignty
(3) Nationalism reframed
C. THE UNION STATE
(1) The state of the Union state
(2) MacCormick and the Union
D. THE FUTURE OF POLITICAL NATIONALISM

A. INTRODUCTION

Neil MacCormick was a committed Scottish nationalist, but a far from dogmatic one. He never stopped reviewing and revising his thoughts about how nationalism should best express itself, and in that spirit he came over the course of his life to believe ever more firmly in independent statehood as the fullest realisation of his political vision. His attachment to the cause of nationalism, and the directions in which it led him, are reflected in his many writings on the subject,[1] just as they are in his lifetime involvement with the Scottish National Party (SNP) and with nationalist political movements more generally.

° Regius Professor of Public Law and the Law of Nature and Nations, University of Edinburgh. As this chapter was completed in late 2011, it was unable to take account of relevant constitutional developments in the early months of 2012, in particular commitments made by the UK and Scottish governments to the holding of an independence referendum within a specified timetable and subsequent bilateral negotiations on the basis of these commitments. Section D below should be read in light of these developments.

1 For a comprehensive bibliography, see Maks Del Mar's chapter in the present volume. The main reference point for the present chapter is N MacCormick, *Questioning Sovereignty: Law, State and Nation in the European Commonwealth* (1999), although a number of other sources are cited where particularly appropriate. *Questioning Sovereignty* may be regarded as MacCormick's central work on these questions not only because it contains a mature statement of his views on the relationship between political identity and constitutional form but also because it collects and revises many of the important pieces he had written throughout his intellectual life.

Yet, philosophically, Neil's nationalism was not a position that could have been easily arrived at or sustained. It seems to sit awkwardly both with his background liberalism[2] and with his so-called "post-sovereignty"[3] perspective, each of which lay as close to his intellectual and political heart as did his nationalism. On one view, indeed, his nationalism is incompatible with these other major themes of his work, and some have even claimed to detect an unease and an ambivalence in MacCormick's own stated views towards political nationalism. According to Andrew Vincent, for instance, "MacCormick himself, at times, gives the impression of being partly surprised by his own nationalism."[4]

In what follows I argue that Neil's nationalist position, far from ignoring these difficult issues or being embarrassed by the challenge they posed, instead sought to tackle them head-on and was refined and enriched through confrontation with them. In particular, his approach sought to use each element in the troika of key concepts to help resolve the tension between the others. So, as we shall see, his post-sovereign position was deployed to soften and resolve the tension between his liberalism and his nationalism, while his liberalism was deployed to soften and resolve the tension between his nationalism and his disavowal of sovereignty.

MacCormick's nationalist position and his treatment of these tensions were further honed by the practical political context in which he lived and with which he was required to engage. Apart from his five-year stint as a Member of the European Parliament, he spent his entire life in the "Union state"[5] of the United Kingdom. This setting not only provided a formative

---

2   For an early statement of his views on the relationship between liberalism and nationalism, see "Nation and nationalism", in C MacLean (ed), *The Crown and the Thistle*, (1979) 97-111 (also published with modification as ch 13 in N MacCormick, *Legal Right and Social Democracy* (1982). See also MacCormick, *Questioning Sovereignty* (n 1), chs 10 and 11.

3   The seminal article here is N MacCormick, "Beyond the sovereign state" (1993) 56(1) *Modern Law Review* 1-18. See also *Questioning Sovereignty*, ch 8; and for his last word on the subject, see "Sovereignty and after", in H Kalmo and Q Skinner (eds), *Sovereignty in Fragments: The Past, Present and Future of a Contested Concept* (2010) 151-168.

4   A Vincent, *Nationalism and Particularity* (2002) 92.

5   Following the introduction of the term by Stein Rokkan and Derek Urwin in "Introduction: centres and peripheries in Western Europe", in S Rokkan and D Irwin (eds), *The Politics of Territorial Identity: Studies in European Regionalism* (1982), the idea of a Union state has been the subject of much recent analysis. See e.g. N Walker, "Beyond the unitary conception of the United Kingdom constitution?" [2000] *Public Law* 384-404; S Tierney, *Constitutional Law and National Pluralism* (2004); C Kidd, *Union and Unionism: Political Thought in Scotland, 1500-2000* (2008); M Keating, *The Independence of Scotland: Self-government and the Shifting Politics of Union* (2009). Other prominent contemporary examples of Union states are Spain and Canada. On the deep historical background of Scottish unionism situated in transnational perspective, see J D Ford, "Four models of union" (2011) *Juridical Review* 45-76. On the idea of union applied comparatively to national and supranational contexts, see M Avbelj, "Theory of European Union"

framework for his views, but also supplied the horizon for his efforts, which continued until the very end of his life, to cash out his philosophical nationalism in political and institutional terms.[6] The shifting political contours of the Union state, therefore, provide a vital context in allowing us to make sense of MacCormick's efforts to square his nationalism with his liberalism and with his post-sovereign stance.

My aim in this chapter is not simply one of critical and contextual exposition of the ideas of a profound thinker in this area. It is, in addition, and building on MacCormick's highly suggestive body of work, to ponder the topical and increasingly pressing question of how, if at all, it would be possible for anyone to reconcile and pursue in tandem the different kinds of positions that he adhered to in the context of our shifting constitutional politics. How might someone who, on the one hand, is sympathetic to the cause of political nationalism, or at least shares (as do I, as a self-defined Scot) a nationalist self-understanding at the cultural level and is prepared to take seriously the aspirations of those who subscribe to political nationalism, and who, on the other hand, subscribes to the sorts of liberal and post-sovereign positions, broadly defined, that MacCormick advocated in the context of the Union state (as I also do) – a combination that, partly through MacCormick's own example and inspiration, is becoming ever more fashionable – plead the cause of independence? What form, if any, might independence take in a world in which liberal values remain important but sovereignty is not what it used to be, and what, if any, continuing accommodation with unionism is thereby implied? In a nutshell, is the increasingly influential brand of nationalism that we associate with Neil MacCormick and his works necessarily against the Union state, or might it instead be for it?

As we shall see, there may be no single or clear-cut answer to this question. Perhaps the achievement of liberal nationalism in a post-sovereign world is one that may reasonably fall on either side of the dividing line of independence vis-à-vis the Union state; one, moreover, that may call into question the very idea of a strict dividing line. And, to bring us back in conclusion to MacCormick the thinker and actor, perhaps this more fluid conception of constitutional possibilities heightens our appreciation of how his own nationalism was of a type that could remain unswerving in principle while displaying flexibility in its expression over time.

European Law Review (2011) 36 818-836.

6   In his last years MacCormick worked as specialist advisor to the SNP leader, Alex Salmond, after he became First Minister of the Scottish Government in 2007. See further section D below.

B. LIBERALISM, POST-SOVEREIGNTY AND NATIONALISM

(1) Liberal nationalism

Let us start with the challenges that both liberalism and post-sovereignty pose to nationalism, and with how MacCormick endeavours to answer these challenges. The older tension lies between liberalism and nationalism. Indeed, for the majority of their conceptual careers these two concepts have generally been seen as incompatible ideals. Crudely, where liberalism is about individualism, reflection and choice, nationalism, as it has developed since the eighteenth century as a cultural support to the emerging form of the modern state, is about collectivism, loyalty and solidarity.[7] This does not mean that the history of ideas is entirely bereft of attempts to reconcile nationalism and liberalism. There were some nineteenth-century liberal nationalists, from Mazzini to John Stuart Mill, while Woodrow Wilson's League of Nations, launched in response to the ravages of the First World War, can be seen as an early template for liberal internationalism. Yet this ambitious project was a conspicuous failure, and given the notorious, and notoriously illiberal, excesses of nationalism that marked much of the twentieth century, the rehabilitation of liberal nationalism for long remained an unlikely prospect.[8] It is only really since the 1980s, and under the pressure of cumulative waves of new forms of post-imperial and post-communist nation-building, that there has been a resurgence of serious thinking devoted to reconciling nationalism and liberalism. In the Anglophone world, Neil MacCormick, alongside such diverse figures as David Millar,[9] Joseph Raz,[10] Charles Taylor,[11] Will Kymlicka[12] and Yael Tamir,[13] became a key character in that revival.[14]

Consideration of the relationship between liberalism and nationalism takes many forms and is connected to a number of key divisions and debates in the literature.[15] However, as Vincent suggests, if we are primarily concerned with the scope for reconciliation of the two concepts, perhaps the key distinction lies between nationalism viewed as merely instrumental to liberalism and

---

7   See e.g. A Smith, *Nationalism: Theory, Ideology, History* (2001).
8   See e.g. Vincent, *Nationalism and Particularity* (n 4) ch 4.
9   D Miller, *On Nationality* (1995).
10   J Raz and A Margalit, "National self-determination" (1999) 87 *Journal of Philosophy* 12-34.
11   C Taylor, "Nationalism and modernity", in R Biener (ed), *Theorizing Nationalism* (1999) 219-246.
12   W Kymlicka, *Liberalism, Community and Culture* (1991).
13   Y Tamir, Liberal *Nationalism* (1993). MacCormick acknowledged a particular debt to Tamir; see e.g. *Questioning Sovereignty* (n 1) 174.
14   See e.g. Vincent, *Nationalism and Particularity* (n 4) ch 4.
15   For example, the debate between civic and ethnic forms of nationalism (see e.g. M Ignatieff, *Blood and Belonging* (1993)), or between autonomy and diversity liberalism (see e.g. W Galston, "Two concepts of liberalism" (1995) 105 *Ethics* 16-34).

nationalism conceived of as embodying the intrinsic goods of liberalism.[16] The instrumental argument, which dominated nineteenth-century liberal nationalist thought, is pragmatic and prudential. It starts from a recognition that nations are often the only political game in town – the sole vehicles at our disposal within which the values of a liberal society (and also, indeed, a social democratic society)[17] may flourish. The instrumental case maintains that nationalism, understood as a collective co-recognition and co-activation of common national identity, is indispensable in providing the cultural glue and in generating and guaranteeing the associated institutional wherewithal to facilitate our mutual engagement as co-members (of the nation state) and collaborators in those relations of equal, autonomy-respecting concern that are central to liberal thinking.[18] Here the relationship between nationalism and liberalism is reduced to one of pure contingency. We need the communal energy and organising frame that national identity and cultural nationalism provide to breathe life into and embed our liberal values and institutions. But the link is one of means and ends, and no internal connection between the two concepts is thereby implied. Indeed, given its double-edged historical record and highly variable sociological implications, nationalism as viewed from this instrumental perspective is apt to continue to be treated with caution even by its supporters, perhaps even as a condition to be tolerated only as a necessary evil.[19]

Even though they acknowledge and accept the instrumentalist argument, many recent liberal nationalist writers, with MacCormick to the fore, have reached beyond its limited and often reluctant endorsement of national identity. In venturing further, MacCormick stresses that nationalism is in

16 Vincent, *Nationalism and Particularity* (n 4) 90.
17 Many liberal nationalist writers also emphasise the link between nationalism and the generation of the culture of mutual concern necessary for social democratic forms of public policy, and, moreover, stress the internal link between fuller forms of liberal autonomy and the forms of social and economic support associated with social democratic policies. MacCormick clearly subscribes to these views; see e.g. *Questioning Sovereignty* (n 1) 172. See also, e.g. Miller, *On Nationality* (n 9).
18 Although liberals differ, sometimes sharply, over whether autonomy and the protection and development of individual life-plans should be defended on perfectionist grounds, because autonomy and individualism are supreme and self-standing virtues and so provide an ideal conception of the good life, as in John Stuart Mill's original formulation (*On Liberty* (1859)); or on anti-perfectionist grounds, the maintenance of an individual sphere of freedom and of a culture of pluralism being necessary precisely because there is no compelling basis for adjudicating between the different conceptions of the good held by different persons, as perhaps most famously argued by John Rawls; see e.g. J Rawls, *Political Liberalism* (1993).
19 For this interpretation of Mill's nationalism against many of the new wave of liberal nationalists who read Mill as a more enthusiastic supporter, see F Rosen, "Nationalism and early British liberal thought" (1997) 2 *Journal of Political Ideologies* 2.

important respects continuous with and evocative of the very values that lie at the heart of the liberal enterprise. For him, the liberal commitment to respect and to promote the autonomy of the individual implies more than simply safeguarding the familiar litany of negative rights: freedom from harmful interference by the state or by other individuals or collectivities in one's personal liberty and security, or in one's speech, association, conscience, privacy etc. Liberalism, expansively conceived, also implies, more positively, recognising and securing the very "social situation where self-aware individuality and self-fulfillment are possible for individuals",[20] including, crucially, what is for many the overarching "social situation" provided by national identity. That is to say, for the individual autonomy so cherished by liberals to be authentically experienced and effectively realised *as* individual autonomy requires the kind of framework of *individuating* collective self-recognition that nationalism can provide. So nationalism is no longer just a causal *precondition* of the life lived autonomously, as in the instrumentalist argument, but a constitutive *co-condition* – supplying the very milieu in which autonomy is apprehended and activated. On this view, our first-order liberal autonomy in our-day-to-day exchanges presupposes and, indeed, incorporates a second-order liberal autonomy according to which we get to choose, or at least get to experience as uncoerced, the broader associative environment of our first–order autonomy – the population of significant others with reference to whom we both develop and pursue our life plans.

Importantly, therefore, from this larger liberal perspective, nationalism, conceived as a prominent manifestation of our second-order liberal autonomy, necessarily has political consequences. It cannot, as some nationalists would suggest, be relegated to a sphere of privatised culture.[21] Rather, it demands a political expression as a mark of the importance of the associative environment supplied by the voluntary national collective – the civic nation – in providing a meaningful and plausible context for our autonomy, which in turn requires an institutionalised measure of recognition of and respect for the national collective by outsiders as well as insiders.

As MacCormick stresses, in all of this it is vital not to repeat the tendency of some strands of the liberal tradition and confuse two senses of individualism. On the one hand, the liberal has to insist upon the primacy of *normative* individualism: on the "distinct individual"[22] rather than groups or other

---

20 MacCormick, *Questioning Sovereignty* (n 1) 176.
21 See e.g. B Yack, "Nationalism, popular sovereignty and the liberal democratic state", in T V Paul, G J Ikenberry and J A Hall (eds), *The Nation State in Question* (2003) 29-50.
22 MacCormick, *Questioning Sovereignty* (n 1) 175.

superhuman entities as the dominant or exclusive morally relevant units within society and as the only centres of consciousness actually capable of enjoying and experiencing the "enhancement of life"[23] that we should insist upon as a criterion of whatever is worthy of value. On the other hand, the liberal must dismiss *methodological* individualism, or social atomism, as an explanatory orientation, and instead endorse the idea that as normatively significant individuals we are also necessarily socially embedded and societally aware and valuing individuals.[24] Why we value certain things and what we tend to value flows from our natural state not as pre-social creatures, as certain social contractarian strains of liberalism would have it, but as "irreducibly social animals"[25] always already implicated in our collective settings and strivings.

Of course, as MacCormick readily acknowledges, nationalism today retains its dark side, much of which may also be characterised as its anti-liberal side. No amount of liberal injunction to the contrary will make this simply disappear.[26] Liberals have to make a stand, and must display constant vigilance against that dark side. In particular, liberals must be universalistic, and not just in the weak sense that the same rights and duties must attach to any and all human beings in like circumstances.[27] That is the barest standard of formal equality, and its prohibition of arbitrary and *ad hominem* distinctions and exceptions in the treatment of the sphere of individual freedom is the absolute minimum for anyone committed, as the liberal must be, to the idea of each and every person possessing an autonomy which demands respect and requires protection. More than this, however, liberals, once they are prepared to accept the basic standard and discipline of generalisable, and so rule-bound, definitions of the circumstances of individual freedom, should also be slow to specify the "like circumstances" that provide any rule's major premise and condition of application in ways that make it easier to discriminate between different groups; for to do otherwise would be to erode the more general sense of the equal moral worth of the individual that underpins the commitment to autonomy. As MacCormick puts it, liberalism supplies "a presumption in favour of more inclusive over less inclusive characterisations of relevant human circumstances".[28]

A number of points follow from this stronger universalistic premise. To begin with, liberals, including liberal nationalists, must presumptively

23 MacCormick, *Questioning Sovereignty* 175.
24 MacCormick, *Questioning Sovereignty* 176.
25 MacCormick, *Questioning Sovereignty* 176.
26 MacCormick, *Questioning Sovereignty* 157-159.
27 MacCormick, *Questioning Sovereignty* 175.
28 MacCormick, *Questioning Sovereignty* 175.

respect the freedom of all within the relevant political community; not just the majority within the nation state but also internal minorities, immigrant groups, denizens and visitors. In addition, and looking beyond the immediate political community, just because the close link between collective and individual self-determination must apply to "them" as well as "us", liberals who are nationalists also have to respect the equivalent desire for national self-determination of other groups. A nationalism that is indifferent to or discriminates against those who share the same territorial space but who are not considered members of that nation or who do not consider themselves members of that nation, or who are otherwise at odds with the dominant form of self-identification or associated values of the nation, is not a nationalism that respects liberal values. Equally, a nationalism that disregards or rides roughshod over other nationalist claims in matters where such claims may contend with one another, whether boundary disputes or other recognition questions between polities or questions of multinational accommodation within a single political configuration, is not a nationalism that respects liberal values.

(2) Post-sovereignty

These are difficult matters for any liberal working within a nationalist frame to address. Let us, however, leave them hanging for now and turn to consider MacCormick's treatment of the parallel tension between nationalism and post-sovereignty. For MacCormick, the idea of sovereignty, at least in its most significant usages,[29] is quite simply no longer well adapted to the conditions of modern legal and political life. There are three main aspects to his critique.

To begin with, MacCormick takes a very particular view of sovereignty considered as an internal feature of a polity. Basically, he believes that our understanding of sovereignty remains in thrall to the early modern absolutist vision of Hobbes and to later, more socially progressive but similarly singular, conceptions of the moral order of the polity such as Bentham's utilitarianism.[30] In the received historical understanding, unless one could identify a single

29 In response to criticism of his earlier position, in some of his last work MacCormick acknowledges that the use of sovereignty may remain defensible in certain limited contexts, with particular regard to the legal dimension of external "sovereignty"; see in particular, McCormick, "Sovereignty and After" (n 4). Tellingly, it is this very external-regarding and external-regarded attribute, which MacCormick accepts may still be described as international legal sovereignty, that he also regards as providing the formal title and key incident of independent statehood, and so as supplying the very basis for the classification of his political aspiration as still one of Scottish independence. See e.g. MacCormick, *Questioning Sovereignty* (n 1) ch 12. See also the discussion in section D below.

30 MacCormick, *Questioning Sovereignty* ch 8.

powerful entity or organ either standing above the law – Austin's uncommanded commander – or constitutionally prescribed as supreme, then sovereignty no longer really existed. So, for example, any modern federal state, such as Germany or the United States, is understood by MacCormick to lack internal sovereignty just on account of its multiple centres of institutional authority.[31]

One may challenge MacCormick's understanding of internal sovereignty as unduly narrow, as impatient to give up on a deeper conception of the coherence of the modern polity – indeed its very internal identity *qua* polity – that underpins the constitutional settlement and underscores any subsequent and secondary dispersal of power achieved by the authority of the constitutional settlement. One may object that such an approach, by focusing too much on the *display* of institutional diversity too readily dismisses what is resilient and what remains distinctive about sovereignty as it is imagined and understood within the polity, namely its very capacity to represent and re-order the manifest and manifold diversity of the political domain *as* a unity.[32] This, indeed, is the main reason why, in my own work, I prefer the terms "late sovereignty" to post-sovereignty in mapping and evoking the decline of the Westphalian order.[33] However, at least for present purposes, that objection, and the difference that underpins the objection, is of little relevance. For the line of argument that equates mere institutional diversity with post-sovereignty, just because in so doing it takes such a historically restrictive and outmoded view of sovereignty, is in fact less significant for MacCormick's reading of the relationship between political nationalism and the erosion of sovereignty than his other two lines of argument.

What, then, of these other lines of argument? As regards external sovereignty, secondly, MacCormick's definition is more in line with conventional understandings in the literature and his challenge is for that reason more compelling.[34] He is of the view that, provided the totality of legal and political powers of a polity, however internally divided, are not subject to a higher power from outside the polity, sovereignty is not lost. Yet even here, sovereignty is viewed as rapidly becoming a thing of the past, certainly for the states of Europe. For this test of wholly self-contained authority is one that

31 MacCormick, *Questioning Sovereignty* 129.

32 See e.g. the writings of Martin Loughlin and Hans Lindahl, including Loughlin, "Ten tenets of sovereignty", and Lindahl, "Sovereignty and representation in the European Union", both in N Walker (ed), *Sovereignty in Transition* (2003), at 55-86 and 87-114 respectively.

33 See e.g. N Walker, "Late sovereignty in the European Union", in N Walker (ed), *Sovereignty in Transition* 3-32.

34 See e.g. MacCormick, *Questioning Sovereignty* 129-130.

is arguably routinely failed by the member states of the European Union. These states, through their participation in the European project over half a century, are in many areas of economic, social and security policy of traditionally domestic jurisdiction already subject to the binding legal effects of EU norms, and remain relentlessly susceptible to the continuing legislative capacity and ever deepening normative encroachments of the supranational authority, exercised through various combinations of Council, Commission and European Parliament. What is more, under the same policy heads, supranational Europe also, and again increasingly, exercises in a pooled or "compendious"[35] fashion much of the traditional external competence of its constituent states vis-à-vis the rest of the world.

Thirdly, MacCormick's sovereignty scepticism is constellational rather than polity-specific. Not only is it true that polities traditionally possessing internal and external sovereignty, namely states, are increasingly bereft of sovereign power, it is also the case that these increasingly post-sovereign states are joined by, and in some respects checked or rivalled by, non-state polities.

This position, indeed, connects closely with MacCormick's more general legal theory, and his view that the "law-state"[36] is only one amongst many applications of the idea of a legal order or system. For MacCormick, wherever there is "institutional normative order",[37] there is law, or at least something genetically similar to law. Institutional normative order "is a pervasive feature of our existence",[38] one that is found whenever judgement moves beyond the purely personal and autonomous and instead becomes conventional and heteronymous – a matter of the recognition and application of general rules or standards, which state of affairs is in turn reinforced (or sometimes inaugurated) through the development of an institutional apparatus for the making, interpretation and enforcement of these rules or standards. By its nature, then, institutional normative order goes beyond the particular, extending over time and space and coming "to be conceived as systemic in character"[39] through possession of the attributes of settled authority, internal coherence and reflexive adaptability.

We may find institutional order in conventionally non-legal or sub-legal contexts such as "churches, sporting organizations, commercial guilds, and

35 MacCormick, *Questioning Sovereignty* 133.
36 MacCormick, *Questioning Sovereignty* 9. See, more generally, his *Institutions of Law: An Essay in Legal Theory* (2008).
37 MacCormick, *Questioning Sovereignty* 6-11.
38 MacCormick, *Questioning Sovereignty* 23.
39 MacCormick, *Questioning Sovereignty* 7.

leagues".[40] More pertinently for present purposes, however, we may also find it in more conventionally juristic or jurisgenerative contexts, including international organisations such as the United Nations and the World Trade Organization, regional organisations such as the EU and the Council of Europe, and of course, infra-state domains such as federal provinces or sub-state nations such as Scotland itself. These contexts can supply their own legal orders as much as can the state itself. And in many cases, importantly, with the dispersal of power below and above the state that we associate with the globalisation wave of the past sixty years, these legal orders, rather like the law-state, increasingly sustain and are sustained by a measure of political authority and legitimacy.

In short, therefore, for MacCormick not only is the state progressively becoming a post-sovereign polity, but increasingly it is joined in the global constellation by other post-state legal and political orders. What is more, the process is a self-propagating one. Where previously the deep structure of the Westphalian order was one in which states recognised and so reinforced each other's sovereign authority in mutually exclusive domains, the deep structure of the new order is quite different. It is one in which the various polities and their normative orders co-exist in mutually overlapping domains, and perforce tend to recognise and reinforce the sense of the authority of the other as something other than and less than sovereign.[41]

The challenge to MacCormick's independence-focused nationalism posed by his post-sovereign position is just as clear as that posed by his liberalism. If nationalism, as it must do in the liberal nationalist view, incorporates a degree of political authority, our received understanding of how that political authority is cashed out is confused and complicated by the rise of both post-sovereign and, as a further extension of this, post-state polities and legal orders. The traditional black box view of political nationalism – for every nation a sovereign state in a world of mutually exclusive nation states – could never promise more than partial success, confounded as it inevitably always has been by the scarcity of territorial resources and the irreconcilability of competing claims. Today, however, it has become quite emphatically outmoded. The sovereigntist vision that has provided the aspirational frame for the strong form of modern nationalism conceived of as political independence is no longer either possible or necessary.

40 MacCormick, *Questioning Sovereignty* 7.
41 See generally MacCormick, *Questioning Sovereignty* ch 8. See also N Walker, "Late sovereignty" (n 33); and "The variety of sovereignty", in R Adler-Nissen and T Gammeltoft-Hansen (eds), *Sovereignty Games: Instrumentalizing State Sovereignty in Europe and Beyond* (2008) 21-32.

It is impossible, at least in the European domain, because of the altered circumstances that have led to the erosion of external sovereignty. External sovereignty, to the extent that the term retains currency in our continent, is now divided and shared between the member states and the EU as a whole – a point that is not gainsaid by the argument, also supported by MacCormick, that the net overall external influence of the member states jointly and severally may thereby be increased.[42] Yet there is also a strong argument that a sovereignty-based conception of independence is in any case unnecessary, and this for both negative and positive reasons. Negatively, because the fact that in a post-sovereign constellation there are no longer any sovereign states in the full sense means that the kinds of claims to or assumptions of second-order collective self-determination which lead, for both strategic and symbolic reasons, to the counter-assertion and counter-aspiration of other, equally categorical sovereign nationalisms tend to be less frequent and more muted. Positively, since the new post-sovereign, post-state world in any case provides a wide menu of new or revamped polity types – federation, confederation, consociation, supranationality and even, as we shall see, union – that might provide alternative forms of political self-determination to the classic model of fully sovereign independence.

(3) Nationalism reframed

We can now begin to see how the challenges of liberalism and post-sovereignty to the kind of nationalism espoused by Neil MacCormick relate to one another. On the one hand, liberalism, while consistent with an inclusive civic nationalism, must be concerned to show due liberal respect and concern for others who do not share in the indigenous national project or who champion other and potentially inconsistent national projects. On the other hand, the condition of post-sovereignty suggests that the traditional expression of political nationalism as consisting of, or at least conducive to, sovereign independence is no longer available, and that new expressions must be found.

On a positive reading of the relationship between these two sets of challenges, the new conceptual and institutional space of post-sovereignty may allow for the kind of other-regarding concern and accommodation that liberal nationalism's liberal credentials require. On a negative reading, the danger is that we discover in exploration of that new conceptual and institutional space that in order to satisfy one side of the argument we have to pay too high a cost on the other side. Either the price of an adequately inclusive and

42 See e.g. MacCormick, *Questioning Sovereignty* ch 9.

other-regarding political liberalism is the disappearance of any meaningful conception of political nationalism, or if we manage to reconstruct such a meaningful conception in the open horizon of post-sovereignty, we continue to do so at the expense of our liberal credentials.

In order to begin to see how nationalism might be reframed to address this concern, and to appreciate how it is reframed in MacCormick's own work, we need to pose the question less abstractly. We need, in other words, to look at the actual environment of opportunity and constraint within which Scottish nationalism emerged and is today pursued. This requires an examination of the peculiar circumstances of the Union state.

C. THE UNION STATE

(1) The state of the Union state

The idea of Scotland as part and parcel of a wider Union has a complex double significance. On the one hand, unionism is a key interpretive category in our active political culture. It is a term of richly variable and continually evolving meaning within a national vocabulary of individual and collective self-understanding, aspiration and critique, and of normatively engaged public debate. It involves a way of thinking that long predated both the regal union of 1603 and the parliamentary union of 1707 and that has embraced ecclesiastical and legal dimensions of identity as much as it has embraced direct questions of political authority. On the other hand, the more specific concept of the Union state is also an important analytical category, detached rather than engaged, operating at one remove from the "lived" social and political culture. It provides a key conceptual tool for making sense, from a disinterested perspective, of the distinctive configuration of power – neither centralist and unitary nor dispersed in accordance with an orthodox federal model – within the British state.[43]

Historically, not least in recent decades, the ideological significance of unionism as a polarising term within our wider political culture has tended to obscure its "in-between" meaning and value as an analytical and explanatory category. In conventional understanding unionism has tended to be treated as the stark opposite of nationalism, as the hegemonic condition of singular "Britishness" set against all politically resonant expressions of "regional" identity. As Colin Kidd reminds us in his excellent recent study, this binary opposition is blind to the many more nuanced streams of unionist thought

43 See references at n 5.

with which it co-exists from time to time, as well as to the actual historical record of the Union state that informs and is informed by these more
nuanced understandings.[44] In particular, the binary approach fails to appreciate that unionism has largely been an indigenous Scottish product rather
than an English "imperialist" import, and that its relationship with ideas of
Scottish national identity has been one of accommodation as well as one of
competition. Indeed, unionist thought, more subtly conceived, has often
been the vehicle through which, whether in matters of church, law or state, a
measure of Scottish autonomy has been asserted or preserved within a wider
British frame. It remains the case, nonetheless, that the dominant versions
of unionism, whether the "banal unionism"[45] that has provided the taken-for-
granted frame of reference for so many within everyday culture – "part of
the wallpaper of Scottish political life"[46] – or the more articulate but equally
categorical defences or critiques of "the Union" issuing from different ends
of the party political spectrum over the last half century, have tended towards
the reductive logic of binary opposition.

What, then, is the nature of that complex intermediate ground occupied
by our "actually existing" Union state, a territory in perennial danger of being
obscured by the dominant narrative? As already noted, we can situate the
Union state negatively, as standing somewhere between unitary and federal
models. On the one hand, and tending in a unitary direction, while the
case for treating the original "Union Agreement"[47] of 1707 as fundamental
law enshrining certain protections of the status of the original parties has
received renewed backing in recent years, according to the traditional and
still dominant "English" understanding of the British constitution there can
in principle be no guarantee of the continuing or renewed authority and
standing of the constituent nations of the UK and of their legal and political
systems. This absence has both a specific and a general aspect. Specifically,
under the various devolution statutes passed over the last dozen years, most
relevantly the Scotland Act of 1998,[48] the UK Parliament retains the right to

---

44 Kidd, *Union and Unionisms* (n 5) especially chs 1 and 8.
45 Kidd, *Union and Unionisms* 23-31. The term is adapted from Michael Billig's study of *Banal
    Nationalism* (1995). As Kidd acknowledges (24, at n 34), another insightful use of the idea of banal
    nationalism in the Scottish unionist context is by James Mitchell, "Contemporary unionism", in C
    MacDonald, *Unionist Scotland 1800-1997* (1998).
46 Kidd, *Union and Unionisms* (n 5) 24.
47 This is the term preferred by T B Smith to describe the totality of instruments, Articles of Union
    between Scotland and England followed by Acts of their respective Parliaments, by means of
    which the new state was created. See T B Smith, "Fundamental law", in *The Laws of Scotland:
    Stair Memorial Encyclopaedia* vol 5 (1987) paras 338-360.
48 Scotland Act 1998; Northern Ireland Act 1998; Government of Wales Act 1998; Government of
    Wales Act 2006.

legislate in devolved matters[49] and, similarly, ministers of the UK Government reserve certain powers to interfere in matters of devolved competence.[50] More generally, the doctrine of parliamentary sovereignty in any case entails that a later UK Parliament can always undo or amend the legislation of an earlier one. Therefore, as a matter of strict law, the dominant view remains that any scheme of devolved powers is in principle susceptible to repeal or modification by the UK Parliament at a later point without the consent of the devolved institutions or the constituencies they represent.

On the other hand, the different parts of the United Kingdom are in fact very differently treated under the existing constitutional structure, and in all cases informal controls provide at least some compensation for the absence of constitutional guarantees of autonomy. Most emphatically in the case of Scotland, to a lesser extent in Northern Ireland, and to a still lesser extent in Wales, the legislative and executive authority devolved is greater in depth and scope than we would expect under the merely "local" government of a unitary state.[51] Furthermore, the political circumstances that precipitated and have continued to accompany these grants of power – namely broad and settled support for at least some measure of political autonomy on the part of the peoples of the constituent nations of the United Kingdom – mean that in practice their reversal or modification could hardly be contemplated in the absence of the consent of the constituent parts themselves. This, indeed, is in some measure recognised in the development of new constitutional conventions governing the terms of adjustment of the devolution settlements.[52]

If we now attempt to move beyond negative to positive definition, the import of the term "Union state" appears to be twofold. First, it suggests something distinctive about the level of integration of the parts within the state. The concept of a Union, unlike "unit" which is the nominal term from which the notion of a "unitary state" is derived, implies the continued existence of the parties to the Union, albeit now joined in a settlement of permanent or at least indefinite duration. Secondly, the idea of a Union makes a historical and politico-sociological point to reinforce the basic conceptual one. Great Britain was created (in 1707) out of the two prior nation states

---

49 Scotland Act 1998 s 28(7).
50 Scotland Act 1998 ss 35, 57, 58 and 93.
51 And much greater than was provided for under the earlier aborted devolutionary scheme for Scotland; see Scotland Act 1978 s 18 and Schs 2,10, 11 and 12.
52 In particular, through the so-called Sewell Convention, which provides that the UK Parliament should not legislate within an area of devolved competence without the agreement of the Scottish Parliament: see CMG Himsworth and CM O'Neill, *Scotland's Constitution: Law and Practice*, 2nd edn (2009) 5.22.

of Scotland and England, and the United Kingdom out of their fusion with a third, Ireland (in 1800). To the (variable)[53] extent that it has succeeded in retaining the support of its constituent nations, the United Kingdom has been required through its general political system and culture to continue to acknowledge that legacy and retain something of these diverse roots. In the Scottish case, however we understand its precise constitutional status, the original Union Agreement remains an important emblem of that constitutive diversity. With its pledge to retain the separate system of courts and of public and private law, the Presbyterian church, the system of education at both university and school levels, and some aspects of the system of local government, it supplies both a record of historical difference and a commitment to continued distinctiveness.

A more detailed consideration of the anatomy of the Union state suggests a number of interconnected characteristics.[54] To begin with, the Union state is one whose constitutional arrangements have evolved slowly over time rather than having been made the subject of a plan or design. At no point has a constitutional system been established from first principles. Much is made of the rarity of the so-called "unwritten" quality of the United Kingdom constitution.[55] What is certainly true is that it has never been "written up" in canonical form, the focus of a comprehensive and integrated vision. Rather, it has been a cumulative achievement, an amalgam of different ideas and institutions continually adapted to new circumstances. As one aspect of this, the Scottish legal and political system, therefore, can be seen as a layered arrangement, embracing the legacy of a fully autonomous pre-1707 legal order, a long and uneven experience of administrative autonomy and executive devolution, and a short post-1998 demonstration of full legislative devolution.

In the second place, and now looking forward rather than backward, we may regard the Union state as provisional rather than final in composition. Its integrity depends upon the negotiated settlement continuing to be both functional for the whole and satisfactory to the various parts. That balance lacks certain important aspects of fixity associated with many unitary and

---

53 Evidently, as is demonstrated by the history of violent conflict between (Irish) nationalists and (UK) loyalist communities, which reached a peak between the late 1960s and mid 1990s, Northern Ireland is the part of the UK where the legitimacy of the Union settlement has been most contested.

54 The following paragraphs are adapted from N Walker, *Final Appellate Jurisdiction in the Scottish Legal System* (2010) ch 2.

55 Other examples include Israel and New Zealand. On the continuing relevance of the unwritten quality of the UK constitution today for many areas of constitutional law other than the distribution of authority between the whole and the constituent parts, see e.g. A King, *The British Constitution* (2007); V Bogdanor, *The New British Constitution* (2009).

federal states. This has both a legal and a political dimension. Legally, the provisional quality of the Union follows from the lack of a settled constitutional law entrenched against reform. Politically, it has to do with the continuing significance of the constituent nations and the inappropriateness of a federal or any other prior template as a definitive container for their unresolved national aspirations.

Thirdly, and in a further break from classical federalism, the Union state is asymmetrical rather than symmetrical in form. As noted above, the Union state incorporates various legal and constitutional elements of the historical nations from which it is formed. And since these historical nations are not themselves identical in legal and constitutional terms, either in their pattern of development or in their current needs and aspirations, we cannot assume that the existing structure of the Union state or its projected design should involve identical treatment of the parts. This is most clearly the case in respect of the comparison between England, as the dominant nation in terms of economy, population and political power, and the three Celtic nations. Historically, in England, unlike in the Celtic nations, there has been little pressure for devolved political institutions – whether internally to the regions or as a distinct national unit – and this continues today.[56] Even as between Scotland, Ireland and Wales, however, the pattern and phasing of institutional distinctiveness has differed greatly. This variety and uneven development makes the kind of common or shared institutions we associate with federal symmetry, most notably a regionally representative legislative senate or upper chamber, inappropriate to the British case.[57]

Finally, the combination of the legacy of pre-Union difference, post-Union intermeshing and lack of constitutional fixity over the terms of accommodation means that the Union state follows no single or dominant dynamic of convergence or divergence, but is an ever fluctuating mix of the two. On the one hand, the absence of an entrenched federal demarcation and protection of local competence has helped to foster convergence of institutional forms, public policy, and even of background politics and culture. Thus, until 1998, with the exception of Northern Ireland for most of its short post-1920 history,[58] the Union as a whole possessed no regional parliaments but only the one central legislature at Westminster. And for all that there was central recognition of separate jurisdictional and administrative needs, inevitably

---

56 See e.g. MacCormick, *Questioning Sovereignty* ch 12; J Mitchell, *Devolution in the United Kingdom* (2009).

57 MacCormick, *Questioning Sovereignty* ch 12.

58 See e.g. C McCrudden, "Northern Ireland and the British constitution since the Belfast Agreement", in J Jowell and D Oliver (eds), *The Changing Constitution*, 6th edn (2007).

much of the legislation that flowed from this single institutional source and site of representative government was common to the different jurisdictions of the UK. Furthermore, the political system more generally, including the organisation of party politics and the concentration of political debate, was primarily (if far from exclusively) located at the wider British level. In the broader cultural sphere, moreover, "Britain" became a focus of national identity to rival that of its Scottish, English, Irish and Welsh constituents.[59] In such a closely intermeshed system, regardless of the formal separation of legal systems, a high degree of substantive convergence is inevitable. For all that Scots law in many areas has continued to plough a separate furrow, in other areas the effect of the common political and cultural space has been to produce a close alignment of laws. The trend in most of public law and an increasing body of statutory criminal law is a convergent one. Even in private law, the effect of a long process of political, cultural and economic convergence, reinforced by the wider union brought about by European integration, has been to generate much commonality in areas such as contract, commercial law and negligence.

On the other hand, the Union state is equally capable of being more diverse than the federal state. The lack of a fixed settlement closely specifying areas of competence within the remit of the different levels of government also supplies a silent constitutional permission for continuing disparity. Although we should be careful not to impose today's categories on yesterday's world, prior to the Union agreement of 1707 Scotland was for most intents and purposes a sovereign state in its own right, with effective control over both internal and external affairs.[60] Scotland also had its own political institutions and other social and cultural institutions typically associated with the civil society of an autonomous state, such as Church, education system, economic organisations and professional bodies. As already noted, with the exception of the old Parliament, these forms and manifestations of autonomy survived the Union and supplied a distinctive juridical, governmental and societal vehicle to carry forward Scottish autonomy to the present day.

This deep well of difference helps to account for the resilient distinctiveness of the Scottish legal and political systems. For all that the Scottish legal system and court structure holds in common with the laws of the other jurisdictions of the UK, it retains a formal identity entirely distinct from these other jurisdictions. And the fact that so much else of the Scottish political and cultural system survived 1707 means that autonomy is by no means *just*

---

59 See e.g. L Colley, *Britons: Forging the Nation, 1707-1832*, 2nd edn (2005).
60 See e.g. C Kidd, *Union and Unionism* (n 5) chs 2 and 3.

a matter of form. Some areas of the pre-1707 Scots law – mainly its common law rather than its statute law – have survived, and for most of the history of the Union, even prior to legislative devolution in 1998, there has been some measure of recognition in Westminster and Whitehall of the need to retain a separate stream of Scottish legislation and public policy and some provision of the procedural means to deliver this.[61] Today, alongside its separate court system, the Scottish legal system continues to express many individuating features. Reflecting their roots in the system of civilian law that has exerted such a profound influence over Scots law, many areas of private law, notably property, succession and family law remain highly distinctive in content from the laws of the other jurisdictions of the UK.[62] Contemporary Scots criminal law, too, both substantive and procedural, remains not insignificantly different from that of its neighbours – the legacy of a distinct society and framework of governance.[63] Even in public law, where the common political system might be expected to provide a remorselessly unifying effect, Scots law remains distinct at the margins.[64] In broader systemic terms too, there is significant evidence of autonomy. Scotland remains a separate jurisdiction for the purpose of private international law, and boasts its own legal profession and system of legal education and qualification.

(2) MacCormick and the Union

It was noted above that there has long been a disconnection between unionism in the vernacular, locked in everyday opposition to political nationalism, and the Union state as an explanatory category depicting the richly blended distinctiveness of the British and Scottish constitutional experience. The "superficial irreconcilability"[65] of the quotidian political culture and of the more sophisticated usages and understandings of unionism is itself of political significance, as it is precisely the dominance of the former that has tended to restrict the horizons of Scottish constitutional debate to a set of stark alternatives – either full independence and sovereign statehood or

---

61 See C M G Himsworth, "The Scottish Grand Committee as an instrument of government" (1996-1997) 1 *Edinburgh Law Review* 79; C M G Himsworth and C M O'Neill, *Scotland's Constitution: Law and Practice*, 2nd edn (2009) 3.15-3.17.

62 See e.g. R Evans-Jones (ed), *The Civilian Tradition in Scotland* (1995); D L Carey Miller and R Zimmermann (eds), *The Civilian Tradition and Scots Law: Aberdeen Quincentenary Essays* (1997).

63 See e.g. L Farmer, *Criminal Law, Tradition and Legal Order: Crime and the Genius of Scots Law 1747 to the present* (1997).

64 For discussion see e.g. C M G Himsworth, "Devolution and its jurisdictional asymmetries" (2007) 70 *Modern Law Review* 31.

65 Kidd, *Unions and Unionism* (n 5) 303.

the accommodation of a (more or less modest) scheme of legislative and executive devolution within the existing United Kingdom. With the higher profile of constitutional debate after 1998, and with the election in 2011 of a second successive SNP government at Holyrood, now for the first time with an overall majority in the Scottish Parliament, there are distinct signs that this binary approach is changing, and that the cross-fertilisation between unionist and nationalist thought and practice over the centuries is beginning to be recognised and drawn upon in serious constitutional debate.[66]

As we shall see shortly, Neil MacCormick's contribution to this recent shift has been significant. But even in his earlier positions, MacCormick offered a bridge between the mainstream political debate and the richer history of constitutional ideas and institutions. From the outset he sought to reconcile his nationalism with at least some features of the unionist tradition described above, and in so doing distinguished himself in ways that he would not always find comfortable. It is worth dwelling for a moment on these earlier efforts. On the one hand, they serve to underline how, even across one political and intellectual life, the projection of nationalism is influenced, and inevitably altered, by political context. On the other hand, they demonstrate the under-lying continuity of MacCormick's efforts to blend liberalism, nationalism and an emerging post-sovereignty in a way that remains mindful of the unionist past, introducing certain themes that were to recur and mature in his later thought.

Two areas of MacCormick's early treatment of the relationship between contemporary nationalism and the unionist tradition stand out. One is his consistent and creative championing of the position that the 1707 Agreement does indeed set fundamental justiciable limits to the terms of Union that remain relevant to current constitutional development.[67] Of course, John MacCormick, the founder of the Scottish National Party in 1934 and petitioner in the most celebrated case of the twentieth century on the constitutional status of the Union Agreement,[68] was Neil's father; if we also take into consideration Neil's own specialist interest as a distinguished public lawyer and legal philosopher, then as a simple question of biography his focus on juridical foundations is hardly surprising. Yet it is remarkable, some might say paradoxical, just how important the Union Agreement – which, after all, did sound the death knell for an earlier and fuller model of Scottish nationhood – has been as a support to nationalist thought in modern times. By no means all

---

66 See section D below.
67 See e.g. MacCormick, *Questioning Sovereignty* ch 4.
68 *MacCormick v Lord Advocate* 1953 SC 396.

modern defenders of the constitutional status of the 1707 agreement against the unqualified doctrine of parliamentary sovereignty have been political nationalists.[69] But many have been, most prominently MacCormick father and son, in so doing emphasising the continuity between the pre-1707 and the post-1707 constitutional landscape and the enduringly conditional quality of the Scottish consent to Union.

In the second place, and more controversially in its time, there is the "unrepentant gradualism"[70] implicit in the early MacCormick's commitment to devolution. As Hector MacQueen points out in his introductory chapter to the present volume, the young MacCormick of 1970, writing before the first wave of modern electoral success for the nationalists in the middle years of that decade, could declare himself "unconvinced" that, even in the long run, independence was the best course for Scotland or Britain, adding that if devolution, considered by him to be a necessary staging-post to independence, "worked well", the very idea of proceeding to independence might be forsaken.[71] Two decades later, and after the aborted devolution project of the Scotland Act 1978 and ten years of unbroken Westminster rule by a Conservative Party progressively bereft of popular support in Scotland, MacCormick was more squarely committed to the ultimate end of independence, even if his was a conception of independence that matured in parallel with and was moderated in the light of his growing commitment to post-sovereignty.[72] In the intervening years he had returned permanently to his native Scotland to take up his Edinburgh Chair in 1972, had become much more active in the SNP, and, indeed had emerged as the key architect of his party's draft constitution for an independent state.[73] Yet he remained convinced of the

69 For insightful discussion of the complex and shifting relationship between legal nationalism and political nationalism in the Scottish context, see L Farmer, "Under the shadow over Parliament House: the strange case of legal nationalism", in L Farmer and S Veitch (eds) *The State of Scots Law* (2001) 151-164.

70 N MacCormick, "Unrepentant gradualism", in L Paterson (ed), *A Diverse Assembly: The Debate on a Scottish Parliament* (1998) 174-182.

71 N MacCormick (ed), *The Scottish Debate: Essays on Scottish Nationalism* (1970) "Introduction" 1-2.

72 The connection between MacCormick's growing enthusiasm for some form of Scottish independence and his increasingly nuanced "post-sovereign" understanding of what Scottish or any other form and locus of independence would entail is clear, but would repay closer investigation than I have been able to make in the context of the present essay. Though MacCormick's first full statement of post-sovereignty is not until his 'Beyond the sovereign state' essay of 1993 (n 3), it was a theme, if not yet a term, that had begun to emerge earlier in his work both on nationalism and the Union state and in the institutional theory of law generally.

73 Initially drafted in 1976-1977, and most recently updated in 2002. For discussion see N MacCormick, "An idea for a Scottish constitution", in W Finnie, C M G Himsworth and N Walker (eds), *Edinburgh Essays in Public Law* (1991) 159-184.

indispensability of legislative devolution as a first and intervening step, and found himself at odds with his party over that preference.

As a signatory to the Claim of Right of 1989, the foundation document of the Scottish Constitutional Convention which helped fuel the political momentum towards the devolution settlement a decade later, MacCormick stood firm against the SNP's decision to boycott the broad cross-party movement for devolutionary reform.[74] To the SNP hierarchy, devolution was the unacceptable halfway-house that would undermine support for more fundamental constitutional change. To MacCormick, the gradualism that devolution represented, and for which he remained forever unrepentant, was instead pragmatically and strategically attractive, half a loaf in his view being better than no bread and helping to keep the independence agenda on the table. Significantly, however, he also favoured the gradualist approach on deeper philosophical grounds. MacCormick's commitment both to democracy and to constitutionalism – conceived of as a limitation on the arbitrary exercise of governmental power – as the twin poles of the structure of collective and individual freedom that sustains liberalism, begot his conclusion that, as a matter of principle, the progress of nationalism should not be "faster than the speed of the greatest majority in promoting constitutional change".[75] Nationalism *in general* might be a suitable vehicle – for MacCormick himself even the optimal vehicle – for a liberal conception of collective self-realisation. Nevertheless, he felt bound to insist that the justification of any *particular* nationalism, even his own cherished Scottish nationalism, depended on the contingencies of popular support. It could *in fact* only provide that self-realising vehicle to the extent that it was freely embraced as so doing and did not ride roughshod over other freely embraced popular or minority conceptions and aspirations for collective autonomy. Political nationalism, therefore, for MacCormick, possessed a virtue that was primarily performative. It was not an ideal we were morally bound to pursue, but a project whose very value depended on the collective will to its pursuit.

What abiding commitments do we find intimated in these areas of MacCormick's early nationalist thought and strategy, and to what extent are they informed by the unionist tradition? In the first place, there is the commitment to gradualism, which appears to be doubly linked to the unionist tradition. On the one hand, the unionist framework represents the point of (gradual) departure for the development of political nationalism – both the source of residual legal commitments to national distinctiveness and the contemporary

---

74 As described and defended in his "Unrepentant gradualism" (n 70).
75 *MacCormick*, "Unrepentant gradualism" 180.

framework from which an institutional bridge towards independence may be built. On the other hand, and more deeply, many of the themes that distinguish the Union state also inform MacCormick's incrementalist version of liberal nationalism. In particular, the idea that the legal and political order should develop through evolution rather than rupture and grand design, and that it should be provisional rather than final in outlook, echoes those parts of the unionist tradition that remain respectful of deep origins and wary of utopian projection.

In the second place, and underscoring McCormick's investment in the presence of the past, there is a sense of the continuity and inextinguishable character of the underlying political right associated with nationalism. For all that MacCormick eschews the language of sovereignty as inappropriate to the contemporary legal and political coding of authority, he often refers approvingly to the underlying idea of popular sovereignty – of "the people" as constituent power whose assent is required for any legitimate system of government[76] – and notes with satisfaction how the 1989 Claim of Right chose to revert to the language of "the sovereign right of the Scottish people".[77] His inspiration here is in part again historical, referring back to pre-Union Scottish authorities such as George Buchanan. But it is once more also philosophical, a necessary incident of the democratic commitment to collective self-determination as an abiding ideal of the liberal polity. Where MacCormick finally parts company with unionism, then, is in his identification of the true roots of modern Scotland's deep political origins. In the last analysis, the Union is for him simply a textual and institutional trace of something more basic – albeit for 300 years a vital trace, perhaps even a lifeline – and it is this more basic and resilient sense of a culturally framed collective political potential that he wants to put at the centre of constitutional debate.

D. THE FUTURE OF POLITICAL NATIONALISM

Earlier it was remarked that the old binary opposition between nationalism and unionism is at last beginning to break down in mainstream Scottish constitutional debate, and it was suggested that the contribution of Neil MacCormick has been an important catalyst in this transformation. In his last years, Neil MacCormick acted as an advisor to the SNP leader Alex Salmond following the historical moment in 2007 when Salmond became the first nationalist First Minister of Scotland. So MacCormick was well placed to

---

76 See e.g. MacCormick, *Sovereignty in Question* (n 1) 55, 130.
77 MacCormick, *Sovereignty in Question* 60.

influence the development of SNP constitutional policy at the dawning of a new political age. In particular, MacCormick's post-sovereign thinking on the detail and trajectory of political nationalism left a significant mark on the key document, *Choosing Scotland's Future*,[78] through which the SNP launched the so-called "national conversation" after their 2007 victory.

Of course, MacCormick did not live to witness the SNP's second and greater electoral triumph in 2011, nor to advise how the constitutional agenda should be adjusted and advanced according to its new position of strength as the party with an overall majority in the Scottish Parliament. Certainly, however, he would have recognised many of the signals to emerge from the new SNP administration and their supporters in 2011 as echoing and building on the earlier policy document to which he had contributed so much. He would also have noted that in 2011 the SNP commitment to a non-fundamentalist conception of independence was tending to be more broadly and more loudly articulated and to generate far more publicity than it had done four years earlier.[79] In large part, no doubt, this was because the SNP's newly found electoral advantage was concentrating the minds of supporters and opponents alike on political independence as a plausible medium-term scenario rather than simply a distant ambition or a remote threat. More pointedly, from the SNP's own perspective, the obstinate gap between its electoral success and the ambivalence or hostility of many of its supporters towards a robust version of independence[80] has made it ever more a priority, as it moves towards its promised commitment to a referendum in the second half of the current Parliament, to underline the extent to which its policy on independence is continuous with constitutional positions with which many of its voters feel more familiar and comfortable.

If we consult the MacCormick-inspired *Choosing Scotland's Future* as the most considered statement to date of the revisionist position, we can discern a dual emphasis on structural and cultural elements of continuity. Structurally, reflecting MacCormick's view of the obsolescence of sovereignty, emphasis is placed on the inevitability of continued international interdependence even if and when formal international legal sovereignty and the independent title in external affairs that accompanies this are obtained. In particular the power-sharing implications are stressed of continued membership of the EU and of

78 *Choosing Scotland's Future: A National Conversation* (2007).

79 In particular, in the immediate aftermath of the election victory on 5 May, many figures within the SNP began to flirt publicly with ideas of "independence-lite", including even the traditionally fundamentalist Jim Sillars; see "Politics of the possible replaces politics of perfection" *The Scotsman*, 14 May 2011

80 For discussion, see M Keating, *The Independence of Scotland* (n 5) 71-77.

participation in other key global organisations such as the Commonwealth, the World Health Organization, the Organisation of Economic Cooperation and Development, and the World Trade Organization.[81] More tellingly, even within the British Isles, the policy document is at pains to emphasis the continuity of SNP policy with certain lateral constitutional initiatives of recent years. Both the Joint Ministerial Committee framework, which presently provides a mechanism for the various governments of the United Kingdom to work together, and the British-Irish Council, established in 1998 under the auspices of the Good Friday Agreement as a co-operative body for all the executives of the two states, are endorsed as models to be retained and built upon as vital confederal supports for a newly independent Scotland rather than rejected as relics of an outmoded settlement.[82] Perhaps most striking, however, is the retention of the language, and indeed upper case of Unionism. "The current parliamentary and political Union ... would become a monarchical and social Union – United Kingdoms rather than a United Kingdom – maintaining a relationship first forged in 1603 by the Union of the Crowns"[83] and the close intermeshing of various policy areas, in particular those aspects of economic and monetary policy governed or influenced by EU membership, is also emphasised.[84] This policy convergence has been further reinforced since the 2011 election, with the prospect being aired of continued close collaboration across the United Kingdoms not only on a generous range of economic matters but also on many areas of security and defence policy and capacity.[85]

Of course, as much of the early response on all sides to the efforts of the SNP to reposition itself after the 2011 election demonstrates, the old ideological tramlines that set nationalism in rigid opposition to unionism are not so easily overcome.[86] There remains a powerful reductive tendency within our political culture, one that dismisses any effort to reframe independence as a matter of more-or-less, as a series of points on a continuum, as simply incoherent, or that seeks to force new positions back into old categories. This kind of reaction can in turn be criticised as cheap political point-scoring, as betraying a lack of imagination, or as displaying a willful blindness before the growing complexities of an interdependent globe. Whatever the motivations for the critique of new forms of political nationalism, however, the question

81 *Choosing Scotland's Future* (n 78) ch 3.
82 *Choosing Scotland's Future* ch 4.
83 *Choosing Scotland's Future* para 3.25.
84 *Choosing Scotland's Future* para 3.25.
85 See, for example, J Mitchell, "Breaking up has become less easy", *The Scotsman* 20 May 2011.
86 Mitchell, "Breaking up has become less easy" (n 85).

of the coherence of the new tendency remains, and the original puzzle of reconciling the different strands of MacCormick's thought returns. Even – indeed, especially – if earlier and more fundamental conceptions of political nationalism are superannuated, how can we square the circle of a liberal political nationalism in a post-sovereign world, and how can we do so in ways that, accord due recognition to the legacy of unionist thought?

The way forward, which is at least implicit in MacCormick's own work, would seem to involve contemplating the mental map of nationalism with a new key. More particularly, it depends upon moving from what we might call a teleological to a reflexive conception of political nationalism. Under the historically dominant teleological conception, political nationalism, conceived of as an active and ongoing project, is typically evaluated, whether positively or negatively, in terms of its relationship to a determinate set of ends associated with the classical form of sovereign independence. So political nationalism may be praised, or may be criticised, for its aspirational quality, its measures short of full independence treated as mere staging-posts towards the ultimate goal. Or, as we have seen in many of the recent reactions to the change of emphasis in the SNP, it may be praised, or it may be criticised, as a form of "independence-lite" – as an approach defined simply in terms of a curtailment of earlier ambition, a refocusing on objectives that fall short of a determinate set of ends associated with full independence. Or, as a variation on these two themes, as Drew Scott points out in his contribution to the present volume, political nationalism may invite scepticism for revealing an "asymptotic" quality, as describing a line that is fated never to reach the destination towards which it tends. On this view, political nationalism is presented as an absolute discourse to prosecute a non-absolute strategy, but one whose impossibility or absence of conviction is exposed the closer it gets to its goal. This very idea of asymptotic nationalism remains in negative thrall to an idea of political nationalism, teleologically conceived. For it only makes sense as a critique of the corruption of nationalism so defined, whether an aspirational nationalism that has come to lack the courage of its convictions, or a form of independence-lite – or an even lesser devolved creature – that seeks to permanently defer its fuller realisation and so deflect the modesty of its ambition.

A reflexive nationalism, by contrast, is one that is by its nature self-referential, an iterative achievement in which consequences repeatedly feed back into developmental causes. More specifically, it has a number of key attributes. First, and negatively, it does not possess a teleological character. It is not judged as inauthentic or strategically inept for its failure to specify or to pursue a utopian end state as its ultimate objective, nor dismissed as unsuccessful for not achieving such an end state. Instead, as with the Union state, but measured against a wider horizon of possibilities, its goals are viewed as provisional rather than final, cumulative rather than predetermined. Secondly, reflexive nationalism presupposes an internal duality – a subject as well as an object. The project of political nationalism is not just about the specification and achievement of a certain objective state of affairs, but about the ongoing relationship between a collective subject – a putative "people", and a set of political institutions and goals. Thirdly, reflexive nationalism, in consequence, emphasises process over substance. Political nationalism does not, on this view, imply a right to any particular outcome, but a standing entitlement to forms of procedural consideration that allow the nationalist cause to be take seriously and, if certain conditions of support and respect for others are met, to be given institutional form. And just as outcomes favourable to the nationalist cause are not guaranteed, so, too, occasional failure or frustration of the nationalist project do not exhaust the underlying procedural right.

Many elements of MacCormick's approach chime closely with this kind of reflexive attitude. His own shifting views on the essential desirability and optimal form of independence, as well as his attraction to the kind of flexible and gradualist development he could see at least modestly reflected in the Union state, speak to a non-teleological approach. His belief in an underlying cultural imagining of popular sovereignty allows him the means to contemplate and appreciate an ongoing relationship between subject and object. His support for and consistent interest in investigating and charting consent-based, co-operative and constitutionally recognised methods of pursuing the nationalist cause as the only and always available such methods, whether through constitutional conventions, referenda, or intra-state and international negotiation, speak to his deep commitment to a process-based conception of nationalism.[87]

Of course, MacCormick's has been by no means a lone voice in this shift, and the SNP is far from the only movement to take seriously this more reflexive conception of nationalism. Indeed, many nationalist and autonomist parties in Europe and elsewhere can reasonably claim to have developed momentum behind this more nuanced approach considerably in advance of their Scottish counterparts.[88] And if we move beyond internal constitutional

---

87 See e.g. N MacCormick "Is there a constitutional path to Scottish independence?" (2000) 53 *Parliamentary Affairs* 721-736.
88 For discussion see e.g. M Keating, *Plurinational Democracy: Stateless Nations in a Post-Sovereignty Era* (2001).

debate to consider the perspectives of international law, and of transnational law more generally, on the question of self-determination, this kind
of process-based approach has also attracted increasing support in recent
years as a new template for change in which internal and external processes
feed off each other.[89] Neil MacCormick, nonetheless, remains a key figure for
the Scottish as well as the wider global cause of nationalism. Unlike many,
he is explicit in his dismissal of a categorical status of sovereignty for the
modern age, and so committed in principle to a more modulated approach.
Unlike many, he neither fetishises nor dismisses the underlying notion of
"popular sovereignty" which drives the process of nationalism. Rather, he
treats this as a shifting, sometimes precarious but always ethically relevant
set of cultural attitudes and possibilities, both acting upon and acted upon
by the institutional forms of nationalist achievement. And unlike many, his
sense of the procedural pathways of reflexive nationalism is informed by deep
liberal sensibilities, by the firm belief that liberalism, operating in a gradualist
manner, must respect and balance all reasonable conceptions of the kind
of collective political autonomy, whether Scottish or British nationalist, or
indeed whether or not primarily national in conception at all, within which
individual autonomy thrives.[90]

So significantly and so sympathetically is it conditioned by his liberalism and his post-sovereignty, indeed, that we are bound to conclude that
MacCormick's brand of political nationalism, notwithstanding his own final
preference for a form of independent statehood,[91] could not as a matter of
principle be *necessarily* either for or against the Union state. Rather, it must
locate itself on an unpredictable trajectory along a continuum that straddles
that distinction and divide. MacCormick's depiction of political nationalism,
then, is one of an unsettled state, one ill-defined within our existing political
and constitutional vocabulary. For some, this will be an unsettling conclusion.
But, as I think Neil MacCormick would agree, it is the price we are bound
to pay for continuing to take nationalist beliefs and aspirations seriously in a
world much and irrevocably altered from that in which the modern idea of
the nation first emerged as a relevant framework for a state-centred conception of political community.

---

89 See e.g. C Bell, *On The Law of Peace: Peace Agreements and the Lex Pacificatoria* (2008); J
    Klabbers, "The right to be taken seriously: self-determination in international law" (2006) 28
    Human Rights Quarterly 186-206.
90 MacCormick, *Questioning Sovereignty* (n 1) ch 12.
91 MacCormick, *Questioning Sovereignty* ch 12.

8 Stateless Nations in the European Union: Two Cheers Not Three

Joanne Scott°

A. INTRODUCTION
B. STATELESS NATIONS AND THE CONSTITUTIONAL CONVENTION
C. JUDICIAL DEVELOPMENTS
D. CONCLUSION

A. INTRODUCTION

Overall, this Draft Constitution ... represents a robustly statist, and to that extent, confederalist, vision of the Union. It is a Union whose powers are conferred upon it by Member States whose internal constitutional arrangements remain entirely their own affair. To the extent that these arrangements empower stateless nations or other territorial collectivities in the form of legislative or administrative regions, the Union's institutions are obliged to take account of these, and of local authorities as well. Linguistic and cultural diversity is more generously recognized than hitherto. Subsidiarity is better defined and will probably be better policed and observed. This is worth two cheers, if not yet the full three.[1]

Neil MacCormick was a committed Scottish nationalist and a committed European. It was not simply that he did not see a contradiction between the two, but that his vision of Europe was such that he believed it could nourish rather than diminish the sub-state sphere. Neil's was an optimistic vision of the EU "commonwealth", but, as we will see below, it was an optimism that was not born only of conceptual clarity but of active engagement in the process of political change.

Neil's understanding of the EU took us "[b]eyond the sovereign state".[2] He accepted the EU as constituting a distinct legal and, indeed, constitutional order that encroached upon both the internal and external sovereignty of the

---

° Professor of European Law, University College London.
1 N MacCormick, "The European Constitutional Convention and the stateless nations" (2004) 18 *International Relations* 331 at 342-343.
2 N MacCormick, *Questioning Sovereignty* (1999) 131.

member states. What he did not accept was that the once-upon-a-time sovereignty of the member states had been ceded *en bloc* to the EU as a hierarchically superior all-powerful super-state. Neil's vision was much more subtle and complex, and it rested upon the often controversial idea that ultimate power, both legal and political, could be, and indeed had been, shared.

For Neil, post-sovereignty was liberating in its implications for "stateless nations",[3] as well as for administrative regions and localities, within existing member states. Pluralism need not stop at the parcelling-out of power between the EU and the member states, but could be generalised and extended to imply also a diffusion of authority below the level of the state.[4] Henceforth,

> [c]hoices between claims of different nations can cease to be choices between rival claims to sovereign statehood … [and] become choices about allocation of levels of political authority within a transnational commonwealth embracing many nationalities and cultural traditions or groupings.[5]

In this way subsidiarity, or level of governance, questions become key.

Subsidiarity requires that "a given public question should be vested in agencies as close to the persons affected as is compatible with acceptable degrees of efficiency and equity".[6] And according to this understanding, subsidiarity is capable of empowering communities constituted at a level below an individual member state. As such, given full and proper expression, subsidiarity is a powerful sword against an over-reaching EU *and* against an over-reaching member state. It can help to guard against "monolithic democracy" or the silencing of peoples under the ideological banner of the so-called nation state.[7] As such, the EU can be viewed as a friend to the politics of identity and to the sub-state (liberal) nationalism to which this may give rise. "The emergent picture is of Europe as a confederation of confederations [or a commonwealth of commonwealths] together with smaller unitary member states of a more homogenous kind".[8]

3 See MacCormick, "The European Constitutional Convention" (n 1) 339 for a discussion of this concept. See also Neil's written contribution to the Convention on the Future of Europe entitled "Stateless nations and the Convention's debate on regions" (CONV 525/03 ANEXO). In this, Neil points out that there are "quite a few nations within states in Europe, many of which possess important institutions of state and display considerable historical continuity", and that in these stateless nations, "the citizens generally consider that their nations are entitled to parity of esteem with others of similar size" (3). He contrasts these stateless nations (or constitutional regions) with regions that are administrative in character, and that do not self-identify as nations.
4 MacCormick, *Questioning Sovereignty* (n 2) 135.
5 MacCormick, *Questioning Sovereignty* 191.
6 MacCormick, "The European Constitutional Convention" (n 1) 335.
7 See MacCormick, *Questioning Sovereignty* (n 2) 134 by way of example.
8 MacCormick, *Questioning Sovereignty* 194.

B. STATELESS NATIONS AND THE CONSTITUTIONAL CONVENTION

If Neil had a worked-out vision of Europe and a strongly held conviction in relation to it, he was anything but complacent in pursuit of this goal. He became a Member of the European Parliament for the Scottish National Party in 1999, and in this capacity was a member of the Convention on the Future of Europe during 2002-2003. As Neil himself observed, he was the only elected representative on the Convention in a specifically "civic nationalist" or "regionalist" guise,[9] and he worked closely with colleagues from the European Free Alliance in developing his contributions to the process of drafting a constitution for Europe.[10]

A quick glance at Neil's contribution to the Convention process is enough to be awed by the breadth and depth of his engagement. His impressive written contributions[11] were accompanied by eighty proposals for amendments to the text.[12] While some operated at the level of high politics, others were technical and detailed and demonstrated a remarkable mastery of many complex areas of contention and debate.

To give just one example that will become relevant to the discussion below; acting alone, Neil suggested an amendment to Article I-12 specifying the competences of the Union. He proposed to delete the phrase that sought to confer exclusive competence to the Union in respect of the conservation of marine biological resources under the common fisheries policy.[13] He argued,

9 MacCormick, "The European Constitutional Convention" (n 1) 336.
10 The EFA is a European political party in the European Parliament constituted as an alliance of regionalist and civic nationalist democratic parties. See: *http://www.e-f-a.org/home.php.* (accessed 25 July 2011.) It stands for the idea of "a true decentralised Europe taking subsidiarity and diversity serious[ly]".
11 Neil made fourteen written contributions, three of them authored by him alone. See "Subsidiarity, common sense and local knowledge" (CONV 275/02), "Stateless nations and the Convention's debate on regions" (CONV 525/03), "Democracy at many levels: European constitutional reform" (CONV 298/02). Other co-authored contributions concerned matters as diverse as environment, the protection of minorities, various aspects of institutional and constitutional reform, transparency and subsidiarity. For the texts of these see the Convention website at: *http://european-convention. eu.int/search.asp?lang=EN* (accessed 25 July 2011) and search under "MacCormick".
12 Neil submitted eighty proposals for amendments to the text of the draft constitution, thirteen of which were authored by Neil alone. These eighty amendments covered an extraordinary array of issues, ranging from the composition and functioning of the EU institutions, EU competence (including in relation to foreign direct investment, for example), the future of Euratom, transparency, subsidiarity, democracy, citizenship, and so the list could go on. See the Convention website (n 11).
13 This was just one of several amendments proposed by Neil in the area of fisheries. He was concerned that the equation of agriculture and fisheries in the treaties failed to acknowledge the specific characteristics of the fishing industry and in particular the fact that it exists only in certain member states, and is as such "strongly regional in its economic and social relevance" (see Suggestion for amendment of Article III-116 (new)).

in keeping with his vision set out above, that "there needs to be much greater decentralisation of the governance of fisheries and marine resources", and that a change of this kind taken with no serious discussion and in a forum in which only a minority of members represents any significant interest or experience of fisheries would lack warrant. In a manner that was both impressive and entirely typical, Neil combined astute legal and political analysis.

Of course, ultimately the Treaty Establishing a Constitution for Europe failed. But its legacy and Neil's legacy within the Convention process remain. The Treaty of Lisbon, which entered into force in 2009, may have eschewed the imprimatur of a constitution, but it incorporated important aspects of the Convention's constitutional text, including in relation to "regions" and stateless nations in the EU.

For example, article 3(3) of the Treaty on the European Union now requires that the European Union respects its rich cultural and linguistic diversity and ensures that Europe's cultural heritage is safeguarded and enhanced. This emphasis on cultural and linguistic diversity, previously confined to the EC Treaty chapter on education (art 149 EC), is a direct result of several amendments proposed by Neil MacCormick, among others.[14] Neil recalled the moment when he challenged the Convention President's dismissal of the notion of encouraging more and more languages in the EU, by pointing out that "we were not seeking to multiply languages but to get fair recognition of the existing languages and the existing linguistic diversity of Europe".[15] "I think", Neil told us, "that was the moment when the point was won".[16]

Also practically and symbolically important are the changes introduced by the Lisbon Treaty to the subsidiarity principle; changes that have their origins in the language of the Convention's constitutional text. The very definition of this principle has been imbued with a strong sub-state theme. Henceforth, EU-level action can only be justified where the objectives of the proposed action cannot be sufficiently achieved by member states, acting "either at a central level or at regional or local scale".[17] While this version of subsidiarity does not regulate the exercise of power by the member states, it does take an important first step in recognising the downwards diffusion of political power within member states and the implications of this for the exercise of competence by the EU.

---

14 See Suggestions for amendment of Article 3(3) and Suggestion for amendment of Article 2.
15 See Suggestions for amendment of Article 3(3) and Suggestion for amendment of Article 2.
16 See Suggestions for amendment of Article 3(3) and Suggestion for amendment of Article 2.
17 Article 5(3) EU (formerly art 5 EC). This wording is the same as that proposed by art III-9 of the Treaty Establishing a Constitution for Europe. This change incorporates the substance of the proposed amendment put forward by Neil in respect of art 8(3).

This is further reflected in the revised Protocol on Subsidiarity and Proportionality, which is now binding on the institutions of the EU.[18] The revised version included in the Lisbon Treaty was drafted during the Constitutional Convention, and Neil played an important role.[19] The revised protocol provides a monitoring mechanism that places "national" (meaning member state) parliaments at centre stage. It will be for the member state Parliaments (capital P) to consult, "where appropriate, regional parliaments [small p] with legislative powers".[20] But in consulting on legislative proposals, the Commission will be obliged to take into account the regional and local dimension of its proposed action,[21] and draft legislation must be accompanied by an assessment of the proposal's financial impact and take account of the need for any burden falling on regional or local authorities to be minimised or at any rate commensurate with the objective to be achieved.[22] Draft legislation in the form of a directive should also be accompanied by an assessment of its implications for the rules to be put in place by member states, including where necessary by regional legislation.[23]

Though Neil was equivocal about the role of the Committee of the Regions, believing that its membership must be based on regions not states,[24] he nonetheless viewed the new powers of the Committee to challenge subsidiarity-infringing legislation before the European Court as constituting a gain.[25] It remained a matter of regret that neither regions nor other territorial entities, including stateless nations, were granted comparable access to the European Court.[26]

C. JUDICIAL DEVELOPMENTS

If the Constitutional Treaty, and ultimately the Treaty of Lisbon, lend some support to Neil's pluralist, multi-level vision of the EU, Neil was equally clear that in important ways they fell short. As he put it in the quotation at the start

---

18 Article 5(3) EU.
19 See in particular Neil's contributions listed at n 11 above.
20 Article 6 of the Protocol on the application of the principles of subsidiarity and proportionality.
21 Article 2 of the Protocol on the application of the principles of subsidiarity and proportionality.
22 Article 5 of the Protocol on the application of the principles of subsidiarity and proportionality.
23 Article 5 of the Protocol on the application of the principles of subsidiarity and proportionality.
24 MacCormick, "The European Constitutional Convention" (n 1) 340.
25 MacCormick, "The European Constitutional Convention" 341.
26 See Suggestion for amendment of Protocol on Subsidiarity, para 8 (MacCormick, Voggenhuber, Lichtenberger) where it was suggested that they should also be entitled to challenge subsidiarity-infringing legislation, subject to their being authorised by the relevant member state. I return again to the theme of standing below.

of this piece, the Draft Constitution merits only two cheers and not more. It is important, however, not to isolate formal treaty-building and amendment processes from EU law and politics as a whole. Elsewhere, and notably at the hands of the European Court, we have seen shifts in the EU's constitutional self-understanding that add substance to his post-sovereign vision which is premised upon a parcelling-out of power both above and beyond the state.[27] This is entirely in keeping with Neil's own perception that improvement would more likely be achieved by "further tinkering and marginal adjustment, than by an attempt at grand re-design and comprehensive constitution-making".[28]

Two recent cases before the European Court stand out as marking a new appreciation of the role and standing of stateless nations or regions.

The first is the *Hovarth* case involving the implementation of agricultural policy in England and Wales.[29] In order to be eligible for direct payments under various income support schemes, farmers are required to maintain their land in "good agricultural and environmental condition" (GAEC). Member states enjoy some discretion in determining what this entails. In the UK, different rules were elaborated in England and Scotland, with the former imposing additional conditions regarding the maintenance of public rights of way. These stricter English standards were challenged by an English farmer who argued, among other things, that the resulting differential treatment of farmers in these different parts of a single member state amounted to a form of discrimination that should be viewed as contrary to EU law.

This was in keeping with previous judgments of the European Court, where it had held that where there is a choice between a number of different ways of implementing EU legislation, member states may not choose an option that is liable to result in discrimination between producers within that member state.[30] However, in the *Hovarth* case, the ECJ back-tracked. Where devolved administrations enjoy the power to implement EU law,[31] and where divergences between the measures adopted by the various administrations emerge, these divergences "cannot, alone, constitute discrimination".[32]

---

27 For a good recent overview and more detailed discussion of these issues see J Hunt, "Devolution and differentiation: regional variation in EU law" (2010) 30 *Legal Studies* 421.

28 N MacCormick, "Democracy, subsidiarity and citizenship in the EU" (1997) 16(4) *Law and Philosophy* 331-356 at 355.

29 See Case C-428/07 R v *Secretary of State for the Environment, Food and Rural Affairs ex parte Hovarth* [2009] ECR I-6355 18.

30 See in particular Joined Cases 201/85 and 202/85 *Klensch and Others v Secrétaire d' Etat* [1986] ECR 3477.

31 In ascertaining the scope of the powers of the devolved administrations, the Court referred implicitly to the Scotland Act 1998 and to the "Memorandum of Understanding" accompanying this which is regarded as a complementary statement of political intent.

32 R v *Secretary of State for the Environment, Food and Rural Affairs ex parte Hovarth* (n 29) para 57.

This finding is of especial importance because of the increasing tendency of the EU to enact open-ended framework norms.[33] Gone on the whole is the vision of the EU as "harmonising" national laws and as an agent of transformation privileging market-driven likeness at the expense of diversity in all its shades. Detailed legislative prescription has given way to framework norms and exhaustive harmonisation is less favoured than minimum harmonisation today. In this situation, the question of where responsibility for implementing EU legislation lies within a member state assumes great importance, as does the issue of the extent to which there may be legitimate differences in approach.

The second case concerns the powers of the Autonomous Portuguese region of the Azores.[34] The Azores region chose to adopt a tax regime that served to reduce the tax burden on all economic operators within its territory. Despite its generality, and the absence of specific advantage for particular firms, the Commission found that this regional tax regime constituted a state aid within the meaning of article 107 TFEU (formerly article 87 EC). Critical to the Commission's conclusion was its finding that, where tax measures of this kind do not *extend to the entire territory of a member state*, they will be viewed as favouring certain undertakings and consequently as meeting the selectivity threshold for state aids. The Commission rejected Portugal's argument that benefits of limited territorial scope become "general measures" when they are adopted by a regional authority and apply throughout the entire territory of the region concerned.[35] On the contrary, the Commission found that in view of the "fundamental role the central authorities of the Member States play in defining the political and economic environment in which undertakings operate", the point of reference for assessing whether a measure is general or selective is that of the entire member state.

However, the European Court did not agree. Adopting a perspective that is much more attuned to the reality of diffuse power, the Court found that where an "infra-state" or sub-state body enjoys a legal or factual status which makes it sufficiently autonomous from the central government of the member state, it is this infra-state body that should be viewed as playing a fundamental role in the definition of the political and economic environment in which undertakings operate.[36] As such, it is the area of operation of this infra-state body that should be viewed as constituting the territorial point of reference for assessing whether or not economic aid serves to favour certain undertakings. This is subject to the condition that the central government

33 R v *Secretary of State for the Environment, Food and Rural Affairs ex parte Hovarth* (n 29).
34 Case C-88/03 *Portugal v Commission* [2006] ECR I-7115.
35 *Portugal v Commission* para 23.
36 *Portugal v Commission* para 58.

in question is not able to intervene directly in shaping the content of the economic aid in question, and to the requirement that the financial consequences of the economic aid are not offset by aid or subsidies from elsewhere within that member state.[37]

While in this case, the regional tax reduction was found to have been offset by centrally managed fiscal transfers and hence as nonetheless constituting state aid, results more favourable to sub-state authorities have subsequently been achieved elsewhere. This has been the case for the government of Gibraltar for example,[38] where even the fact that the United Kingdom government retains a residual power of last resort to legislate for Gibraltar was not enough to stand in the way of a finding that it is sufficiently politically autonomous to act as the point of reference for assessing the selectivity of economic aid. The European Court emphasised here that this residual legislative power has been exercised only exceptionally, and even then never in relation to taxation. "No United Kingdom law in respect of fiscal matters applies, or has ever applied, to Gibraltar".[39]

Each of these two cases represents an important step in recognising the policy autonomy of stateless nations or regions within EU member states. Whereas the former acknowledges regulatory autonomy in the implementation of EU law, the latter provides additional freedom to distribute economic aid in a manner that is distinct and independent from the economic or fiscal policies of the member state. They attest to an important shift in the jurisprudence of the European Courts and offer support for Neil's vision that there is nothing inherent in the concept of the European Union that would lead it to suppress a vibrant local politics below.

I want to conclude, however, by discussing a case that would offer support for Neil's overall conclusion that while good progress has been made, ultimately the EU still falls short. Two cheers not three. This is a case that was decided on appeal by the European Court some months after Neil died, and it is (I think) a case that would have disappointed him in many different respects. It is a case about fisheries and it is testimony to Neil, as that rare legal theorist, that he would nonetheless (or therefore) have been engaged!

In a different case from the state aids case highlighted above, the Autonomous Region of the Azores brought an action for judicial review to challenge

---

37 *Portugal v Commission* para 67.
38 Case T-211/04 *Government of Gibraltar v Commission* [2008] ECR II-3745. See also Joined Cases C-428/06 and C434/06 *Union General de Trabajadores de La Rioja* (UGT-Rioja) [2008] ECR I-6747.
39 Case T-211/04 *Government of Gibraltar v Commission* para 95.

the legality of an EU fisheries regulation.[40] The Azores is an autonomous region of Portugal which has legal personality under Portuguese law and significant legislative power, including in relation to fisheries. The Azores is also classified as one of the "outermost" regions of the EU.

In this case, the Azores alleged that the contested regulation would lead to an increase in the fishing effort for deep-sea species in the waters of the Azores and that it would in addition permit trawling, including bottom-trawling, for the first time. It also argued that the result of the regulation would be to open up the waters of the Azores beyond 100 nm to Spanish vessels fishing for tuna, and that moreover it would create a legal vacuum for a period during which there would no restrictions on fishing in the waters off the Azores. All in all, the applicants alleged that the contested regulation would lead to the removal of too many fish and to the rapid and irreversible depletion of fish stocks.[41] They argued further that it would generate significant collateral environmental damage, by destroying the seabed, reefs and coral, and lead also to the collapse of local industry in the Azores, which is highly dependent on fishing.

The Council, supported by the Commission and Spain, raised a plea of admissibility that was upheld by both the Court of First Instance (now the General Court) and the European Court.[42] The ECJ stated that an action brought by a regional or local entity cannot be treated in the same way as an action brought by a member state. To do so would risk undermining the institutional balance provided by the Treaty.[43] Moreover, "the nature of the harm purportedly suffered by the [region or locality] can have no bearing on whether the [region or locality] is individually concerned by the provisions which it seeks to annul".[44] Even where the contested regulation falls within the scope of a regional or local authorities powers under national

40 Case T-37/04 *Região autónoma dos Açores v Council* [2008] ECR II-103° and on appeal Case C-444/08P [2009] ECR I-00200. The contested measure was Regulation 1954/2003. For an overview of the grounds raised, see the Order of the President of the Court of First Instance in respect of the application for interim measures, [2004] ECR II-2153.

41 The best overview of the legal and factual background to this case is provided by the President of the Court of First Instance in his Order on interim measures. On the alleged factual consequences, see especially paras 85-89.

42 In the application for interim relief, the President of the Court of First Instance found that there were serious doubts as to whether the applicant was individually concerned, it could not be excluded that the Region of Azores would be affected by the contested measure in a different manner than the other outermost regions, and therefore he declined to dismiss the application for interim measures on the basis of inadmissibility alone (see Case T- 37/04 Order of the President of the Court of First Instance [2004] ECR II-2153, paras 121-125).

43 Case C-444/08 (n 40) para 31.

44 Case C-444/08 para 45.

constitutional law, "national constitutional rules which confer powers cannot determine the standing of regional bodies to bring proceedings".[45]

The European Court's judgment suggests that there may be two situations in which the nature of the regional authority's legislative powers may have a bearing on standing in such a case. First, where that authority enjoys powers that have been conferred by EU law, and where these powers are subsequently reduced by the contested act, the regional authority may enjoy standing to bring an action in judicial review.[46] Second, where the regional authority has adopted a specific legislative measure while acting within the scope of its own powers, the validity of which is called into question by the contested act, again the regional authority may enjoy standing to sue.[47] Outside these narrowly drawn situations, and regardless of the factual impact of EU law, the voice of administrative regions and stateless nations will be silenced in the European courts.

There is one additional question highlighted, if only indirectly, by the Azores case. This concerns the entitlement of sub-state actors, including administrative regions and stateless nations, to invoke safeguard powers conferred by EU law. In an Order refusing to partially suspend the operation of the EU's new fisheries regime, the President of the Court of First Instance addressed the question of whether interim relief was required to prevent serious and irreparable damage arising.[48] He concluded that it was not. He did so on the basis that the interim measures requested were not

> necessary to avoid damage to the marine ecosystem from materializing within the relevant timeframe given that there are several other more proportionate and appropriate avenues … which can be pursued rapidly and effectively to address such damage".[49]

45　Case C-444/08 para 63.

46　Case C-444/08 para 62, where the ECJ notes that the relevant EU legislation only confers power on the member states.

47　Case C-444/08 para 65. Here the ECJ seems to confirm the case law of the CFI (now the General Court) in Case T-214/95 *Het Vlaamse Gewest v Commission* [1998] ECR II-717 and Joined Cases T-366/03 and T-235/05 *Land Oberosterreich and Austria v Commission* [2005] ECR II-4005. In the former case, the Flemish Region challenged a Commission decision that was addressed to Belgium, but which found that a loan granted by the Flemish Region contravened EU rules on state aid. In the Austrian case, the Austrian Region was the author of the act that was impugned by the EU measure it contested in the case. The issue of standing was not addressed by the ECJ in the appeal in the Austrian case (Joined Cases C-439/05P and C-454/05P [2007] ECR I-7141) though as K Lenaerts notes, the ECJ could have raised the admissibility issue of its own motion (see his "Access of regions with legislative powers to the European Court of Justice", on file with the author). The implication of the Azores case is that there must be a specific act adopted by the regional authority in question, and that it is not enough to confer standing that the contested EU measure prevents the region in question from exercising the powers conferred upon it by the member state constitution (see para 28 of the CFI judgment, Case T-37/04 (n 40)).

48　Case T- 37/04 Order of the President of the Court of First Instance (n 42) para 140.

49　Case T- 37/04 Order of the President of the Court of First Instance para 157.

The other avenues that he had in mind were the safeguard clauses included in the EU fisheries regime. These permit the adoption of emergency measures where there is evidence of a serious threat to the conservation of living marine resources or to the marine eco-system resulting from fishing activities and requiring immediate action.[50] The President observed that "the applicant has taken no action in order to secure any such measures",[51] pointing also to evidence suggesting that the Commission would be unlikely to object to the adoption of such measures.[52] Given the availability of these alternative avenues, the requested interim measures were not regarded as necessary by the President of the court.

What is striking about this discussion is the absence of any reflection on the fact that safeguard clauses may only be invoked by member states. There is nothing in the language of the specific clauses included in legislation or in the general clauses set out in the TFEU to suggest that they may also be invoked by sub-state authorities within the member states.[53] As Jo Hunt has recently observed, the power to exercise the art 95 EC (now art 114 TFEU) safeguard clause is reserved to member states.[54] It would be up to the legal order of an individual member state to decide how to treat requests for derogations from EU law emanating from an administrative region or stateless nation within that member state. Yet there is no discussion of this issue by the President of the CFI in the Azores fisheries case, a fact that is all the more striking given that the interests of Portugal and the interests of the Azores did not wholly coincide in the circumstances of this case.[55]

In the context of Scotland within the UK, the issue is addressed in the Concordat on Co-ordination of European Union Policy Issues.[56] While, in keeping with the statist nature of the EU framework, this provides that requests for derogation emanating from Scotland will be routed through the UK Permanent Representative's office in Brussels, involving the lead Whitehall authority as required, there is equally no suggestion that any such

---

50 Case T- 37/04 Order of the President of the Court of First Instance para 158. See in particular arts 7 and 8 of Regulation 2371/2002 (the base regulation).

51 Case T- 37/04 Order of the President of the Court of First Instance para 159.

52 Case T- 37/04 Order of the President of the Court of First Instance para 161. The CFI President also suggested that it was unlikely that the Commission would fail to intervene itself if this were necessary to prevent damage.

53 See especially art 114 TFEU (formerly art 95 EC).

54 Hunt, "Devolution and differentiation" (n 27) 438.

55 One result of the new fishing regime is that the access to Azorean waters of Portuguese vessels not registered in the Azores or traditionally fishing there would be improved.

56 See B-1 (Scotland) at *http://www.ofmdfmni.gov.uk/memorandum_of_understanding_and_ concordate_on_co-ordination_of_eu_issues_-_march_2010.pdf*, accessed 25 July 2011. See in particular B4.19.

Scottish request may be blocked at this stage. The lawfulness of any attempt to do so would depend ultimately on the interpretation of the Scotland Act 1998, and of the scope of the UK's reserved powers.[57] The relevant part of the act provides that "Foreign affairs etc" are reserved matters. While this is stated to include international relations, including relations with the EU, it does not extend to "observing and implementing international obligations" including obligations arising under EU law.[58] It is certainly possible to argue that a decision by Scotland to seek to rely on an EU safeguard clause with a view to justifying stricter protective measures as a matter of EU law should be construed as pertaining to the observance and implementation of EU law, and hence as falling within the scope of its devolved powers. That said, in the event that the UK government were to refuse to act as a conduit for the submission of any such Scottish request, it seems unlikely that the Commission would be willing to liaise directly, and accept the petition of the Scottish government instead. Ultimately, in this regard, it is probably the Concordat rather than the constitutional framework of the EU that protects the interests of Scotland as a stateless nation in the EU.

D. CONCLUSION

Neil MacCormick was one of the first legal theorists to accord serious attention to the EU. It is only in re-reading his work that one comes to appreciate just how many of the key ideas that we take for granted today have their origin in arguments that he developed or applied. Neil offered to us, first during a lecture I organised in London, a vision of the EU as a commonwealth, supported by the existence of a common weal, based not on ethnic association but a product of deliberation in Europe's organised political space.[59] Neil MacCormick has been an inspirational figure for me ever since that day, and at a distance he also became a friend. He was one of the only legal theorists I have known who was as happy discussing the intricacies of the Water Framework Directive as he was theorising about European constitutional law. With his passing, we have lost an extraordinary scholar, and an extraordinarily kind man.

---

57 See Sched 5 of the Scotland Act 1998. Note, though, that the Concordat requires the devolved administration to consult with the lead Whitehall department (and vice versa) in relation to any such request, to ascertain whether there are wider UK policy implications. The clear hope is that any disagreements can be resolved through consultation at this stage.
58 See Sched 5, s 7 of the Scotland Act 1998.
59 See N MacCormick, *Questioning Sovereignty* (n 2) ch 9.

The Scottish Public Intellectual

9 Neil MacCormick: Public Intellectual

Drew Scott°

A. INTRODUCTION

For this volume I was invited to consider Neil's contribution to Scottish public life. Undoubtedly Neil made a range of important and distinguished contributions to public life in Scotland, and I reflect on elements of this aspect of his life later in this chapter. But Neil's intellectual footprint extended well beyond the geographic border of Scotland, and it would do a disservice to his influence in this wider sense to restrict an appreciation of this sort to a particular jurisdiction – albeit one which shaped much of his thinking. So rather than focus exclusively on Neil's contribution to Scottish public life, in this contribution I reflect on Neil's broader impact in his capacity as a "public intellectual". As he was a man of considerable modesty, such a description would have caused him some unease. Nonetheless I think there is little doubt that Neil warrants this designation, such was the significance of the contributions he made to what we generally term "the public sphere".

Reflecting on Neil as a public intellectual is both an exciting and a daunting task. And it is an important one. It excites because it provides a different perspective to that which a more conventional assessment of his scholarly work might reveal. Indeed a core theme running through this chapter is that

° Professor of European Union Studies, University of Edinburgh.

it is in his later writings and activities in particular that one encounters the "public" aspect of Neil's extraordinary intellectual versatility. It is daunting in that, while he speaks strongly and passionately to "the public sphere" in many of his contributions, in none more so perhaps than the collection of essays he published as *Questioning Sovereignty*,[1] he resisted the temptation to deliver a running commentary on day-to-day aspects of contemporary society. Instead Neil provided us with the conceptual apparatus – the philosophical principles – that, if applied properly, will better equip *us* – the reader, the policy-maker, society – to contribute to the public good in the actions *we* undertake. As I discuss later, nowhere was this more evident than in the various contributions Neil made to the EU governance order during his time as a Member of the European Parliament (MEP).

The investigation of Neil as a public intellectual is an important task. It provides an opportunity to reflect on the role that the intellectual can, and should, play in informing and shaping debates in the public sphere in today's society. If Posner is correct in describing the task of the public intellectual as being to contribute to "social betterment",[2] the opportunities and obstacles to achieving this have never been greater. Whereas the challenge for public intellectuals in the past was to ensure their message extended beyond the local intelligentsia to the wider public, the onset of the internet era has given the intellectual access to a virtually unbounded global public sphere. For the contemporary intellectual the potential to influence events across the world is, in this sense, seemingly limitless, and it is one that has certainly been exploited, with the emergence of a new cadre of internet commentators. But the emergence of this opportunity to inform and influence on the global stage has created its own challenges. One is simply the absence of any quality control over those regarding themselves as public intellectuals and engaging in (global) social commentary. A second – and doubtless more serious – challenge is the presumption that the capability for the internet to transcend territorial, political and cultural divides necessarily means that intellectual comment itself is immune from the territorial, political and cultural prejudices of the commentator.

Of course, pointing to the changing context in which today's "public intellectuals" engage the public sphere does not in itself undermine the significance of their contributions. However it may require us to re-think the attributes that are generally associated with *being* a public intellectual – in other words,

---

1 N MacCormick, *Questioning Sovereignty* (1999).
2 See generally R Posner, *Public Intellectuals: A Study of Decline* (with a new preface and epilogue) (2003), e.g. at 6.

being "public" perhaps may have become a more important aspect of the endeavour than being "intellectual". As my own reflections of Neil MacCormick indicate, he was the quintessential intellectual who assumed a public persona, and not a commentator who sought the status of intellectual. To my mind this is the proper ordering of qualities, although it is one that is being challenged in this internet age.

So if there is a sub-text to this contribution, it is to encourage discussion about the role the public intellectual can play in this globalised, internet age in which comment is free, motives are unknowable, and influence can be instantaneous.

B. THE SCOTTISH INTELLECTUAL

Scotland is a country with a rich intellectual history. The Scottish Enlightenment of the eighteenth century remains one of the defining moments in the birth of modernism and, in many respects, it laid the foundations for the emergence of the intellectual as a contributor to, and participant in, debates conducted within the public sphere. By virtue of a command over knowledge and a capacity to deploy reason and judgement, the intellectual progressively assumed an independent moral responsibility as the protector of individual and collective social justice against attack from those who otherwise would abuse positions of power or ideological conviction for reasons of narrow self-interest. The territory the emerging public intellectual would come to occupy therefore was that which straddled the normative or moral ground of the orthodox philosopher and the quite separate and more challenging arena of politics and power in which decisions taken by "the few" determined the individual and collective rules which formed the legal and social constructions within which ordinary people lived their lives.

The role of the public intellectual therefore was to represent notions of justice and fairness to those in positions of power, to develop and apply criteria against which public policies could be assessed, and generally to be a guardian of the "public good". Chomsky expressed it in typically forthright manner: "Intellectuals are in a position to expose the lies of governments, to analyze actions according to their causes and motives and often hidden intentions."[3]

From the eighteenth century therefore, Scotland developed as a country in which the intellectual would play an important role in shaping the emerging

3 N Chomsky, "The responsibility of intellectuals" (1967) *New York Review of Books*, 23 February, available at *http://www.nybooks.com/articles/archives/1967/feb/23/a-special-supplement-the-responsibility-of-intelle/*, accessed 24 July 2011.

social order – an order to be based on knowledge and scientific understanding rather than superstition or indeed Calvinist-inspired religious belief.[4] One of the principal characteristics arguably shared by all Scotland's Enlightenment thinkers was a commitment to "universalism" – that is, a view of the social world that ignores status or class and regards each individual as essentially equal.[5] Unsurprisingly, in no field was this basic tenet of universalism more widely applied than with respect to the Scottish education system. Education was the foundation from which intellectual thought developed, and universal education was therefore the basis from which a just, fair and self-governing (democratic) society would evolve. Universalism in education therefore was a pre-requisite for, and an essential condition of maintaining, a self-governing society.

As we will discuss later, this Enlightenment idea of *self*-government represents one of the strongest intellectual threads connecting MacCormick the legal and political theorist and advocate of Scottish self-government in the twentieth century to the traditions of eighteenth-century liberal thought as expressed in the writings of Scotland's Enlightenment thinkers. It is no exaggeration to suggest that the relationship of Scots with power and authority has – since the eighteenth century – been, and continues to be, infused with a strong sense of universalism and egalitarianism. It is precisely this aspect of Scottish civil society that is celebrated in much of the eighteenth-century poetry of Robert Burns – most famously of course in "A Man's a Man for A' That" – and it is one that continues to have a powerful resonance in today's Scotland.[6]

Against this backdrop, it is not at all remarkable that Scotland developed as a society not only comfortable with the idea of the public intellectual, but one in which education and intellectualism were regarded as fundamental to the evolution of a fair and just society. Those who sought to challenge power and question the exercise of authority were viewed not with suspicion, but instead were welcomed as necessary and desirable counterweights to those who might otherwise seek to exploit high office to their own advantage. The public intellectual is there to promote the cause of social justice, and to speak on behalf of those lacking the capacity or opportunity to represent themselves. And while this depiction of the role of the public intellectual is

---

4 C Camic, "Experience and ideas: education for universalism in eighteenth century Scotland" (1983) 25(1) *Comparative Studies in Society and History* 50-82.

5 Key intellectuals in the Scottish Enlightenment include Adam Ferguson, David Hume, William Robertson and Adam Smith. See further, Alexander Broadie's contribution to the present volume.

6 It is no coincidence that this poem was the centrepiece of the ceremony marking the opening of the re-convened Scottish Parliament in 1999.

true across the world, it is one that has very deep roots in Scotland's social and political traditions and practices.

The picture being painted here is of a country in which the public intellectual emerges as the guardian of the *normative* order within which society develops and which directs its collective actions and the individual actions of those in positions of power and authority. And of course this is precisely the terrain which Neil MacCormick occupied, especially in his later work – perhaps nowhere more completely and elegantly than in *Questioning Sovereignty*. Here we find Neil engaging the fundamental normative issues that must underpin the assignment and exercise of power in the complex interdependent world in which we live in order for that power to be legitimate in the eyes of the citizen. Certainly Neil the legal theorist is much in evidence in these essays, and they reveal his lifelong dedication to the study of law and the institutions of law. But equally in evidence here is Neil the public intellectual who, like all public intellectuals across the world, is engaged in a discussion about the fundamental nature of power, governance and government.

It is worth pausing briefly to reflect on the wider "intellectual" Scotland in which Neil was raised and worked. To my mind it was a rather remarkable place. Neil was one of a number of Scots of his generation, albeit intellectually the most gifted, who contributed significantly in different ways to Scottish public and intellectual life, following closely in the tradition sketched above. Of the same, or almost the same, generation as Neil were John Smith, Neal Ascherson, Tom Nairn, John P MacIntosh, Donald Dewar and Ken Alexander. These were individuals of considerable presence in Scottish public life during the second half of the twentieth century. In Smith, MacIntosh and Dewar Scotland produced three outstanding politicians, each of whom made significant contributions to the development of modern social democracy in Britain, and in so doing paved the way for a fundamental shift in the nature of British politics. Ascherson, Nairn and Alexander, on the other hand, are more properly recognised as public intellectuals in the orthodox sense. Once again their writings are firmly located in the tradition of egalitarianism, and are always informed by a concern for the disenfranchised and vulnerable in society. Indeed, the collective contributions these individuals made to the intellectual history of Scotland from the mid-1950s ultimately may come to be recognised as an intellectual renaissance in much the same way that the disparate writings of Hugh McDiarmid, Sorley McLean, Lewis Grassic Gibbon, Edwin Muir and Naomi Mitchison from the 1920s much later came to be recognised as having constituted a

Scottish literary renaissance – the impact of which continues to be felt within Scotland's literary circles today.

Of those who shared Scotland's intellectual stage with Neil MacCormick, few if any commanded the same capacity in their work as did Neil to distil lessons that have universal application from considerations that, at first sight, appear to have only local significance. I would suggest that in this facility Neil excelled. Unsurprisingly the universality of the underlying message in his writings is a characteristic that Neil shares with many other leading public intellectuals, past and present, for whom "locality" or "place" may initially have provided the intellectual stimulus for, or arena in which, their thinking developed and to which their contributions initially were addressed, but whose impact and meaning ultimately had relevance in a much broader setting. Indeed I would suggest it is this very fusion between the intellectual resource at the command of the scholar and its subsequent application and relevance in a virtually universal sense that distinguishes the public intellectual from other contributors.

In the remainder of this chapter I will gather my general remarks around three themes: first, the public intellectual and the Scottish nationalist; secondly, Neil and the "public" quality of the public intellectual; thirdly, the public intellectual at work, in the context of the EU Constitutional Convention.

C. THE PUBLIC INTELLECTUAL AND THE SCOTTISH NATIONALIST

The argument I want to advance therefore is that beyond the many things that Neil did in, and for, public life in Scotland – especially of course as a teacher and politician – to my mind his lasting legacy will be the intellectual contributions he made to Scottish public life, and our understanding of public life in Scotland. To appreciate the richness of that legacy, we have to look beyond his activities and recognise his role as a public intellectual of international standing.

The term "public intellectual" clearly requires a definition of sorts. Even a cursory glance at the literature reveals a plethora of competing definitions of the term, and there is no consensus on the necessary or sufficient conditions that have to be met before one can be regarded as a public intellectual. So bearing that in mind, I want to simply state two definitions that I think are reasonable, both in general and in the specific context of Neil.

In *Public Intellectuals: A Study of Decline*, Richard Posner defines a public intellectual as "a person who, drawing on his intellectual resources, addresses a broad though educated public on issues with a political or ideological dimension".[7] An alternative, and pithier, definition comes from the late Tony Judt who describes a public intellectual as "a person who is engaged in an ethical conversation with the public".[8] What these two definitions provide is a *sense*, although not a definitive statement, of what the public intellectual is, and what he or she is not.

For instance, not all intellectuals necessarily are *public* intellectuals. Even an intellectual equipped to do so may be unwilling to engage in public discourse about ethical or ideological issues. Nor are public intellectuals necessarily academics or experts in the subjects on which they pronounce, although they must command the requisite intellectual resources to render their comment meaningful.

A particularly interesting question is whether a public intellectual can be politically aligned. Or indeed aligned in any meaningful sense? To many, being a public intellectual is very much a solitary pursuit. Edward Said, for instance, insists it is not something that can be pursued from a position of membership of an advocacy or partisan group: this is the intellectual as the passionate yet independent "outsider". Given his role in the Scottish National Party (SNP), this, of course, raises interesting questions about Neil's credentials as a public intellectual. But Said also goes on to assert that *he*, as a public intellectual, "is moved by causes and ideas that I can actually choose to support because they conform to values and principles that I believe in".[9] So the public intellectual as advocate, as activist, is partially redeemed, although allegiance to a particular political party doubtless remains a conundrum.

This, I think, points to one of the most interesting aspects of Neil's role as a public intellectual. Despite what one might expect, I detect no tension in the relationship between Neil as a *party* political activist and as a public intellectual. In fact, quite the opposite. Instead it is a relationship that I think sits entirely comfortably with Said's own intellectual self-portrait. The hypothesis therefore becomes that Neil's brand of Scottish nationalism – his "cause" if you like – is a function of the "values and principles" he holds as an intellectual rather than being an aspect of his life that he just kept separate from his intellectual endeavours.

I think this is a hypothesis with which most of us intuitively would agree, but it does raise interesting questions about the type of nationalism to which Neil subscribed. By that I do not mean was he an "ethnic" nationalist or

---

7   Posner, *Public Intellectuals* (n 2)170.
8   See generally, T Judt, *The Burden of Responsibility: Blum, Camus, Aron, and the French Twentieth Century* (1998).
9   E Said, *Representations of the Intellectual* (1994) 65.

a "liberal" nationalist. That is a question that Neil directly addressed in an article in which he both in large measure defined, and then claimed membership of, the liberal nationalist camp. [10] But the more interesting aspect of his – and indeed the SNP's – politics that I see his intellect speaking to is his long-term adherence to "gradualism" as the necessary and desirable progression through which Scotland *should* achieve independence.[11] I would assert that he did not adhere to this approach out of any acute sense of political strategy, though he might have subscribed to that as well, but rather because gradualism played to his intellectual approach to the nature of the state, to his conception of sovereignty, to his determined views on legitimacy while never losing sight of his conviction that the "submerged constitutional tradition of a distinct Scotland" should be resurrected.

But to take this one step further, did Neil's "gradualism" ever *need* to reach its logical conclusion with the emergence of a separate Scottish state at least in the classical sense? Or was it what I rather inelegantly term an *asymptotic* nationalism – that is, one that while progressively approaching comprehensive independence by ever smaller increments, never actually gets there. And in which, indeed, if the final destination ever were to be reached, the very ethos that had fuelled the journey might be undermined.

In my newly defined category of asymptotic nationalism, then, it is the journey that matters, often more than the final destination, provided that the journey itself is guided by appropriate values and principles. Neil's gradualism was designed as a journey that would, by its very nature, ensure this was the case. And it was a journey that had to conform to these values and principles, which is why he championed gradualism – often in the teeth of considerable opposition – within the SNP.

It seems to me that gradualism played to Neil's intellectual preoccupations in another sense. Namely, it provided an opportunity for the interests of the "minority" to be fully protected during, and following, the construction of an independent Scotland. Gradualism is often perceived to be desirable simply because it offers the SNP an opportunity to demonstrate their "fitness" for government ahead of full independence. And certainly this is one appeal it holds. But perhaps it offers another advantage – namely the opportunity for the non-nationalist citizen to come to terms with the transition to independence and for the nationalist to prepare to govern for all in the society and not just for the supporters of nationalism. In that sense the gradualist approach is

---

10 N MacCormick, "Liberalism, nationalism and the post-sovereign state" (1996) 44 *Political Studies* 553-567.

11 N MacCormick, "Unrepentant gradualism", in O Dudley Edwards (ed), *A Claim of Right for Scotland* (1989) 99-109.

more likely to be one that embeds within the emerging polity a full respect for the rights and interests of minorities, along with the necessary institutional bulwarks against any potential encroachment of these rights and interests.

So the argument is not that Neil was led inexorably to SNP membership because in the SNP he found a political movement whose objectives chimed with his values and principles. What I am suggesting is that once he had arrived at the SNP, and throughout his time in the SNP, his contributions were fundamentally informed by his values and principles. I never asked Neil why he joined the SNP, although family connections presumably offer one reason. But I did observe some of the contributions he made within it and these are entirely consistent with what Posner describes as the "intellectual resources" of the public intellectual.

D. THE "PUBLIC" QUALITY OF THE PUBLIC INTELLECTUAL

I said earlier that Neil's legacy to Scotland's public life would be through his role as a public intellectual. I briefly want to offer two illustrations of that legacy – that is, hia legacy as a person who had an ethical conversation with the public.

(1) Neil and the democratic intellect

The first example was very neatly packaged by Neil in a form ideal for my purposes. It is the article he published in *Legal Studies* in the mid-1980s entitled "The democratic intellect and the law".[12] Here Neil consciously invokes the terminology of George Elder Davie to argue that part of the duty assigned to legal educators is to prepare their students to take their place as, essentially, tomorrow's deep thinkers, and to equip them with the intellectual resources they will need to discharge their duties because of their proximity as professionals to the ethical questions that, as members of the legal community, society will challenge them to answer.[13] The element that Neil draws upon from Davie's study of the distinctiveness of Scotland's universities is the commitment within the universities to teach a range of subjects in a way that is infused with a "strongly philosophical bias".[14] Davie's implicit argument, endorsed by Neil, is that Scotland's education was, and must remain, an open intellectual system.[15] This is, of course, the only environment in which the

12 N MacCormick, "The democratic intellect and the law" (1985) 5(2) *Legal Studies* 177-183.
13 MacCormick, "The democratic intellect" 180.
14 MacCormick, "The democratic intellect" 173.
15 See G Elder Davie, *The Democratic Intellect: Scotland and her Universities in the Nineteenth Century* 2nd edn (1964, repr 1999).

public intellectual can flourish. It also, at the same time, defines the very essence of public intellectualism, which is an ability to engage in public dispute both over the nature of ideas and their application to the pressing ethical questions confronting society.

Needless to say, in this article Neil underscored the central role that legal theory should play in the education of successive generations of lawyers, and the centrality of philosophical reflection to the theoretical study of law. He wanted the teaching of law to exist within the type of open intellectual system that Davie has identified as distinctively Scottish. That legal study should be considered "a fit subject matter for an academical system of liberal education"[16], invoking another phrasing to be found in Davie.

As an educator, therefore, Neil recognised both the essentially public nature of the legal profession and the public eye in which those dispensing the law will find themselves, but also the importance of ensuring those so tasked are fully aware of the nature of law itself as a "philosophical enterprise". The democratic intellect in this sense then becomes an intellect fashioned by its exposure to the "academical system of liberal education" of which Scotland was justifiably proud. Of course the charge to which Neil was responding in "The democratic intellect and the law" was the counter proposition: that a lawyer did not require to be so grounded in legal theory.

What the article reveals is Neil's recognition that in some sense it is within the discourse and practice of *the law* that we find the origin of the public intellectual. And if we are to follow tradition and identify the Dreyfus Affair as marking the birth of the modern public intellectual – in the shape of Zola publicly railing against the injustice meted out to Dreyfus – then we can accept the force of Neil's argument.

So Neil was more than the public intellectual. He was a teacher who recognised the importance of equipping those for whom ethical questions would arise in their daily lives with the intellectual resources they would need. This is quite a large legacy to bestow on future generations.

(2) Neil and subsidiarity

To my mind Neil's contribution as a public intellectual is defined in his writings on, and around, the theme of subsidiarity and sovereignty. I do not need to go into any detail on the substance of his argument, not only because it is well enough rehearsed in this collection and elsewhere[17] but also because it is not

---

16 Elder Davie, *The Democratic Intellect* 120, quoting Sir William Hamilton.
17 See in particular the contributions by Neil Walker (ch 7) and Joanne Scott (ch 8).

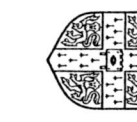

The Cambridge Law Journal
University of Cambridge
Faculty of Law
10 West Road
Cambridge CB3 9DZ

Telephone: +44 (0)1223 330042
Fax: +44 (0)1223 330055
Email: lawclj@hermes.cam.ac.uk

With the Compliments of the Book Review Editor

the content of the academic discourse that I want to focus on. Rather it is that Neil's writings on subsidiarity and also on the nature of sovereignty exemplify precisely why Neil deserves the accolade of public intellectual. There is little doubt that Neil's work on subsidiarity, and indeed on sovereignty, is directly linked to his ethical and ideological views on the nature of liberal democracy. That is, on the organisation and legitimacy of government, and on the fundamental principle that sovereignty resides in people and is not some inviolable right that belongs exclusively to the state. This takes us to Neil's many contributions to the notion of a world "beyond the sovereign state", and its legal philosophical adjunct in the conception of overlapping normative orders.[18] It provides insight into the relationships between the architectures of government and its legitimacy.

The beauty of the lasting significance of the literature that Neil contributed around these closely related themes is its universality. As in the contributions of so many other leading thinkers and public intellectuals, "place-location" is crucial in the selection of the subject matter. There is no doubt that the ethical and ideological challenges facing Scotland as part of the union that is the United Kingdom figured heavily in his treatment of sovereignty, while in the union of the twenty-seven countries of the EU we find the key puzzles to which he applied his conception of sovereignty in order to confront real political problems. But again like those of many other public intellectuals, the intellectual contribution has a universal resonance. The analysis can be applied to any country or group of countries anywhere in the democratic world.

E. NEIL – THE PUBLIC INTELLECTUAL AT WORK: THE EU CONSTITUTIONAL CONVENTION

My final section addresses Neil as a public figure in which his engagement with the Scottish public was direct. Once again there are many aspects of his role in this regard that one could draw upon, but unsurprisingly I want to look at Neil the Member of the European Parliament. It was in that role, which he occupied between 1999 and 2004 on behalf of the SNP, that Neil had his most direct involvement in Scottish public life in the widest sense.

Of course, on a practical level, engaging the public in Scotland on matters European is no easy task, even if one was an elected politician. Neil was well aware of this. I remember convening a private seminar to discuss the state aid

18 See N MacCormick, "Beyond the sovereign state" (1993) 56(1) *Modern Law Review* 1-18.

problem that then threatened the provision of CalMac's ferry services to the Western Isles, which Sir David Edward chaired and Neil attended. Because of the personnel gathered to discuss the question, I stated at the outset that the proceedings would be held under the Chatham House rule, meaning that what was said might be reported but that no direct attribution could be made. Neil immediately asked that his comments not be subject to this rule and should be as widely reported as possible on the basis that it was difficult enough for him as an MEP to get any press coverage without his consenting to any further gagging order!

Of course, Neil being Neil, it was insufficient to be involved only in Scottish public life, it was the whole of the European Union that was to benefit from the application of Neil's intellectual resources in a very direct and immediate way – namely as an alternate member of the Convention on the Future of Europe. It is difficult to imagine a more appropriate time for Neil to have been an MEP or a more appropriate forum than the Convention for Neil's public intellectualism to come to the fore. Here he was directly involved in a public debate about the future constitutional architecture of the EU, and the position of states and sub-state nations within it, to which he was uniquely qualified to contribute. Indeed, I think one can assert with confidence that no other member of the Convention was better qualified to address the very foundational questions of legitimacy, representation and governance that were at the core of the deliberations of the Convention.

It is impossible in this setting to do justice to the various contributions that Neil made to the work of the Convention, formally through written interventions and informally through discussion and debate. I doubt there were many more significant individual contributions from "the floor" than those made by Neil. If you do have the occasion to talk to other members, including Lord Kerr who headed the Convention's secretariat, you will be left in no doubt about the significance of Neil's work in that regard. It is possible to get a flavour of the manner in which Neil brought to bear on the Convention his unique intellectual resources. A couple of short quotes from written contributions he made to the Convention testify again to the *"public"* intellectualism that marked his life:

> September 2002, commenting on democracy at many levels:
>
> In drawing up a Constitution ... for the European Union, the Convention ought to direct attention to the manifest truth that European Democracy must operate at many levels, and that a concern for subsidiarity cannot be exhausted by reflection merely on relations between member states and union institutions.[19]

19 N MacCormick, "Democracy at many levels: European constitutional reform" (CONV 298/02) 2,

This is an intellectual argument grounded in classical liberalism to which most would subscribe. But then Neil transforms this ethical, even ideological, proposition into a statement about the "local" in arguing that a governing principle for a European democracy is that of "self-determination for the peoples of Europe, including the possibility of internal enlargement",[20] and then calling for "full recognition of the right to self-government of all those territorial entities in the Union whose citizens have a shared sense of national, linguistic or regional identity".[21]

We can all recognise this as the intellectual conclusion to the strap-line the SNP had by then adopted of "independence in Europe", a strap-line that appealed because it no longer conjoined independence with isolation. In other words, while the setting of the EU represented a threat to fundamental principles of democracy through any tendency it had to centralise political authority and policy competence in Brussels, in countering that tendency the EU provided a framework in which its constituent elements both could and should be reconfigured wherever the applications of the fundamental principles of democratic government – including the notion of subsidiarity and, consequently, legitimacy – decreed this was appropriate.

It was Neil the public intellectual who was speaking in the Convention, not Neil the politician, for whom the slogan "independence in Europe" was actually the very tip of an iceberg that was constructed on very firm intellectual argument. And of course Neil's contributions – all of which are brilliant statements of the practical application of challenging intellectual principles – had a resonance that extended way beyond Scotland.

Neil was both representing his, and his political party's vision of a Europe of the peoples, and at the same time attending to the issues facing his constituents, but it was a vision which by dint of his intellectual resources could be shared by many others from different parties and different countries. I doubt there was any written submission comparable in its rich versatility to one with a title reading "Subsidiarity, common sense and local knowledge" which begins with a recital of the principle of subsidiarity, cites the relevant Treaty articles, and then morphs into a discussion about the movement of waste water on Islay and Jura.[22]

However Neil's experience in the Convention ultimately must have been a disappointing one, although he never stated it so. While firmly of the view

available at the Convention website: *http://european-convention.eu.int/search.asp?lang=EN* (accessed 25 July 2011).

20 MacCormick, "Democracy at many levels" 2.
21 MacCormick, "Democracy at many levels" 2.
22 Conv 275/02.

that such a Constitution was desirable – he always argued (1) that de facto EU already had a constitution and (2) so did his local golf club – and a proponent of the Constitution that did emerge from the Convention, the failure in that document to explicitly address internal enlargement and elevate the rights of sub-state governments along the lines he advocated must have left him with a sense, if not of regret, then certainly of "missed opportunity". Of course some progress was made in enhancing the rights of sub-nation states in the draft Constitution, and some of these survived into the new Treaty. Subsidiarity as both principle and practice has been buttressed, though it remains essentially ill-defined in any legal sense. So progress was made but the basic architecture of the Union remains that of the nation states.

Any such sense of missed opportunity that Neil might have had did not prevent him from publicly supporting, and campaigning for adoption of, the draft Constitutional Treaty that emerged from the Future of Europe Convention. Indeed in the very best traditions of the pamphleteer he produced his monograph *Who's afraid of a European Constitution?*[23] which sought to explain the content and context of the prospective constitution and persuade others of its merits – if not in an absolute sense, then certainly as an improvement over what currently existed.[24]

Although Neil stood down from the European Parliament in 2004 after one term, he had by then made a considerable contribution to debates about the EU, both in terms of its governance arrangements and direct application of the Treaty provisions in Scotland. For all his involvement in the heady atmosphere that was the Convention, Neil never neglected in the slightest his duties, as an MEP, to his constituents.

Despite standing down in 2004, and doubtless believing his active participation in European politics and policy to be at an end, Neil was to return to the European action in 2007 following the SNP victory in the Holyrood elections in what was to be, arguably, the most appropriate afterword in the biography of this most astonishing Scotsman.

Flora, Neil's widow, recounted to me that days after the result was announced and the new First Minister installed, she and Neil returned from a few days' break only to receive a phone call from Alex Salmond asking Neil to become his special advisor on EU issues – a role that Neil accepted, albeit unpaid. It is Scotland after all! As has been recounted to me by a wide range

23 MacCormick, *Who's Afraid of a European Constitution?* (2005).

24 His support for the Draft Constitution did not, however, carry forward to the Lisbon Treaty. The principle objection he had was the proposal formally to declare the protection of marine life to be an exclusive competence of the EU.

of politicians and officials at various times, and as was so movingly reflected at Neil's funeral, in that capacity Neil excelled. I suspect it was with enormous pride that Neil took his place as a servant of the first SNP government in the history of his country. But this was no footnote. Neil worked as hard in the capacity as special advisor as he had in any of the many other roles in academic and public life that he had played in the past. And as I mentioned, his counsel in that capacity was as wise and engaging as we all experienced it to be in the various capacities in which we encountered Neil MacCormick.

(1) Concluding remark

In conclusion. Neil's role in, and contribution to, Scottish public life was remarkable. He was unique in the manner in which he combined his two professional lives as a world-class legal theorist and intellectual and as a polit- ical activist. But I hope I have demonstrated why these roles were not actually – or indeed ever perceived to be – in contradiction to one another. The bridge was provided by his public intellectualism. Public intellectuals are defined both by their preparedness to engage in the important ethical debates of the day, and by their ability to marshal their intellectual resources to that end.

To my mind, public intellectuals must be players in the democratic process. If they are not, that process will be all the weaker and more vulnerable to attack. Neil was a public intellectual who took on that role in Scotland and for Scotland, but who in doing so contributed directly to advancing the broader liberalism to which he also subscribed.

10 Scotland's Meridian: A Memoir of Neil MacCormick in the Scottish Public Sphere

William Storrar°

A. INTRODUCTION
B. THE SCOTTISH PUBLIC SPHERE
C. A PUBLIC-SPIRITED INTELLECTUAL
D. SCOTLAND EXPECTS
E. SCOTLAND'S CITIZEN
F. SCOTLAND'S MERIDIAN

A. INTRODUCTION

It was a great honour to take part in the celebration of "Neil MacCormick's Scotland" that took place in the School of Law at the University of Edinburgh in 2010. My contribution on that occasion was a personal memoir of encountering Neil MacCormick in the Scottish public sphere over four decades. Jürgen Habermas has famously defined the public sphere as occurring whenever and wherever people meet to exchange views on public issues and influence public opinion, whether over a drink in the bar or in a debate in some public forum.[1] The Scottish public sphere has a character all of its own, perhaps not one envisaged by Professor Habermas, but certainly one enjoyed by Professor MacCormick.

B. THE SCOTTISH PUBLIC SPHERE

The distinctively Scottish approach to public life was brought home to me again en route to the MacCormick celebration at Old College in 2010. I arrived at Edinburgh Airport on a plane from New York full of my fellow Scots. I have done that journey many times since moving to Princeton from Edinburgh University in 2005. There are always two queues you have to

° Director of the Center of Theological Inquiry, Princeton University.
1 See J Habermas, *The Structural Transformation of the Public Sphere*, trans T Burger (1989) 27.

negotiate: the queue for the toilet before landing and the queue through immigration on arrival. On this occasion, somewhere over Ireland, I joined the queue for the toilets at the back of the plane. One man was ahead of me but did not seem to be taking the toilet that declared itself vacant. "Aye," he said, seeing my puzzled look, "she hisnae locked the door. Mind you, I cannae blame her. Ah dae it ma'sel!" Here we have Adam Smith's theory of moral sentiments, alive and well at 35,000 feet: to pee ourselves as others pee.

On landing at Edinburgh Airport, I stood in line to have my passport checked. At the head of the queue was a young man in a wheelchair, bedecked in a Scotland football shirt, kilt and obligatory sombrero. Suddenly, moved by the prospect of entering his native land, he burst into song:

> Scots, wha hae wi' Wallace bled,
> Scots, wham Bruce has aften led,
> Welcome tae yer gory bed,
> Or tae victorie.

His douce fellow passengers moved silently away from the wheelchair, now turned into one of Bruce's bristling schiltrons at Bannockburn, startled and alarmed at this bellicose outburst from the man in the kilt.

There you have it, the Scottish public sphere, caught between moral sympathy and native aggression. The poet Alan Jackson conveyed our national condition perfectly in two short lines, quoted from memory:

> I long to embrace you, my darling,
> But you seem to be covered in harling!

At the celebration of MacCormick's Scotland in Old College, one of the participants captured this binary patriotism in the more sober terms of the penal law of Scotland. In our criminal policy and attitude to children, it was remarked, we are caught between our vaunted Enlightenment tolerance and our punitive default mode. No one did more to heal this split in the Scottish public psyche than Neil MacCormick. By the acuity of his intellect and the generosity of his character, he transformed the Scottish public sphere into a more humane place of possibility. He did so by embodying his own distinctive philosophy of liberal nationalism, practising what I would call his "patriotism of the person", a love for neighbour in his country and every country.

As a contributor to this volume of essays, I wish to offer a personal memoir of Neil in the Scottish public sphere during a momentous period in its history, the debate on our constitutional future in Scotland and Europe. As these reflections were first presented at an event to remember Neil among his ain folk in Old College, my selected memories are of Neil in Edinburgh and at the University over that period, from the late 1970s to the opening decade of this century.

C. A PUBLIC-SPIRITED INTELLECTUAL

Memory plays tricks. Preparing my remarks for the Old College event, I had thought that my first public encounter with Neil had been at a conference in February 1989, marking the tenth anniversary of the 1979 devolution referendum and organised at Edinburgh University by its Unit for the Study of Government in Scotland. The event was called: "What Scotland Wants: Ten Years On". As the title suggests, it was more than an academic conference. On that February day in Edinburgh, it was the epicentre of the Scottish public sphere. Not only was the fateful course of the 1979 referendum being re-contested, ten years on, the route to a Constitutional Convention was also being hotly debated, in light of the then recently issued *Claim of Right for Scotland*.[2]

As David McCrone, the conference chair, later wrote in his Introduction to the published papers from the event:

> This was the political context in which the conference to mark the 1979 Devolution Referendum took place on February 25 1989, on a wet and windy Saturday in Edinburgh. Over 120 people attended, a major turn-out from all over Scotland, from Oban to Galloway, from Aberdeen to the Borders. The conference drew party activists, academics, journalists, all interested in the constitutional issue of Scotland.[3]

There was only one person who could open that day's deliberations on the constitutional issue of Scotland, and command universal respect from devolutionists, federalists and nationalists alike: Neil MacCormick. In his opening lecture, as a co-author and signatory of the recently issued *Claim of Right for Scotland*, Neil gave his characteristically European account of an ideal constitution for Scotland, and then made his compelling argument for adopting a gradualist approach to attaining an independent Scotland, challenging what he saw as the "elective dictatorship" of the British government under Margaret Thatcher, and advocating the participation of his own Scottish National Party in the proposed Constitutional Convention.[4] In that

---

2 "A Claim of Right for Scotland", Report of the Constitutional Steering Committee presented to the Campaign for a Scottish Assembly, July 1988. Published in O Dudley Edwards (ed), *A Claim of Right for Scotland* (1989) 11-51.

3 D McCrone, "Introduction", in D McCrone (ed) *What Scotland Wants: Ten Years On* (1989) 1-2 at 2.

4 N MacCormick "Constitutionalism and constitutions", in McCrone (ed) *What Scotland Wants: Ten Years On* (n 3) 3-8 at 7-8.

one 1989 lecture at Edinburgh University, we have all the key elements in Neil's approach to public life and politics: principled, internationalist, gradualist and pluralist.

It was a spellbinding lecture, vintage MacCormick, brilliantly delivered before the gathered elite of the Scottish political class: Neal Ascherson, Tom Nairn, and leading lights from all the airts. Unfortunately, I had arrived halfway through Neil's talk, having driven through a snowstorm from Lanarkshire, where I was then a parish minister. As I sat in the back row, taking in Neil's closing remarks but preoccupied with the weather on the road home, somewhere on the edge of consciousness I heard the conference chair say, "And now the Reverend Willie Storrar will reply to Professor MacCormick's lecture."

Anguished questions seared my addled brain: "What did he just say? The Rev Willie Who?" Amid rising terror and panic, a terrible memory flashed into my mind of a passing conversation months before with one of the conference organisers, Allan Macartney: "Why don't you take part in the conference, Willie?" As I had heard no more from Allan, I had thought no more about it, only that I would try and attend the event. But now, somewhere on the edge of public oblivion, I found myself standing up before the swivelling heads of the Scottish intelligentsia, turning in disbelief to see what on earth an obscure minister could possibly have to say in reply to the constitutional colossus in their midst, the Regius Professor of Public Law and the Law of Nature and Nations. After a few rambling remarks, I slumped back into my seat in the back row, desperate to slink out of the proceedings at the first opportunity.

Tom Nairn's prophecy had come true.[5] As Scotland contemplated its rebirth that day, the latest copy from its finest mind had duly strangled its least impressive minister! Or rather, it had not quite strangled me. With characteristic kindness of thought for his less able interlocutors, Neil respectfully paraphrased my poor response, thus turning it into a cogent criticism of his own position, before rebutting it with graceful ease. Here we have Neil MacCormick in the public sphere, not so much the spirited public intellectual as the public-spirited intellectual. He never made his case for the public good at the expense of his critic's public dignity, while always relishing the absurd in the human condition, not least his own.

As it turned out, my memory had played a trick on me. This was not my first encounter with Neil. Straight off the plane from New York for the 2010

---

5 "Scotland will be reborn the day the last minister is strangled with the last copy of the *Sunday Post*." T Nairn, "Three dreams of Scottish nationalism", in K Miller (ed) *Memoirs of a Modern Scotland* (1970) 34-54 at 54.

Old College event, I went to the National Library of Scotland to look up the published proceedings of that 1989 conference. Not only had the publication of *What Scotland Wants* given me the opportunity to redeem the nightmare and write a more considered response to the entire text of Neil's lecture, but to my surprise, it also revealed the true date of our first conversation on Scottish affairs, ten years earlier than I had thought. This is how I opened my published response to his 1989 address:

> My abiding memory of Neil MacCormick and the 1979 Referendum Campaign has him in his native setting, professionally and temperamentally – the cool, rational Enlightenment proportions of a room in the Old College, Edinburgh University. We were sitting in a University committee room on the Friday afternoon following the referendum vote on the previous day. A student official kept bringing in the regional results from a radio in the anteroom outside. Neil noted them down on a piece of paper and added up the totals. A majority in favour but not a majority in practice under the notorious 40% rule. What kind of Alice through the Looking Glass constitution do we have in Britain, I remember wondering, that one of the country's finest minds should have to engage in such nonsense political arithmetic?[6]

So that was my first meeting with Neil in the Scottish public sphere, not the moment of my own public embarrassment in 1989 but the forgotten memory of sharing our national embarrassment in 1979. On both occasions, he expressed his convictions with unfailing courtesy in the face of folly, whether personal or political. I continued to be impressed by this public style, as I observed it at first hand in the turbulent decades of Scottish and European constitutional debate that followed the first referendum in 1979. Three further public encounters with Neil from those years stand out in my memory as typical of this brilliant thinker and generous colleague.

D. SCOTLAND EXPECTS

Despite my stumbling public dialogue with Neil in that 1989 Edinburgh University conference, he graciously agreed to be interviewed shortly afterwards for an educational film I was making for the Church of Scotland. It was on the distinctively European idea of sovereignty in the history of church and state in Scotland and its relevance to the contemporary constitutional debate on a Scottish Parliament. Returning to his room in Old College after a good lunch, Neil sat back in his chair and answered my amateur questions with the same respectful attention he showed to his ablest peer and weakest student. Two phrases stand out in my memory, as in the film. Developing

---

6 W Storrar, "Response to Neil MacCormick's paper", in McCrone (ed) *What Scotland Wants: Ten Years On* (n 3) 8-10 at 8.

an elegant argument in support of a constitutional settlement for Scotland that was grounded in this national and European notion of sovereignty, he declared, "I would expect it. It is what it ought to be."

Personal attention. Logical argumentation. Moral conviction. Convivial luncheon! Here are the characteristic features of Neil's style of engagement in the public sphere, as I was to witness it in his quest for a Scottish Parliament and a European constitution over the next two decades. It was as if he could perform all the noble characters in the medieval *Satire of the Three Estates*[7] simultaneously on the thrust stage of contemporary Scottish public life. Time and again he showed a Charity of heart and Clarity of mind in public debate, leading to the Sanctity of conscience, with Hilarity at frail Humanity not far behind.

E. SCOTLAND'S CITIZEN

My next public encounter was in the mid-1990s, when the Tory government relented on its earlier ban and allowed the Home Rule movement to hold a public event in the old Royal High School on Edinburgh's Calton Hill. As one of the organisers, I had invited Neil to speak. He had turned up looking rather pale, and quietly explained that he had been in bed with flu. But, he said, looking round the elliptical debating chamber prepared in 1979 for the expected Scottish Assembly but mothballed ever since, nothing would have prevented him from being there and speaking in that hallowed hall on such an occasion. This was the Neil MacCormick I saw that day, standing in quiet awe before the public arena; not only an outstanding philosopher, dedicated to reasoned argument in making the case for a Scottish Parliament, but also an ordinary citizen with a deep reverence for the public sphere.

Standing beside him in that once and future temple of democracy, as we all thought then, I sensed the ancestral roots of his unfeigned humility. This was to be the public assembly of his own ancient European nation, already possessing its continental systems of law, religion and education. This was to be the public voice for justice he first heard from his mother, a dedicated social worker among the poorest women and families in Glasgow. This was to be the Parliament his father had spent a lifetime campaigning for in harder times for the home rule cause. This was to be the legislature he had spent his own lifetime trying to persuade his fellow citizens to vote for in countless draughty halls and election meetings across Scotland. He was just proud to be there.

7 D Lindsay, *A Satire of the Three Estates*, ed by R Kemp (1968).

F. SCOTLAND'S MERIDIAN

My final public encounter is from the opening decade of this century, the time when Neil was an MEP and playing a prominent part in preparing a new Constitution for Europe. I had invited him to speak on that topic at the Centre for Theology and Public Issues in Edinburgh University. He had brought along with him from the European Parliament Giorgio Napolitano, then chair of its Constitutional Committee and subsequently President of Italy. Neil and Napolitano arrived at New College on the Mound for what was to be a public seminar on yet another wet and windy winter's night in Edinburgh.

Before he got up to speak, I apologised to him for the size of the audience, about forty people when we would normally have expected 100 or more for such an occasion. Neil was not disappointed, far less annoyed that he had brought his distinguished colleague from Brussels to address such a small audience. This was the Scottish public sphere, discussing a constitution for Europe, and whether there were forty people or 400, it did not matter to him. What mattered was that we were engaging in a thoughtful, civil conversation about the public good. He considered it a privilege to be invited to be part of it, even on that cold winter's night in Edinburgh. As Robert Louis Stevenson put it, "To none but those who have themselves suffered the thing in the body, can the gloom and depression of our Edinburgh winters be brought home."[8] Or, indeed, the gloom and depression of our Scottish political winter before home rule finally came in 1999.

Neil was always the sun at midday in the midst of that Scottish gloom, shedding intellectual light and personal warmth wherever he spoke. He was Scotland's meridian, aligning us all in our disparate political views and loyalties along the line of wisdom that ran in his person through the Scottish public sphere from his student days in Glasgow to his final days in Edinburgh. Decade on decade, he illuminated the Scottish and European constitutional debate and expanded its circle of conversation to bring many opponents in from the cold. My cold Edinburgh evening with Neil and Napolitano ended in a basement restaurant on the High Street of the Old Town. As I sat at dinner with them, the future president of Italy and the finest son of Scotland, Neil's laughter and wit echoed round the stone cellar, awakening the shades of his forebears, the great thinkers of the Scottish Enlightenment who gathered in such howffs and would surely have welcomed him as one of their own. Neil

8 R L Stevenson, *Edinburgh Picturesque Notes* (1879, repr 2004) 34.

MacCormick is still the meridian line of enlightenment running through the Scottish public sphere, and as his colleagues and fellow citizens we can do no better than to align ourselves along it, whatever our differences. It is what he would expect. It is what ought to be.

Afterword

11 Neil MacCormick: An Epilogue

Zenon Bańkowski°

A. TEAM SCOTLAND
B. A JOURNEY WITH THE PARABLE
C. THE PARABLE: DEFINITION, LAW AND IDENTITY
D. PERFORMING THE PARABLE: RECOGNITION AND
   TRANSFORMATION
E. SYMPATHY AND THE INTELLECTUAL LIFE

Es ist nichts gross als das Wahre und das kleinste Wahre ist gross. (Goethe)

A. TEAM SCOTLAND

Dundee, 1965. I was in a small classroom listening to an introductory lecture in Jurisprudence, it was a hot and sticky afternoon, the classroom was hot and not well ventilated, the lecturer was interesting but not *that* interesting, and I was dozing off. Suddenly, and with a great clatter, I woke up with a start, finding that I had kicked the desk in front of me. I threw my hands up in the air – I had dreamt that I had scored the winning goal for Celtic in the Scottish Cup Final. I looked around, found I had not, and went back to the lecture and sleep again. That was in the semi-public sphere that is the University, my first irruption into the life of Neil MacCormick. I was one of his first pupils. He taught me Jurisprudence when he began teaching at the Law School in Queen's College at the University of St Andrews (Dundee University as it now is). I have known him as teacher, senior colleague and mentor, collaborator and friend. My intellectual and personal debt to him cannot be measured.

But it is not that which I want to talk about here. This volume, and the seminar that preceded it, looks at the more specifically Scottish dimensions of Neil's work. We have looked at his work on the legal system in Scotland and more generally his examinations of the Union and sovereignty vis-à-vis both England and beyond. We have also considered his more specific work

° Professor of Legal Theory, University of Edinburgh.

on nationalism and Scottish nationalism in particular, and on how this fits into the humanist and intellectual traditions of the Scottish Enlightenment. Finally, we examined Neil's role in the public life of the Scottish polity and beyond with reflections on the role of the public intellectual. In short, we examined the way that the *Scottishness* of Neil coloured his work – we have looked at him through distinctively Scottish lenses. I do not intend to go over this ground again but to bring this work to a close and, through those lenses, talk about, to use a phrase of Neil Walker's, MacCormick the Scottish "cosmopolitan local".[1]

In the Centre for Legal Studies (CLS) at Edinburgh where he and I ended our careers, we had a tradition of a virtual football team where colleagues were given a position and the name of a philosopher whom they represented. The idea was to match the position to the philosopher and to the colleague. When colleagues left they were given a football shirt with the name of that philosopher on it. When Neil left, he was given the shirt of David Hume and his position was that of a holding midfielder. Someone who holds the team together and, thus firmly grounded, sparks its and his creativity. It was inevitable that he would have that shirt and that position. His team was Scotland, but from that he extended way beyond.

B. A JOURNEY WITH THE PARABLE

I am going to do this in a somewhat unusual way. Neil, when he knew that his time was limited, began planning his own funeral. He asked me to read at the memorial service the parable of the Good Samaritan. He wrote to me, not to be impersonal but in his characteristically sensitive way, "so you could think it over before replying and not feel inhibited if it is something you would rather not do, for any reason":

> I very much want there to be a reading of the Parable of the Good Samaritan as part of this service … It is a theme we have puzzled over for many years, since away back trying to make sense of *Donoghue v Stevenson* … I won't be there to hear you, but it will be a great blessing to know in advance that you will be heard on my behalf, if you find it possible to agree to doing this.

> How sad to write on a theme like this to a very dear and old friend, an absolutely oldest former student, and a longest-standing Edinburgh colleague in jurisprudence. But it comes to us all one day, and I am, as you know, content with my lot and cheerfully resigned to subsequent phases of development. It is a mercy to feel that I have had an enjoyable and reasonably constructive and outgoing life, so that its coming to an end does not bring a sense of frustration about things not done,

---

1 N Walker, "The cosmopolitan local", in A J Menendez and J E Fossum (eds) *Law and Democracy in Neil MacCormick's Legal and Political Theory* (2011) 3-16.

much though I would have liked to do more things, usually in a context of having chewed the fat over them with you.

The Divine Parables are, as Roger White argues,[2] not like some religious Aesop's fables, meant to teach us one moral precept with their story, nor are they something that is meant to explain or define the Divine. They are rather to be viewed as an invitation to explore the Divine. They do not give us an answer; they invite us on a journey in an unknown, mysterious World. The beauty of the parable is that it takes you to places you cannot know. As you follow and explore the often twisting paths of its meaning, you end up in places that sometimes surprise, sometimes delight, and always challenge you, although you might not know it at the time. We will be full of wonder at what we see there, but it will never exhaust the meaning of the places we go to and the journey we make. And this was characteristic of Neil. For him the scientific life was a journey and he always reacted and changed in response to the mysterious, wonderful and challenging things that came along on that journey. Always moving forward, but always rooted in where he had been.

Perhaps for him the journey is over and he has finally arrived. Neil was not a believer in any conventional sense. He variously told me that he was a "Presbyterian agnostic" or a Deist, and without doubt Scotland's national Church was important to him as part of the tradition of Scottishness. I do not want here to imply anything about his beliefs – all I want to do is to prolong that journey for a while. In meditating on the parable of the Good Samaritan, and why it was that Neil wanted it to be read at his funeral or to "chew the fat over" it with a "dear friend", I would like to see what it might be able to tell us about him and his work and how, so guided, it might lead us to unexpected places in our scientific lives.

C. THE PARABLE: DEFINITION, LAW AND IDENTITY

Famously the "Good Samaritan" first makes his appearance in law in the case of *Donoghue v Stevenson*,[3] a case that founds an aspect of the law of negligence in the UK. Mrs Donoghue, in a cafe in Paisley, has a concoction of ginger beer and ice cream which appears to have a decomposing slug in it. She feels ill and sues. She does not, however, sue the cafe owner with whom she has a contractual relation, but rather sues the manufacturer of the ginger beer. The question then arises whether he can be said to have any legal

---

2 R White, "MacKinnon and the Parables", in K Surin (ed), *Christ, Ethics and Tragedy: Essays in Honour of Donald MacKinnon* (1989) 49-70 at 52-53.

3 [1932] SC (HL) 31.

relationship to her. Part of the reasoning was to do with the parable of the Good Samaritan which was seen as illuminating our response to the question "Who is my neighbour?". The court, in giving judgment for Mrs Donoghue, tried to define "neighbour" so that it could be used in law. Lord Atkin said:

> The rule that you are to love your neighbour becomes in law: You must not injure your neighbour, and the lawyer's question: Who is my neighbour? receives a restricted reply. You must take reasonable care to avoid acts or omissions which you can reasonably foresee would be likely to injure your neighbour. Who then, in law, is my neighbour? The answer seems to me to be persons who are so closely and directly affected by my act that I ought reasonably to have them in contemplation as being so affected when I am directing my mind to the acts or omissions which are called in question. This appears to me to be the doctrine in *Heaven v Pender* as laid down by Lord Esher.[4]

Neil used this case in his seminal work, *Legal Reasoning and Legal Theory*.[5] This book, as he said, originated in a set of lectures that he gave in Dundee. I remember them and what struck me was the *Scottishness* of them, although coming from someone who was educated in English law. Though dealing with general issues of reasoning they were rooted, at least as I heard them, in Scotland and its system. Though Neil was not educated as Scots lawyer, he was at home in that system. An incident early on in the then Faculty of Law will illustrate this. In those days many Scots lawyers had a view that one could not really know Scots law unless educated in it. They therefore could not accept that Neil could really be a Scots lawyer since he did not have that almost mystical inculcation in the system.[6] One day in the staff club they were making this and similar points when Neil finally got exasperated and asked them to question him on any aspects of Scots law. He surprised them with his knowledge, and they "were astonished at his understanding and answers".[7] They saw that he really was a Scots lawyer, as they were.[8] And his writings, from his inaugural lecture *Law as Institutional Fact*[9] to his penultimate book *The Institution of Law*[10] betray this fact. For Neil was strongly embedded in the eclectic interdisciplinary tradition of Scots law, and his work on the idea of systems helped to describe the Scottish system and show how it could be considered separate but also connected.

4 *Donoghue v Stevenson* [1932] SC (HL) 31 at 44-45.
5 N MacCormick, *Legal Reasoning and Legal Theory*, 1st edn (1978), 2nd edn (1994).
6 To the extent that a wild anarcho/Marxist (as I was then) was treated with less suspicion because I had a degree in Scots law!
7 Luke 2:47.
8 Luke 2:39-52.
9 N MacCormick, *Law as Institutional Fact*, Edinburgh University Inaugural Lecture No 52 (1973), also published at (1974) 90 *Law Quarterly Review* 102-129.
10 N MacCormick, *Institutions of Law: An Essay in Legal Theory* (2007).

But describing rigorously and in a nuanced way what it means to be a system and its operation in this Scottish context is not all. For, in looking at the legal system in this way, one interrogates questions of identity and what it means to be a Scottish state. Neil's work points the way in terms of the "cosmopolitan localism" that Neil Walker talks about,[11] and it cashes out as a wider definition of what it means to be Scottish. Though rooted in its ethnic and territorial soil, Scottishness spreads out beyond that. We can see this in the SNP slogan in the 1992 general election, which owed a lot to him, namely "Scotland in Europe". This was not meant to be just an image of concentric circles where the more local identity is subsumed by the larger one, but one that is more nuanced and horizontal. So it could be more inclusive while still encompassing the exclusion that is inherent in nationalism. In the context of that electoral slogan then, to say that you are Scottish means to say that you are not English, but the English are not thereby excluded. This is so because it also implies we are in some sense English because we are European Scots and, as the English are European English, then in that sense we also have that Englishness within us – the Englishness is a part of our Europeanness. And this can be taken more broadly in the European context to show how sub-national groups can claim identity and representation without necessarily falling foul of the problem of excessive nationalistic demands; how European identity becomes an immanent process, a product of a never-ending set of complex negotiations.

This became an important theme in Neil's work, starting from the seminal article, "Beyond the sovereign state"[12] where, in the context of showing that traditional legal theory would fail to account for the *sui generis* of the European Union, he began to develop a theory of polycentric "interlocking normative orders".[13] On this view, multiple sites of validity could interlock and make a coherent system without being locked in the traditional statist view of legal theory, which demanded one site of validity for one system and which would make the EU either a set of states, each joined by treaty, or one super-state. His article was the start of important work that widened the way in which validity was seen in legal theory and in legal theoretical work in European Union studies.

So, as in the parable, here we have a widening out of the definition of neighbour. But for him it was not just a question of definition. Again, it is

---

11 Walker, "The cosmopolitan local" (n 2).

12 N MacCormick, "Beyond the sovereign state" (1993) 56(1) *Modern Law Review* 1-18.

13 See further Z Bańkowski and E A Christodoulidis, "The European Union as an essentially contested project" in Z Bańkowski and A Scott (eds), *The European Union and Its Order: The Legal Theory of European Integration* (1999) 17-30.

instructive that Neil used that case and that parable and indeed the parable form. One way of looking at what Jesus did in answer to the lawyer who was trying to test Him is that He gave a rather larger definition of neighbour than the prevailing narrow one – so neighbour did include Samaritans. So Scotland and Scottishness, both in terms of the legal system and citizenship, are wider than any current narrow definition. Neil's way of demonstrating this, especially through the idea of the system of interlocking normative orders that can be linked both to legal systems and identity, shows us how people who might have been thought of as different have in them some of our identity, and can thus be seen as neighbours.

D. PERFORMING THE PARABLE: RECOGNITION AND TRANSFORMATION

But one can also think of the parable, as Peter Winch did,[14] as something performative. Looked at in that way, what Christ is doing is not commanding you to "Love Thy Neighbour" and simply giving a rather wider definition of "neighbour". Rather, He commands you to make someone your neighbour by dealing with them as one. You, by your actions, constitute the neighbour relation. And so Neil in his work, both scientifically and as an MEP, was concerned to do just that. This meant that he was one of those who worked for the opening to the East and the South, that for him Europe was not some *Festung Europa* retreating back into itself and its own fixed identity, but that it was always to be seen as a place of transformation, one that reaches out and in doing so transforms itself and those to whom it reaches out. And this was consistent with his views on nationalism and identity; which he saw as something that could never be static but was always in flux, transformed and transforming – a profound sense of multiculturalism indeed.

We can see this as the way that the parable is about the *recognition* of someone. In having compassion and acting as he did, the Samaritan recognised he who had "fallen among thieves" and made him visible in his vulnerability and need. That love, as Simone Weil[15] says, makes the invisible visible and subject therefore to political action. Rai Gaita[16] supplies a startling image. When he was a young man he worked in a mental home where, he says, most of the staff treated the inmates as worse than animals. There were some doctors and himself who, he hoped, tried to treat them with some concern

14 P Winch (1987), "Who is my neighbour?", in *Trying to Make Sense* (1987) 154-166.
15 S Weil, *Waiting For God* (1951) 149.
16 R Gaita, *A Common Humanity* (2000) ch 1.

and kindness. But there was a nun whose interaction with the inmates put them all to shame. This did not stem from, he claims, any rule system, but was something that came from the love of that nun. The point Gaita is trying to make here is the following. Of course, as Kant and others have said, you cannot expect to found and organise a society, to protect the poor and vulnerable, with only this "law of love". Love is not all, and you do need institutions such as law and the like. But why, he asks, would you even begin to build those institutions unless you saw and recognised that vulnerability and need in people and were moved by compassion as was the Samaritan. Those institutions are the social side of our love. People like the nun in Gaita's image are the secular saints who model and show that need for us – they make visible what we tend to hide away. This is not a hagiography, and Neil was no saint, but there was something in the quality of his engagement that always reminded me of that nun. Will Storrar alludes to it in his contribution and it is this aspect of the parable that I think is relevant to two of the key themes of this book, that of the Enlightenment and that of the public intellectual in Scotland.

The parable of the Good Samaritan was the favourite of Simone Weil. For her what the Samaritan did was an act of "creative attention":

> Christ taught us that the supernatural love of our neighbour is the exchange of compassion and gratitude which happens in a flash between two beings, one possessing and the other deprived of human personality. One of the two is only a little piece of flesh, naked, inert, and bleeding beside a ditch; he is nameless; no one knows anything about him. Those who pass by this thing scarcely notice it, and a few minutes afterwards do not even know that they saw it. Only one stops and turns his attention towards it … The attention is creative.[17]

This attentiveness brings to life by mutual engagement. One has to engage with the other in a way in which you embrace their vulnerability and pain. Again, I think that an image from Simone Weil[18] is appropriate. She answers the question "why should we struggle for justice" with a story. Well-fed people, she says, do not stand pressed outside the windows of restaurants looking at the food therein. Only the hungry stand there desperate. So also we will only work for justice if we hunger and thirst for it. We who are well fed and not in pain will only hunger and thirst if we have the grace to allow the injustice in the cry of pain, wherever it comes from, to lacerate our soul because of its existence. The point is that it is not your pain I feel, but I have pain that, even though it is because you have pain, is my own. In some respects what we have

---

17 Weil, *Waiting For God* (n 15) 146-7: see J Grote, "Prestige: Simone Weil's theory of social force" (1990) 42 *Spirituality Today* 217-232.
18 S Weil, "Are we struggling for justice?" trans by M Barabas, (1987) 10(1) *Philosophical Investigations* 1-10 at 4.

here is the difference between sympathy and empathy. The former, "I feel your pain" is empathetic, whereas the latter is more sympathetic. And from the latter, says Weil, stems the desire to help the unfortunate and to enable them to participate in the fullness of life that we have. The former is in some respects rather cool and can sometimes exhibit a sort of Kantian rationalism.

But this is not to denigrate the rationality in morality but rather, to pick up the point from Gaita, to claim that the urge to act, and to choose those modes of acting, both personally and in the way we design institutions in a society, will only come from the desire to connect – that ineffable moment that is shown in the story of the nun and is modelled to us by her and other "secular saints". It is in this sense that we can have rational institutions of love; otherwise we have something like the "liberalism of fear"[19] which does not connect but rather builds institutions to protect our own autonomy and affords no connection. We become like ships passing in the night. Again, this is not to denigrate the "liberalism of fear", but to suggest that it would be a different kind of society generated by the engagement that the nun had and that I recognised, at least partially, in Neil.

But there is another problem also. We must not let this rationality slip over into that ineffable moment, for if this happens we get what one can see in many of the contemporary approaches to disability, which are keen to let people live a full and normal life but not in the end accepting of the disabled life as a life as something that you can learn from. For they do not embrace the disabled. Rather they want to make them like themselves – they have a cool rationality, albeit one which is full of compassion – their religion is Kant. They are not mutual partners in vulnerability and suffering, they are there to help from their superior position, but in doing it this way they cannot see. They "feel your pain" but have none of their own.

E. SYMPATHY AND THE INTELLECTUAL LIFE

Neil in his last book *Practical Reason in Law and Morality*[20] tries to bring together the rationality of Kant with the sympathy of Smith in morality and practical reasoning. And in it one can see him dealing with the sorts of issues I have talked about above, struggling with his affective and rational sides, trying to come to a position where he could embrace both. This is perhaps his most personal book, written as he was dying with not much time. But perhaps

---

19 M Krygier, "Four puzzles about the Rule of Law: Why, what, where? And who cares?" [2010] UNSWLRS 22, available at *http://law.bepress.com/unswwps/flrps10/art22/* (accessed 25 July 2011) at 25-26.

20 N MacCormick, *Practical Reason in Law and Morality* (2008).

that was no bad thing. He did not have time so he could say what he felt and it was good for that. He did not let the rational overwhelm the affective – it is true to him and the parable. For the point about the parable is that, in the act of helping, the Samaritan opens himself out with his gift and thus shares a mutual vulnerability. He gives life to him who had "fallen among thieves", but at the price of receiving his vulnerability. But of course this is exactly what makes the way the nun acts special. The way she acts makes no distinction between her and the inmates; she does not give help from a superior vantage point, a "Lady Bountiful" wanting to bring them to her elevated position. Instead, they learn from each other in mutual openness and vulnerability. The nun at a deep level recognises she is not special, and she is not only helping and teaching but open to what they can give her.[21]

It is this that I think that Neil exhibited in his academic life. Neil was always prepared to engage with others in the academy, his colleagues and his students. And this was a passionate and moral intellectual engagement. For him that was part of the vocation of the academic life and something internal to it. He took his responsibilities seriously not because they were part of the job. He did not see these responsibilities as criteria in some modern job and grade-matching exercise so beloved of (In)human Relations. He did not see what he did as a job but as a vocation, and that he was lucky to be paid for pursuing it. He was extraordinarily open and generous. He was an inspiring teacher and saw it, unlike many in these research-oriented times, as an important part of his academic vocation. He had time for everyone, from the first-year student to the most senior member of the Faculty. His door was always open and he would always offer constructive and careful criticism. He was a master of the difficult art of being critical but also positive. He found it difficult to be entirely negative. He was relentlessly optimistic and always able to find worth in someone or something because he always thought there was. He was always able to couch even far-reaching critical comments in a positive and encouraging way. This is what made him an exceptional academic, and wonderful colleague and teacher. When he engaged with you he brought you and your halting ideas to life, he transformed you and them not necessarily into something better but into something that you could be proud of, partly because he made you a fellow traveller in the precarious search for truth which Simone Weil called "food for the soul".

When I came to teach at Edinburgh, I was a radical anarcho-Marxist,

---

21 See for example the model adopted by the L'Arche Communities, which is premised on the "common humanity" of all people, and aims to allow "members with and without disabilities get customised support to discover, develop and share their unique – and often hidden – talents." See *http://www.larche.org/home.en-gb.1.0.index.htm* (accessed 25 July 2011).

someone hardly willing to listen to what I considered the bourgeois philosophy of law that Neil propounded. But Neil read my work, engaged with it and took me seriously. Of course this made it much better than it might otherwise have been, but that was not the point. He took it and me seriously and I became that fellow traveller. But more than that. He gave me his own work to read and he took my criticisms and arguments seriously and we both moved and changed in various ways as we worked together to the extent of sometimes finding ourselves espousing the other's views. There was never a "School of Legal Philosophy" emanating from Edinburgh, though I have often been asked for the defining characteristics of it. That was because of the tone set by Neil; the passionate engagement and journey was all. He gave the same time to students and treated them in the same way. From the cleverest to the ones who were barely going to pass, he co-opted them all into the journey for truth and they touched him as he touched them. One image can stand as a metaphor for this; one year, instead of the usual end of the academic year party for his honours class, he organised a Jurisprudence walk in the hills where we walked (he in his kilt) and talked in the hills and ended up in a pub where we drank and talked some more! For him the concept of a university is of a place where one reflects on the life of the mind and engages with all those members of it. Take that away and it becomes something less than a university, and he always fought against that.

I have been talking of Neil's engagement as an academic and intellectual in the semi-public sphere of the University. In moving as well to the more public sphere, he embodied the best Scottish traditions of the "democratic intellect",[22] tirelessly pursuing an engagement with the outside world. He was constructive, welcoming and inclusive. This showed in his politics, where he vigorously espoused in his writings and public interventions a nationalism that was not narrow-minded and xenophobic but inclusive and open. At base it was an extension of his vocation as an intellectual in the academy and he brought the same qualities to it. In the sense I have described, he was a public intellectual because he was a private intellectual.

No journey is ever over but this particular journey and the route the parable has taken me has come to an end. I welcomed the opportunity to "chew the fat" with my dear friend even if he is perforce a silent interlocutor. I am not sure what he would have said but I am sure that he would have listened and engaged and transformed that journey – he would never forget that you were there. He would have made that journey come to life.

---

22 See G Elder Davie, *The Democratic Intellect: Scotland and her Universities in the Nineteenth Century*, 2nd edn (1964, repr 1999). See also Drew Scott's contribution to this volume.

Index